Have You Seen the Lamb?

Have You Seen the Lamb?

THE STORY OF
THE FIRST PASSOVER AND THE LAST SUPPER

Robert F. Wolff

Based upon an historical view of the Holy Scriptures

Copyright 2005 – Robert F. Wolff

All rights reserved. This book is protected by the copyright laws of the United States of America. This book may not be copied or reprinted for commercial gain or profit. The use of short quotations for personal or group study is permitted and encouraged. Permission will be granted upon request.

Unless otherwise identified, Scripture quotations are taken from the New King James Version. Copyright © 1982 by Thomas Nelson, Inc. Used by permission. Some Scripture quotations are taken from the Complete Jewish Bible, Copyright 1998 by David H. Stern. Published by Jewish New Testament Publications, Inc. All rights reserved. Used by permission.

Previously published as Have You Seen the Lamb by Xulon Press
ISBN 1-59781-593-4

Drawbaugh Publishing Group
444 Allen Drive
Chambersburg, PA 17202

ISBN paperback 978-1-941746-13-4
ISBN eBook 978-1-941746-14-1

For Worldwide Distribution, Printed in the U.S.A.
1 2 3 4 5 6 7 8 9 10 11 / 17 16 15

Majestic Glory Ministries

The mission of Majestic Glory Ministries is to encourage Jews and Gentiles to join together as One New Man to advance the Kingdom of God. When people of faith serve side by side in the Spirit of Lovingkindness, all humanity will be the blessed.

As we study the Passover, we discover God wants all of His children to be free of slavery. The Lord orchestrated these miraculous events to help us reach this inevitable conclusion.

It is for freedom that Messiah has set us free.
Stand firm, then, and do not let yourselves be burdened again by a yoke of slavery.
[Galatians 5:1]

The truth of God's Word is here for all to see. Come, drink from the fountain. See the Light. Discover God's treasures, as the Lord speaks to you from the realm of His Majestic Glory.

History awaits to teach us our future.

Majestic Glory Ministries embraces vital ministries. The *Every Tribe Every Nation* Project joins the First Nations of America and the Nation of Israel to develop agricultural expertise. Majestic Glory also fights slavery via the O.A.T.H. Project (One Against Trafficking Humans). Please join us at: SigntheOATH.org

Other books available through Drawbaugh Publishing and Majestic Glory Ministries include:

UNITY Awakening the One New Man;
My First 40 Days with the Lord;
Catch and Release

Awakening1.org

Table of Contents

Acknowledgements xi
Introduction xiii

PART I
THE FIRST PASSOVER 1

And the Land Was Dark 3
Moses Is Coming 5
The Good News 8
The Prophet and the Priest 12
The Mountain of God 18
Called by a New Name 23
Aaron Remembers 27
You Will See My Face No More 36
The Gathering of Elders 40
People Get Ready 45
Plundering Egypt 47
A Lamb Is Chosen 52
Joshua Suffers Silently 55

The Faith of Avraham 59
A Night To Be Remembered 62
The Passover Lamb... 65
The Angel of Death 73
The Exodus... 79
South to Succoth... 84
The Fiery Pillar 89
Revenge!... 95
Walls of Water... 98
A New Dawn 103

PART II
THE LAST SUPPER 109
Jerusalem.. 111
The Triumphal Entry 116
The Temple 123
On Top of Mount Zion... 126
How Will We Know the Messiah?.. 129
Cleansing the House of God 132
Evil Plans Are Laid 137
A Test of Faith 141
Benjamin's Surprise Announcement..................................... 144
The Upper Room.. 146
Yeshua's Miraculous Works... 149
Farewell to Moriah... 156
Sacrifice of the Lamb.. 159
Choosing Sides 164

Yeshua Arrives	167
Washing Their Feet	171
The Four Questions	174
Betrayal	178
Breaking Bread	181
Do Not Let Your Hearts Be Troubled	186
Hearing the Word of God	188
Back to the Garden	192
The Sheep Are Scattered	198
Man, Monarch, and Messiah	204
Roman Justice	210
Stepping into Eternity	214
"It Is Finished"	217
Have You Seen The Lamb?	219
Resurrection Power	224
The Witnesses	228
"Peace Be With You"	231
Epilogue	237
Family Trees	239
Glossary	240

Acknowledgements

I wish to thank my beloved wife Wendy, and our loving children Luka, Kai, and Lee for standing by me; Hilary Clay Hicks, for his countless hours of editorial and creative contributions; Baruch Greenstein, for his inspiring artwork; Dr. Arthur Glasser, whose wisdom and insight suggested this vehicle, and who guided me through its every stage; Moses and Esther Rosenberg, for teaching me the foundations of my faith; Benjamin DeLaine, who impressed upon me that this book needed to be written; Pastor Carleton Lincoln from The Dwelling Place, who taught me about reconciliation by loving and accepting me; Dr. Jack Hayford and Dr. Scott Bauer from The Church On The Way, who tirelessly poured their hearts into their flock; the pastors and staff at The Malibu Vineyard, for permitting me to pursue my dream; my proofreaders, Gaylord Wagner, Carol Izad, Sharon Dittrich, and Jackie Arthur, who gave of their time to review the manuscript; my teachers, who have directed me during my spiritual pilgrimage; my many friends, who have never stopped encouraging me; my parents and family, who loved me and raised me to love God; my aunt Jean, who inspired this work by challenging my faith; the many who have prayed for this manuscript; and Amanda, the boss.

I thank God for each and every one of you and for the opportunity to offer this manuscript to the community of believers both known and those yet to come to faith, for the glory of our Lord.

Peace be to you. Shalom aleikhem.

Introduction

Have You Seen The Lamb? illuminates and illustrates the parallels between the two most famous and defining events in the Hebrew Scriptures. As you will discover, the sacrificial lamb of Passover is a profound common denominator, which inextricably links our historical and traditional faith in God's carefully recorded plan for the salvation and redemption of all humanity.

This is not intended to be a definitive history of events, however great effort has been made to be historically and scripturally faithful. Whenever possible, The Holy Scriptures have been quoted or paraphrased. Wherever possible, actual Scriptural personalities have been utilized, with the addition of realistic new characters to help present the stories. This is to say, much of the dialogue and fictional elements are projections to facilitate the telling.

For context, please read and refer to the Torah account of Exodus (Sh'mot) Chapters 1-15 and The New Testament (B'rit Hadashah) books of Mark (Markon) and John (Yochanan).

A glossary and family trees are provided at the conclusion to aid in interpretation. Enjoy your journey.

PART I

The First Passover

And the blood shall be a sign for you
On the houses where you live;
And when I see the blood
I will pass over you,
And no plague will befall you
To destroy you
When I strike the land of Egypt.

EXODUS (SH'MOT) 12:13

And the Land Was Dark

Blackness hung like ink. Gloom invaded the atmosphere. The air was clammy and dank. It clung like black chalk. A vaporous cloud of utter darkness covered the empire. Even with a torch, it was impossible to see beyond an arm's length. This abnormal absence of light enclosed the kingdom in endless night.

Nothing stirred. The oppressive haze resisted all movement. The only sounds heard were the occasional moaning and lowing of the surviving animals. Of these, most suffered from a pestilence that inflicted painful oozing sores. No one tended the livestock. No one cared. The people were hiding in their homes. Food was not even a consideration. Everything tasted like death.

Egypt was enduring her ninth plague.

Pharaoh brooded alone, a prisoner in his own palace. He ate not. He slept not. He spoke to no one. He asked for nothing. In this land he was considered a god, but now he was powerless. Even his sorcerers were impotent. His enemy was invisible, beyond his control.

His mind screamed, "When will this longest night end? If the light ever returns, what will I see? My livestock are decimated. Locusts have consumed every edible crop that the hail has not smashed. The darkness serves only to hide the devastation brought on by this ceaseless succession of plagues. My once fruitful land is ruined."

He could only wonder: "How can there be day without daylight? Where is Amon-Ra, our god of the sun? Is this, in fact, the final judgment of the God of Moses?"

Again and again, Moses had foretold calamity if Pharaoh would not let the Israelites go. As promised, the Hebrew prophet's every warning had been followed by a supernatural judgment. Each plague stopped only when the monarch pleaded with Moses for its removal. This time, however, even Pharaoh's own advisors had petitioned him to let the Israelites go. But again he resisted.

Now, his Egypt was made blind. One more time, the king's heart turned to stone. What had once seemed implausible was actually taking place. He fumed, "How could I have allowed these insolent slaves to grow so powerful?"

And then he was gripped by suffocating fear. "Could Moses have an ulterior motive? Perhaps he wishes to reclaim his formal standing in the royal court? Will he even seek the throne of Egypt?"

Pharaoh gnawed on his lips. He dug his fingernails into the palms of his hands, trying to find some sense of himself through the pain. It was useless. Anxiety choked the ruler. He was desperate. He tried to cry out, but the ashen air dampened his voice.

At last, remembering his position, pride welled up within him. He refused to believe he was beaten. No matter what the cost, he would protect his precious throne, his absolute power. How absurd to think Moses would win the contest. He would trick Moses into lifting this horrible plague of darkness. He would find a way to stop this madness.

He called out for his messenger. A moment later the servant arrived. Pharaoh could barely see him. How the king hated to speak the inevitable words once again, "Bring me Moses!" The ruler's muffled voice did little to hide the savagery of his spite. Obediently, the slave slipped away into the mist.

Pharaoh paced restlessly about his shadowy chamber, snarling like a caged beast. His eyes glowing in the dark like burning coals. Foaming hatred frothed on his lips, his mind contemplating revenge.

Like a reptile lurking in the shadows, coiled, ready to spring, the oppressor crouched beside his throne as if preparing to encounter his adversary. Seeking some sign of weakness, the predator imagined himself lunging from his royal hiding place to mercilessly devour his prey!

Moses Is Coming

In the heart of Goshen, the territory reserved by the pharaohs for their Hebrew slaves, there stood a village bazaar. At the edge of the marketplace, Jephunneh the baker glanced out of his stall. For three days, the skies over Pharaoh's city of Zoan had been an impenetrable pitch black. But today, the silver-haired elder of Israel noticed something was changing. He called to his son Caleb and grandson Iru, who were working in the back of the stall. "The darkness upon Egypt is lifting!"

They came to the front to see for themselves. It was true. Others in the bazaar were also taking note. The sound of hundreds of bartering voices paused momentarily while they looked to the west.

Without warning, a young man raced into the middle of the marketplace. His sudden entry caught the attention of all present in the square. Dodging animals and shoppers, he skidded to a halt in front of Jephunneh's stall calling out, "I have news!"

Jephunneh craned his head out from behind stacks of fresh loaves. He reached across the bread grabbing the young man by his sleeves. Almost whispering, "Joshua, you're back. Where is Moses?"

Caleb and Iru rushed out from under the covering, joining the elder, eager to hear Moses' recently appointed aide.

Trying to catch his breath, the young man proclaimed, "Moses is coming. The plague of darkness is ending. You're the first to know."

"Moses is coming!" shouted Jephunneh to the gathering crowd, joyfully repeating Joshua's words. "The plague of darkness is ending."

The people fell silent at the news. From experience, they knew that whenever Moses had an audience with Pharaoh, something incredible and unpredictable was going to happen.

"The time of our deliverance is at hand!" Jephunneh bellowed.

Pandemonium broke loose in the market as if it had been struck by lightning. Even the eldest of the elders were energized. They yelled at one another, waving their arms in animated gestures. Awnings and tents collapsed left and right. Vendors shut down their scales and closed up shop. Fruit stands were abandoned. Costly trading goods, hastily jammed into sacks, were splayed over camels' humps, their owners goading the complaining desert beasts into motion with their cargo only partially secured. Donkeys brayed in dismay, resisting the tugging and cajoling of their owners. Sheep bleated and bolted, trying to flee the onrushing mob. Merchants shouted as they shoved the confused woolly animals aside in their efforts to haul their own hurriedly stuffed carts. Like a startled flock of doves, everyone took off every which way.

Caleb and Iru stayed put, not wanting to miss anything Joshua had to say. Iru was poised to seize Joshua's every word. As a lieutenant in the Israelite messenger corps, Iru was among those responsible for memorizing any message from Moses and then to proclaim it throughout the neighborhood.

Jephunneh continued to repeat Joshua's report out loud to the fleeing tradesmen, "Moses sends word: The elders meet tonight."

By this time, there was no one left to listen. Jephunneh, Caleb, and Joshua stood alone in the bazaar. What had been a bustling place of trade moments before was now a dusty, deserted lot with no signs of life, barring a few squawking chickens and the remnants of several squashed vegetables that had been trampled underfoot.

Jephunneh turned to his grandson and said, "What are you still doing here? On your way."

Iru took off to run his preplanned circuit throughout Goshen to alert as many as possible and to notify other runners so the word would spread throughout the city.

Still gasping for air, Joshua paused and looked around at the empty square. Never in his seventeen years had he experienced anything like this.

"We must hurry home to prepare for the council meeting," said Caleb.

"I must keep on running," said Joshua as he took flight. "I can't wait to tell my family."

Despite his speed, the news was already spreading before him like wildfire. The streets were filled with commotion. The journey home was clogged with rejoicing Hebrews, so Joshua found himself sidestepping donkeys and ducking beneath tent ropes to avoid the celebrants.

While he ran, Joshua's mind also raced. He wanted to believe, as Jephunneh had claimed, that this was the time of Israel's predicted liberation. His people had endured more than 400 years of slavery. The prophetic words of his father Nun rang in his ears: "The day will come soon, my son. The Lord will free His people. He will guide them to the Promised Land. You may see it happen in your lifetime."

Was it true? Was this the time?

The Good News

Joshua staggered around the last corner, his heart pounding in his chest. Though his legs ached, he pressed on. Thankfully, the road ahead was clear. Word had not yet reached his quarter of the city. He would have the privilege of being the first to tell his own family.

Joshua shouted, heralding Moses' words as he ran, "Moses is coming! The plague is lifting!" His lungs burned for air, begging him to slow down, but the news could not wait. His face was bright with excitement and exhaustion. His dark hair was tangled from his frenzied dash back home. He had no time to celebrate his proclamation with his neighbors. In his wake, the children of Israel joyfully thronged into the streets.

The thick rope around his waist had worked its way loose, forcing him to clutch the hem of his flopping garment to avoid getting it tangled and twisted around his legs. Finally spying his family's dwelling, he sprinted the last few yards.

His sister, little Rachel, sat in the front yard, playing with her doll. Joshua swept past her like a whirlwind scurrying along the sandy walk. She jumped up to tag along.

"What's going on?" she demanded. "Tell me, please!"

Ignoring her, Joshua burst into the house exclaiming, "Moses is coming! He'll be back before sundown." He collapsed on the kitchen bench, trying to catch his breath.

His parents were startled. Nun's jaw dropped open. He turned to Deborah, "Mother, do you hear?"

The answer was written upon her face. Both were taken by surprise. Covering her mouth with her hands, Deborah fell to her knees by her son. Nun knelt beside her as they overwhelmed Joshua with a flurry of questions:

"Where is Moses now?"

"Did he see Pharaoh?"

"Was he successful?"

"Were you with him at the palace?"

"Is there yet darkness over Egypt?"

Joshua could only hold up his hands in a vain attempt to get them to listen. He was trying to recover his wind and talk at the same time. His only sounds were frustrated wheezes and gasps. He could barely contain his story. His hands shook as he gestured exuberantly for them to calm down.

Deborah offered a small cup of water to him. "Drink this."

Joshua gulped it down. Swallowing too quickly, he choked and sputtered. He bent over the table and tried to inhale. Nun laughed as he slapped him on the back.

Despite his coughing, Joshua spilled the details. "The plague of darkness is ending," he managed to exclaim. "Moses has finished talking to Pharaoh. He is coming back today! He's called a council meeting!" Joshua located a bucket of fresh water and doused himself in an effort to cool down.

Nun turned to look out the window, witnessing the dissipating shadow over Zoan.

Joshua studied his father. Nun was not an outwardly emotional man except when it came to his zeal for God. The announcement and the sight of diminishing darkness began to stretch the wrinkles of his face with enthusiasm. A widening smile erased all signs of fatigue. Years working in the sun had weathered his brow. His appearance was intense, almost stern, and yet compassionate. Lines of age added to his imposing presence. His lengthy hair and beard were salt and peppered with acumen. There was a distinctive streak of gray at his chin and temples. His hands were unusually strong and large; his arms well developed and taut, not betraying his gentle touch.

Nun was a surveyor's assistant in servitude to the Egyptians. He was widely recognized and respected in the community of Hebrews due to his keen insight. Although he was just forty years of age, he had the stamp of a wizened elder.

Nun beckoned Joshua to come near. Deborah stood behind her husband, her hands on his shoulders. They did not want to miss a word. "Joshua," he said, "We want to hear everything."

Drawing another breath, Joshua continued, "Moses and Aaron made demands of the Pharaoh."

Nun covered his mouth with his forearm. Deborah bit her lip. "Such conduct before Pharaoh is unheard of. Why was he not killed?"

Joshua shrugged. Nun said, "Perhaps it is because Moses was raised in the royal palace. Or maybe God withheld Pharaoh's hand because Moses spoke on His behalf."

Still gulping air, Joshua continued, "You're right. I'm sure no one has ever spoken to Pharaoh like that. But, Moses did! Aaron told me that even he was impressed with his brother's courage."

From the corner of the room a voice softly said, "Amen." No one realized that Grandfather Elishama had entered the room.

Seeing that Joshua was soaked, Elishama spoke to his daughter-in-law. "Deborah, can't you see that the boy is sweating through his clothes? Fetch him a ladle of water."

Joshua chuckled. "That's not sweat, Grandpapa, it is water." Barely able to contain himself, he addressed the family's patriarch, "Moses has called for the leaders to assemble at the lodge of meeting tonight."

"Father, he's expecting you and grandfather to be there. As I left Zoan he shouted after me, 'Tell Elishama to wear his robe.'"

The family looked at each other. This meeting would be crucial.

Nun replied, "Moses wants my father to stand next to him formally dressed as council leader of all the tribes." He rubbed Joshua's shoulders and then patted him on the back. "Good, good. Well done, young man. You have brought good news."

Joshua bounded over to the corner where his grandfather stood. "What do you think, Grandpapa?"

Elishama closed his eyes, looking within, "My heart is filled with joy!"

"Joshua," said Nun, "Bring the robe of authority."

Within moments Joshua had retrieved the robe out of the family cedar chest. Reverently, Nun and Joshua assisted the elder of their family by guiding his arms through the sleeves and sliding the robe up over his shoulders. The fabric was painstakingly crafted from the finest of wools and dyed with many colors. Around the neck of the garment were prominent markings in Hebrew. Scarlet and purple borders flanked the chest. The belt was tasseled. Its ribbons of woven gold braid shone in the firelight. Elishama looked very dignified.

Outside the wind carried distant sounds of jubilation caused by Moses' imminent return. "Hear that?" said Elishama. "This is a rare and wonderful thing in Goshen!"

The air was electric with anticipation. Above the clamor of the city the blast of a shofar, the ram's horn, could be heard. Hah-rooot! Hah-rooot! Hah-rooot!

The Prophet and the Priest

Seeing Elishama in his robe of authority sparked Joshua's memory. Not many days before, he had seen his grandfather dressed in this same robe. So much had transpired since. His entire life's course had been radically altered. He would never forget that glorious night, when Moses had changed his name from Hoshea to Joshua.

* * *

Ever since Moses first returned to his people, council meetings had become more frequent and purposeful. Elishama and Nun had just come home from one. The plague of darkness had only begun that fateful morning in Egypt. The elders had been called to meet with Moses and Aaron at nightfall.

Darkness — what a terrible curse. The Children of Israel had light over their land, but Egypt was enveloped in a supernatural shroud of blackness, deeper than any natural night. From sunlit Goshen, it was possible to look out and see night smothering Egypt just a few short miles away. Sitting on a stone outside the door of their hut, Hoshea thought to himself how miserable the Egyptians must feel.

His father and grandfather were returning from the council lodge. Both men were particularly exuberant. Even while they described the gravity of the plague, Hoshea sensed something else. Nun and Elishama kept looking at him and grinning.

At first he wondered if he had spilled food on his clothes, but upon inspection, he realized their mirth was not related to his appearance. The men's behavior had Hoshea quite unsettled. Deborah, too, picked up the expressions on their faces.

Finally, Nun turned to Deborah. "We will be having guests for dinner tomorrow night." Deborah's hearing perked. This was not a common occurrence among the Hebrew slaves.

"Is it anyone we know?"

"Well, I'm sure you have heard of them," hinted Elishama.

"Are they important people?" she asked.

"I'd say so," Nun said with a big smirk as he arched an eyebrow.

Nun could hold back no longer. "It's Moses and Aaron!" he blurted.

Hoshea looked closely at his father's eyes and realized he wasn't joking. Then he looked at his grandfather and confirmed that it was true. Hoshea was thrilled beyond compare. Nun nodded agreeably at his wife. Deborah muffled a cry in her apron, not wanting to wake their daughter.

"And Hoshea," added Nun, "Moses said he would like to meet you."

Hoshea was dumbstruck. This was an honor surpassing his wildest dreams. The great prophet, as well as his spokesman brother, was coming to his humble home to dine. This was the most amazing thing that had ever happened to any of them.

In the blink of an eye, Deborah was on her feet. If they were entertaining guests, there was much to do. She immediately became concerned about the evening meal. Fortunately, her hearth was always kept ready and there was plenty of dough on hand.

But this was a special occasion. Hebrews seldom had the opportunity for luxuries. Fine food was rare, since their taskmasters controlled much of their provisions. With the onset of severe economic depression due to Pharaoh's obstinacy toward Moses, living in Egypt had been reduced to mere existence. Resourcefulness had become a way of life.

Deborah dug through her scant supplies for any delicacies she could find. Sometimes tasty treats were shared at special festivities such as marriages or the birth of a child. This time it would be to serve the prophet of God.

Early the next day, the household was abuzz as the entire family prepared for the special visitors. Nun and Elishama went out and traded some grain for poultry. Hoshea helped his mother. Everyone was elated except little Rachel. They were too busy to pay her proper attention.

She became perplexed. Several times she demanded to know, "What's going on?"

Upon his return, noting that his daughter was in a flux, Nun scooped her up and held her over his head. "Rachel, my precious jewel, today you will meet a great man."

"Who is he?" she asked, starting to snicker and relishing the attention.

"Moses," said Nun smiling. "Do you know who he is?"

"I remember." she replied. "He's the man who saw the flaming bush that was not burned up."

"That's right my little one," said Nun. "Out of the countless thousands and thousands of Hebrew families in Egypt, Moses has chosen to come to our house for dinner. Such an honor."

He lowered Rachel to his waist and handed her to Deborah. His gaze drifted far, far away as he became preoccupied with hope of the fulfillment of God's promises.

Rachel's face turned red with frustration. If this was going to be fun, she wanted to be part of it. At six years old, she always found too many questions left unanswered.

Rachel had already received some instruction about her heritage. She knew, for instance, that she had been named after the patriarch Ya'akov's wife. She had also been told a little about Moses — that he had warned the Egyptians before God sent the nasty plagues to hurt them. Even so, the idea of encountering the prophet of God in person meant little to her. She decided to find something nice to wear.

The hour arrived. Voices in the street drew their attention outside the house. Sure enough, Moses and Aaron were drawing near. Their neighbors were in the street greeting them, wondering where their leaders were going. Nun lifted the thick flap of hide covering the doorway and welcomed the celebrated guests. He nervously ushered them inside, then followed after. Once within, he stood stiffly, wringing his hands.

Moses sensed the family's uneasiness. He looked at Deborah and the food on the table. Sniffing the air, he turned his palms upward and shrugged playfully. His greeting was warm, polite, and cheerful. "What's for dinner?"

All the tension in the room evaporated. Everyone laughed. Already, Moses was like an old friend.

Rachel volunteered, "You better like the food. My mother has spent all day cooking it." The entire family was somewhat embarrassed by the outburst.

Moses tilted his head back and roared with joyful abandon. His voice was full and kind. He turned and handed his rod to Aaron. Still chuckling, he stepped into the middle of the room, his arms extended, his hands still open as if he was introducing himself. "We are honored to be your guests." He hastened to place a stout arm around each of Hoshea's parents and hugged them both. The man of God was at home.

Hoshea scrutinized the prophet. Moses exuded merriment. The hood of his robe fell back, allowing his lengthy hair and bountiful beard to tumble free. His tousled hair sported lofts of curls divulging telltale signs of graying. The distinguished beard, streaked with silver and gray further displayed his maturity. The next thing he noticed was the prophet's forehead, which stood prominently, slightly protruding above the eyes and slanting backward toward a gently receding hairline.

His look was focused and steady. His eyes were bright yet set back in their sockets. At the outside edges, wrinkles fanned out toward his temples. Dark, bushy eyebrows framed brown pupils reflecting pools of golden light. Large and somewhat elongated ears bordered his head. His nose was straight and strong; it stood wide and flared at its base. Deep lines were etched from the borders of his nose to the corners of his mouth. His teeth were well preserved and punctuated by a small space between the front incisors. His skin had the color of dark sand, displaying obvious signs of extended exposure to the harsh desert climate.

He was a big man. His shoulders were powerful, expressing his authority as he gestured. His feet were sandaled with a broad single strap over the arch. His legs were well muscled, his calves well defined. His robe had oversized sleeves, large enough to hide a young lamb inside their protective covering.

Upon closer examination, his complexion revealed small scars where it had been pierced by the cruel spines of plants inherent to the great wilderness east of Egypt. In his shepherding days, many were the times he had been forced to retrieve a lost sheep trapped in the entangling thorns of acacia trees.

One could detect a certain toughness, but at this moment, joy flowed from him like the morning sun. His demeanor revealed both his wisdom and his quick wits.

He reached into the recesses of his robe for a hidden pair of gifts wrapped in parchment. He handed one to Hoshea, the other to Rachel. The youngest members of the household esteemed him instantly. Each of them echoed, "Thank you."

Rolled inside the parchment were charcoal sticks that could be used for drawing or writing. The young people were thrilled. Soon Hoshea was showing his sister how to hold the instruments without breaking them. The grown-ups appreciated Moses' gesture. They knew this was a precious and rare gift.

Aaron gave a handful of fresh herbs to Deborah. He simply spoke, "For your kitchen." His voice was resonant and impressive. Deborah smiled gratefully.

Moses and Aaron then paid their respects to Elishama, who placed his hands on their shoulders in welcome. Then Elishama gently grasped the prophet's garment in both of his hands and said, "I thank God for sending us such a deliverer."

"I'm only a servant of the Most High, just like you," said Moses. Hoshea was surprised at the humility of the mighty Moses. He had heard that the prophet was so, but it was not what the young man had expected from a performer of miracles – the one who had defied Pharaoh, the most powerful man alive.

The whole family beamed with joy at having these great men in their home. Now that all were comfortable, Elishama asked the best question, "Shall we eat?"

"Yes." the visitors accepted eagerly. Everyone laughed. Elishama motioned them to the dining area. Moses added his compliments. "What a handsome table you have prepared. Now, what is that savory smell?

Deborah uncovered the food and announced proudly, "Fresh desert quail and leeks with seasonings from far-off lands."

"This is an unexpected blessing," said Aaron. "I hardly know what to say."

"The blessing would be fine," said Deborah.

Aaron called upon the Almighty to bless the food and their home. Once the meal had begun, Moses spoke freely. In his glee, he seemed to trip over some of his words and phrases. "The years in the desert have caused my lips to work like a camel's."

Rachel giggled with delight. Hoshea laughed so hard his stomach ached. Nun and Deborah politely tried not to laugh, but couldn't help themselves.

"That is why God chose Aaron to speak so often for me," added Moses quickly.

Elishama leaned back and took in the entire scene with a contented look. "I wonder if the heaviness that has overshadowed every Hebrew home is soon to be lifted?"

No one responded. They were all too busy enjoying the company and fine food.

The Mountain of God

After the meal, Deborah and Rachel cleared the remains of what Moses and Aaron had called "a feast from heaven." The men turned to talk. It struck Hoshea for the first time that the two guests were there with a purpose. He wondered what it could be.

It was not unusual for a meeting or a conversation with an elder to begin with a question, but Hoshea was surprised when Moses turned to him and asked, "Hoshea, may I tell you a story?"

Hoshea eagerly approved. He noticed that Elishama and Nun were smiling broadly. "They must know something I don't," he thought.

"Perhaps you have heard what the people say about me," said Moses. "Most of it is true, including the worst of it. But let me tell you, as I have told the elders of Israel, how the God of Avraham, Yitzchak, and Ya'akov can recover one who has failed and call him to service."

"As you have no doubt heard, I am a Levite, born of Amram and Jochebed, slaves in Egypt. By edict of the Pharaoh, in those days male Hebrew children were to be killed, but my mother set me adrift in a papyrus basket among the reeds of the Nile. There I was found by Princess Hatshepsut; who begged of her father the Pharaoh to keep me. Thanks to the cleverness of my sister Miriam, my mother was asked to help nurse the very child she had brought into the world, after being forced to release me to an unknown fate.

"As a member of Pharaoh's family, I was schooled in the arts and sciences. I was trained in military matters. I was raised as a proud Egyptian prince. Unfortunately, it was a long time before I began to see the world through my people's eyes. It took me forty years to become fully aware of the injustices and cruelty which were ceaselessly heaped upon my fellow Hebrews. I did not know then what I know now — that it was our God stirring me to take action.

"I began to try to find favor with my Hebrew brethren. Believe me, young Hoshea, they did not want any part of me. They only saw me as a member of the aristocracy, not one of their own."

Aaron added, "There remain some who are suspicious of you now."

Moses acknowledged the remark with a nod. "In times past, I gave them good reason to distrust me. One day, I saw an Egyptian taskmaster mercilessly beating a defenseless Hebrew. It was more than I could bear. I attacked the Egyptian and struck him down, snuffing out his very life."

Hoshea was shocked. He had heard the story before, but he was amazed to hear it from the mouth of the prophet himself. He could not imagine Moses doing such a thing.

"I hid his body in the sand — as if to hide my sin," continued Moses. "But soon, everybody knew about it. After the murder, Hebrews and Egyptians alike rejected me. Pharaoh sought my life, and the Israelites offered no protection. In fear, I fled Egypt.

"I roamed deep into the wilderness. After some time, I came to a well in Midian where I met the seven lovely daughters of Jethro the priest, who eventually became my father-in-law.

"I remained there for forty years, a simple shepherd, and nothing more. You know, forty years is a very long time. I learned many things about life and meditated on the history of my people. I grew to appreciate our heritage and our special relationship with God. I thought I would live out the rest of my days in Midian. Then something unexpected happened that turned my life inside out."

"I had led my flock to the far side of the desert where I came to what I now call The Mountain of God.

"One day as the sheep were grazing, I saw a bush that was on fire, but it was not being burned up."

Everyone around the table oohed and aahed as they pictured the fabulous sight in their minds. All of them had heard this story, but it was different with Moses relating his experience firsthand.

"I said, 'I will go over and see this strange sight.' Imagine my fright when the Angel of the Lord appeared to me in flames of fire. He called to me from within the bush. He spoke my name: 'Moses, Moses!'"

"All I could say was, 'Here am I.'"

"'Do not come any closer,' God spoke. 'Take off your sandals, for the place where you are standing is holy ground.' He said, 'I AM the God of your fathers, the God of Avraham, the God of Yitzchak and the God of Ya'akov.' At this, I hid my face, because I was afraid to look at God."

"And wise you were not to do so," said Nun.

"The Lord said, 'I have seen the misery of my people in Egypt. I have heard them crying out because of their slavemasters, and I know their suffering. I have come down to rescue them from the hand of the Egyptians and to bring them up out of that land into a good and spacious country, a land flowing with milk and honey. I am sending you to Pharaoh to bring my people out of Egypt.'

"I was so astounded I could hardly speak. When I mustered up the courage, I said to God, 'Who am I, that I should go to Pharaoh and bring the Israelites out of Egypt? I am nobody.'

"I said, 'Suppose I go to the Israelites and say to them, 'The God of your fathers has sent me to you,' and they ask me, 'What is His name?' What shall I tell them?'

"God told me, 'Say to the Israelites, The Lord, the God of your fathers — the God of Avraham, the God of Yitzchak and the God of Ya'akov — has sent me to you. Tell them I AM THAT I AM has sent me to you. This is My Name forever, the Name by which I AM to be remembered from generation to generation.'"

Hoshea knew, as did every Hebrew, that the purpose of one's name was to identify one's character and reputation. God Almighty had declared to Moses that He stands alone, eternal. He is before, after, and beyond all time. He had revealed Himself as the God of the nation of Israel. Furthermore, His identity could only be found within Himself. This was beyond marvelous.

"The Lord told me, 'Go back to Egypt, for all the men who wanted to kill you are dead. Assemble the elders of Israel and say to them, The Lord, the God of your fathers, appeared to me and said: I have watched over you and have seen what has been done to you in Egypt. And I have promised to bring you up out of your misery in Egypt to the land of the

Canaanites, Hittites, Amorites, Perizzites, Hivites and Jebusites—a land flowing with milk and honey.'"

All those under the sound of Moses' voice pictured a country rich and beautiful.

"I answered, 'What if they do not believe me, or listen to me and say, The Lord did not appear to you?'

"Then the Lord said to me, 'What is that in your hand?'

"'A rod,' I replied.

"The Lord said, 'Throw it on the ground.'

"I threw it on the ground and it became a snake, and as you might well expect, I shrank back from it. Then the Lord said to me, 'Reach out your hand and take it by the tail.' I can tell you that I wanted no part in what He instructed."

Hoshea remarked, "If you must pick up a snake, you don't grab it by the tail."

"But I had to do it. I reached out and took hold of the snake. Once I grabbed the creature, it turned back into a rod in my hand.

"'This,' said the Lord, 'is so that they may believe that I have appeared to you.'

"Then the Lord said, 'Put your hand inside your cloak.' So I put my hand into my cloak, and when I took it out, it was leprous, white like snow. I was terrified.

"'Now put it back into your cloak,' He said. So I put my hand back into my cloak, and when I took it out, it was restored, and like the rest of my flesh. This too was fearful.

"The Lord said, 'If they do not believe you or pay attention to the first miraculous sign, they may believe the second.' Then He told me about the plagues he would bring upon Egypt.

"He said, 'When you return to Egypt, see that you perform before Pharaoh all the wonders I have given you power to do. But remember, I will harden his heart so that he will not let the people go.'

"I tried to get out of it. I said, 'O Lord, I have never been eloquent. I am slow of speech and tongue.'

"The Lord said to me, 'Who gave man his mouth? Who makes him deaf or mute? Who gives him sight or makes him blind? Is it not I, the Lord? Now go; I will help you speak and teach you what to say.'

"But I said, 'O Lord, please send someone else to do it.'

"Then the Lord's anger burned against me. He said, 'What about your brother, Aaron? He speaks well. He is already on his way to meet you, and his heart will be glad when he sees you. You shall speak to him and put words in his mouth; I will help both of you speak and will teach you what to do. He will be a faithful spokesman for you.'

"No sooner had I stepped off the mountain than I encountered Aaron. What a joy to see him again! He advised me that the Lord had directed him to be my spokesman.

"I went back to Jethro, my father-in-law, and said to him, 'Let me go back to my own people in Egypt.' Jethro said, 'Go, and I wish you well.' So I took my wife and my sons, put them on a donkey, and started back to Egypt. I took the rod of God in my hand.

"You have seen what has happened since I returned from the Mountain of God," said Moses with a sweep of his arm. "Have any of God's words fallen to the ground? Not one. This is not my doing; it is His. Is it not clear, Hoshea, that I have been called to service?"

"Oh, yes," replied Hoshea, "you have been called."

Called by a New Name

"Now, tell me about yourself, Hoshea," asked Moses, glancing at Aaron, Nun and Elishama. "In what manner has God gifted you?"

"Let's see," said Hoshea. "I love to run..."

"He's the fleetest of foot in all of Goshen," said Nun proudly.

"He can run all day," said Elishama.

"I can memorize anything," said Hoshea. "I know the story of Job word for word, and the genealogies and oral histories of my people, just as my father and grandfather learned them and taught them to me."

"He has the gift of recalling messages and conversations exactly as they are spoken," said Deborah, adding her support. Nun could see that his wife had a hunch where this was leading.

"I also read and write hieroglyphics and cuneiform, and I know how to compose text in our Hebrew language," continued Hoshea.

"Excellent. These abilities will prove invaluable," said Moses with a knowing smile. "How do you like to spend your time?"

"I like being with my friends," answered Hoshea.

"He's a natural leader," said Elishama.

"He's respected by everyone in Goshen," said Nun. "He's known as trustworthy, hard-working, polite." Hoshea covered his ears and shook his head. He was unaccustomed to this much tribute.

"Let him speak for himself," said Moses, raising a hand. "What is your military training?"

"I have trained in the militia since I was thirteen," said Hoshea. "And I have been well-taught with sword and spear."

"He's first in his troop," said Nun.

"He's truly outstanding in every way," added Elishama.

Hoshea turned red, embarrassed at all the praise. He could feel the eyes of Moses and Aaron examining him.

Seeing his difficulty, everyone quieted down. Moses gestured to Elishama, who said, "Hoshea, our guests came for more than just dinner."

"So we have gathered," interjected Deborah, her voice revealing concern.

Hoshea felt his heart start to thump in his chest. His premonition that something was up was being confirmed. Moses arose from the table. "Hoshea," he said with a smile, "You have found favor with God."

For a moment, Hoshea was relieved, then he became puzzled as to what that meant. Moses' next statement caught him completely unprepared.

"Young man, God has instructed me to call you to serve as my aide."

Hoshea could hardly believe his ears. He looked past Moses at Aaron. Aaron tilted his head toward Hoshea, peering at him wide-eyed. Turning to Nun and Elishama, Hoshea found them grinning in anticipation.

"Father, may I?" he asked.

"I believe it is God's will, my son," said Nun.

Hoshea looked to his grandfather. "You have my blessing," said Elishama.

Deborah nodded her approval. Hoshea was too excited to note a certain sadness in her. She knew this was a turning point in his life.

"But the final decision is yours," said Nun.

Hoshea looked back at Moses. "Yes. Yes! It is an honor beyond compare."

"It is a calling," said Moses solemnly. "Now listen to me, Hoshea. Serving the Lord is not anything a person rushes into. We in leadership are charged with matters affecting the fate of the entire Hebrew nation. The responsibility is greater than you can imagine, and it does not come without travail. But the most fulfilling thing one can do in life is to answer God's call. Do you still wish to serve God at my side?"

Hoshea grew serious, recognizing the weight of this decision. He knew that it would alter the entire outcome of his life, but he could think of no better way to spend his days than as God's servant.

"I will serve the Lord," said Hoshea.

Moses placed his hands on Hoshea's head. Aaron, Nun and Elishama gathered around and laid their hands upon the young man. "And now we do honor the will of our great God, commissioning you to His service." He paused. Hoshea realized that God was speaking to Moses. Finally, the prophet opened his eyes. "In our language, your name, Hoshea, means Salvation. You are no longer Hoshea. Henceforth you will be called Joshua."

Everyone stepped back and smiled. Deborah was clearly filled with emotion. The newly renamed Joshua lifted his head. He knew from the histories of his people, especially those of Avraham and Ya'akov, that a new name ordained by God portended great things. The word *Joshua* meant, "The Lord is Salvation." He could not help but wonder what God intended for him by this.

"Well that's settled," said Aaron.

Unexpectedly, a knock came at the door. Nun answered it. Young Caleb and a black-skinned stranger stood outside. "Please excuse our intrusion," said Caleb. "Pharaoh's servant has a message for Moses."

Nun did not know what to do. He looked to Moses for direction.

"The man is not an enemy," said Moses. "Let us invite him in."

Everyone was confounded by Moses' willingness to receive an Egyptian into a Hebrew home, but Nun trusted Moses. He ushered Caleb and the dark Egyptian within. The stranger was attired in royal crimson, indicating he was a person of importance. However, he bore the customary slave's large earring (though his was of gold, for he belonged to the king).

He was powerfully built, and so tall he stooped to enter the room; nor could he stand fully upright inside. His skin glowed like polished ebony. Despite his sizeable, intimidating appearance, one could sense gentleness within the man. He was not one of Pharaoh's bullies. Moses and Aaron seemed pleased to see him. Even more surprising, the servant waited for permission to speak, a sign of high regard for Moses.

"Tukoh, what brings you here this time?" said Moses with a laugh.

"Ah, Lord Moses, I think you can guess," replied Tukoh in the deepest voice that Joshua had ever heard.

"How goes it in Egypt?" Aaron asked.

"Sheer terror struck Egypt when the sun, moon, and stars stopped shining," said Tukoh. "She is filled with utter darkness and gloom. We cannot see our own families standing in the same room with us. As far as I'm concerned, it is a foretaste of the dreaded place of the dead."

Moses tilted his head slightly as he inquired, "The night is a bit too long for your lord?"

"I am sure it is so," said Tukoh. "You have been summoned to Pharaoh's presence once more."

"Here we go again," said Aaron. "Maybe he will let us go this time."

"You would hope," said Moses.

"That would be the miracle of all miracles," said Elishama.

"Pharaoh is unstable as the great sea," said Moses. "We must go and find out what his pleasure is at the moment. But I know in my bones that God is not through with him yet."

Moses turned to his new assistant. "Joshua, it seems your service begins at once. We go to Zoan in the morning."

Joshua was noticeably confused.

Moses caught the puzzlement on the face of his newly appointed apprentice. He was stunned at Moses' boldness. To speak in front of a servant of the Pharaoh and to even delay responding to Pharaoh's command was unprecedented. Noting his aide's mystification, Moses explained, "We go when the Lord leads us to, and not a moment sooner." And to the visitor he added. "Thank you, Tukoh."

"I take my leave. I will await your arrival at the launch," said Tukoh. He backed out of the doorway as a sign of respect.

After he was gone, Moses said, "Tukoh can be trusted. He has been present whenever we have addressed Pharaoh. He knows firsthand that we speak the truth."

Nun said, "We will look forward to your return with eagerness."

"Be careful," said Deborah.

"The Lord watches over us," responded Moses. "He will not allow any harm to come upon us. Be of good cheer."

Aaron Remembers

At dawn the next day, Moses and Aaron came calling for Joshua, who was just beginning to get used to his new name. Deborah had packed a lunch of figs and freshly baked bread for the three of them to enjoy along their journey.

Joshua was filled with anticipation. There was so much he wanted to know.

Moses had not said, but Joshua suspected, that they would enter the royal palace together. Such a visit would be fraught with danger, but Joshua understood that they were under divine protection. He felt safe with these two godly men.

Aaron walked with the rod that he shared with Moses. They were but a few yards down the road when Aaron began to talk. He chose his statements carefully, using them to expertly craft his meaning. Joshua knew he would remember every word and nuance.

"The land has been blighted with repeated waves of destruction. Egypt's culture has been up-ended." Moses' orator gestured toward the ominous darkness ahead, "The nation is now in total turmoil."

Joshua thought to himself, "His voice is so penetrating and powerful that each remark and phrase he speaks is indelibly marked on my mind."

"Moses has told you how the Lord called him to service on the mountain and sent him to Egypt. We met that day at the foot of the Mountain of God. As soon as we and the rest of Moses' family returned to Goshen, we went before the elders of Israel."

"As God directed, I served as Moses' spokesman, telling the council exactly what the Lord had told him. There were those who were highly skeptical, especially those fear-mongers Dathan, Korah and Abiram." Joshua was familiar with these rebels.

"You should have heard their slanders," groaned Aaron. "'He'll get us all killed,' warned Korah. 'How do we know he's heard from God?' was Dathan's objection. 'We're hardly a match for the armies of Canaan,' Abiram complained.

"Moses barely took note of their protests. He cast his rod before the council and it turned into a snake, which he then picked up by its tail. Right before their eyes the serpent turned back into a rod. Next he put his hand into his cloak and when he withdrew it, it was leprous. I am sure Nun and Elishama have told you how the elders leapt back in fright. When Moses repeated the motion, his hand was healed!"

Joshua remembered the excitement this demonstration of supernatural power had stirred up throughout Goshen the day Moses first returned.

"These signs convinced the council elders that Moses was truly God's elect to lead their nation out of bondage," Aaron continued. "We all humbled ourselves and bowed down before God and worshipped the Almighty.

"The next day, Moses and I went to Pharaoh's palace in Zoan. We were in danger for our lives, to be sure. Nonetheless we told him, the Lord God of Israel says, 'Let My people go into the wilderness that they may hold a feast unto Me.'

"Pharaoh's face revealed his disdain," said Aaron. "He brayed, 'How dare you challenge my authority! You Hebrews are my slaves, my property. I have no regard for any god but those of Egypt. Who is the Lord that I should obey his voice and let Israel leave? I don't know the Lord of whom you speak. I will not let Israel go.'

"Of course, we told Pharaoh, 'We have to obey our God and make sacrifices to Him, lest we be struck with pestilence or violence.'

"But the king of Egypt accused us, saying, 'You just want to keep the people from their work." He commanded us, 'Go, leave my presence.'

"You know what happened next."

"I sure do," said Joshua. "Pharaoh made us work harder. We had to make bricks without straw. Then Pharaoh summoned our Hebrew foremen and placed the blame on Moses, calling God's words vain and meaningless."

"Pharaoh was spiteful," said Aaron. "He declared, 'Slaves who have enough time to plan a festival in the desert must be lazy.'

"Imagine saying that, after we have built cities, fortresses and pyramids for him. So our taskmasters drove us to work harder and our foremen were beaten. The people cried unto Pharaoh for mercy. Pharaoh told them, 'You have Moses and Aaron to thank for this.'"

"When that happened, I had to plead with God," offered Moses. "I didn't understand what He was doing. Then He commanded me to speak to the people." The prophet eyed Joshua, "Do you recall what I said to the congregation that day?"

"Yes," said Joshua, applying his gift of memory. "You quoted the words of God. 'I AM the Lord. I appeared unto Avraham, Yitzchak, and Ya'akov and revealed Myself to be God Almighty. I established a covenant with them, to give them the land of Canaan where they were once pilgrims themselves. I have heard the grieving of the Children of Israel whom the Egyptians have enslaved, and I have remembered My covenant. Tell them I AM God and I will bring you out from under the bondage of the Egyptians and will redeem you with great judgments. I will be your God and you will be My people, and you will recognize that I AM the One bringing you out of bondage.'"

Moses smiled in appreciation of Joshua's well-developed gift of recall.

"God also impressed upon Moses that he must threaten Pharaoh with plagues," said Aaron. "God wanted Pharaoh to be warned in advance of the calamities to come."

"God told me again that Pharaoh would not listen," Moses added.

"We went back before Pharaoh," said Aaron. "As revealed before Israel's elders, Moses had me cast his rod as a sign before Pharaoh. Again it became a serpent.

"Pharaoh was incensed. 'That's nothing but a cheap trick. Moses, you and I were schooled together in the learning of the Egyptians.' Pharaoh pointed at his crown, 'You see the snake over my brow? It represents the authority of Amon-Ra. You're insulting me and my god.'

"Then Pharaoh called out, 'Bring forth Jannes and Jambres.' His two most prominent magician-priests came immediately. What a sham they put on. Those charlatans also turned a rod into a snake and then gave credit to their gods.

"'Pharaoh sneered, 'See. I am not impressed.' His heart was hardened."

"But this was what God wanted," said Moses. "It set His plan in motion."

"Now Joshua, you know that the Nile River with its annual floods brings fertility to this land," said Aaron. "The Egyptians worship it like a god. So the God of Israel told Moses to stretch out his rod over the water while meeting with Pharaoh. In an instant, all the water in Egypt turned to blood. The river became a gushing crimson current that horrified the people. Even the water stored in buckets of wood and pitchers of stone turned to blood. There was no water to drink or use. All the fish died. Everyone remembers the vile stench that lasted for weeks."

"Who can forget? That was appalling," said Joshua.

"Egypt was no longer a fragrant paradise," said Moses. "But more importantly, it made the river an affliction rather than a blessing. God knows how to make His point."

"Indeed He does," said Aaron. "We went before Pharaoh again. Moses told him, 'The Lord says you must let my people go that they might serve Me. If you refuse, I will smite your land with frogs.'

"Moses instructed me to call out frogs from the water," Aaron recalled. "I didn't know what to expect. But in no time at all, frogs carpeted the land. You saw them. Every nook was squirming with them. They invaded the Egyptian's homes, even their beds, their ovens, and their kneading troughs. No place was unsoiled.

"Then Pharaoh's magicians also called forth frogs. That impressed him, but was he happy with the result? I should say not. Now there were even more uncountable multitudes of croaking creatures. He wanted it to stop, but Pharaoh's magicians couldn't make it end. So he blamed us for the whole mess.

"However, as a sign to Pharaoh, God permitted the king to choose the hour this plague would cease. He told Moses the time. The next day, at the appointed hour, the frogs died. They raked them into large heaps that dotted the land. Before long, the stink was worse than that of the fish."

Moses added, "The Egyptians have always worshipped frogs. The goddess Heqt, the one who assists women in childbirth, is represented as a frog."

"And now they hate them," concluded Joshua.

Aaron asked Joshua, "When Pharaoh saw that it was over, what do you suppose he did?"

"He hardened his heart," answered Joshua. "He should have given in right then."

"That's right," said Aaron. "But Pharaoh is not one to relent. So the Lord decided to send a plague of tiny insects down upon the delta. Moses ordered me to strike my rod upon the dust of the land. When I did, the dust changed into lice and gnats. They covered man and beast alike. No part of the land was safe."

"I know," said Joshua, itching at the very memory. "The bugs even infested our homes in Goshen."

"For the first time," said Moses with a smile, "Pharaoh's sorcerers could not match a miracle despite all their incantations. Even the magician Jambres had to admit, 'This plague is the finger of God.'"

Aaron continued, "So much for the Egyptians' worship of insects, which symbolize rebirth, regeneration and transformation. Nevertheless, Pharaoh remained stubborn. He still would not let us go.

"Then came the fourth plague," said Aaron. "To further display His power, God sent forth more insects — dense hordes of flies that swarmed into Pharaoh's palace, the houses of his officials, and throughout the land, tormenting everybody and every beast. This plague was unique because, as Moses foretold to Pharaoh, 'God will differentiate between Egyptians and Hebrews.' True to His word, this plague did not affect our homes in Goshen. But all the rest of Egypt was assailed."

"They soon detested their death-god of the flies," Joshua laughed.

"Pharaoh then tried to bargain with us," Aaron confided. "The king of Egypt said, 'I will permit you to worship the Lord by making sacrifices at your homes in Goshen.' But Moses told him, 'This is not acceptable to God. Moreover, our sacrifices would be abhorrent to the Egyptians and they would stone us. We cannot settle for anything less than our release to the wilderness. We have been commanded to separate ourselves from your people and from your culture to worship our God.'

"Pharaoh was obviously quite irked that the Israelites did not recognize Egypt as superior in all things. However, having had quite enough of the flies and the other plagues, he said, 'Against my better judgment, you may go. And if indeed you have favor with a god, then as my subjects, you must pray for me.'

"So Moses replied, 'Very well, I will pray to the Only God that the flies will leave you and your officials and your people alone. But be careful that you are not acting untruly again and go back on your word.' Pharaoh said nothing in reply, but he stiffened with resentment. Moses knew what that meant. Nevertheless, he asked God to call off the flies. Graciously, the Lord did so. By nightfall, there remained not one. What do you suppose Pharaoh did this time?"

"He hardened his heart," said Joshua. "Such pride."

"Exactly," said Aaron. "So Moses and I approached the ruler again. Moses demanded of Pharaoh, 'Do you not understand yet? Let my people go!' He described the coming plague in detail, how Israel would be immune from it. He even gave Pharaoh a day to consider the risk he faced. You would think that Pharaoh had learned his lesson. No, he just sat there in stony silence. He wouldn't even talk to us.

"You know that the people of this land worship Hathor, the mother goddess of Egypt? You have seen how she is portrayed as a cow? They also bend their knee to Khnum, the ram-god. Well, the fifth plague was aimed at their livestock, their cattle, horses, donkeys, camels, and goats. As everyone knows, many poor beasts died in agony. This time the hand of God alone accomplished it; He did not order me to raise His rod of authority to signify the judgment.

"Once again God distinguished between Egyptians and us. Our cattle were not attacked. Pharaoh sent men to investigate this. I'm sure he was as astounded as his examiners that not even one of our animals had died. Still he would not let us go.

"God followed that curse with the sixth anathema. Even before Pharaoh called us back into his court, God had told Moses what to do. The Lord directed us to gather ashes from a furnace. The Egyptians thought we had lost our minds, digging around in the soot. But they found out.

"In the very presence of Pharaoh, Moses threw the ashes into the air. As the dust dispersed, it spread over the land and rained down like fire upon every living creature. Festering and oozing boils broke out on men and animals alike. Pharaoh's henchmen, including his mighty magicians, were soon unable to stand due to their own agonizing sores. Egypt's remaining beasts took sick and were covered with ugliness. They became even more unworthy of worship.

"The Egyptians were forced to realize that their sacred cow-god could not save them. But again, by the grace of God, none of us or our own animals were touched."

"Once more, the Lord hardened Pharaoh's heart and he still would not listen to me or Moses, just as the Lord had foretold. My brother warned him, 'There is none like God in all the earth,' and that God was angry."

"Moses told Pharaoh and his officials, "God says, I'm giving you notice. Get ready for the greatest storm Egypt has ever experienced. Any man or beast that is out-of-doors will perish. If you have any sense, you will shelter your livestock and yourselves.'"

"Why didn't they obey?" asked Joshua.

"Some of them did. But the most powerful man on earth is also the most stubborn man on earth," said Moses. "There was no official warning or recognition of what was to come."

"Hail fell like rocks," said Aaron. "Lightning bolts crisscrossed the sky."

"I saw the storm clouds from the distance in Goshen," remarked Joshua. "I could hear the thunder and I saw the heavens ignite with fire. It was terrifying."

Aaron shouted dramatically, "In a land where rain seldom falls, God sent a torrential downpour and huge chunks of hail, unparalleled in all history, crashing down upon Egypt's crops! It shattered every tree and mashed every plant — all the rye, flax, cotton, and barley that were ready for harvest were all ruined. And of course, many of the remaining animals and scores of people died also."

"Remember that the Egyptians revere Set, god of protection, who is supposed to guard their crops," said Moses. "Some protector he turned out to be. The hail crushed all trust in their god, Set—along with their crops."

"And with uncanny precision. Our lands in Goshen were left untouched," said Joshua. "A mighty miracle indeed."

"Pharaoh asked Moses to make the Lord stop it. Pharaoh even admitted, 'I have made a mistake. Your God is righteous, and we have underestimated Him. You can go.'

"But Moses told him, 'I know you do not yet respect the Lord.' Moses went outside the city and called upon the Lord. Soon Pharaoh and his officials saw that the catastrophic storm had stopped. The king didn't even wait until we were out of sight. He hardened his heart again and sent word that he would not let us go."

"How could Pharaoh let this happen?" asked Joshua. "Egypt was being destroyed."

"We wondered about that ourselves," said Aaron. "We went back to the palace. The Lord had Moses lecture Pharaoh, 'Even though you believe you are an all-powerful master, you are actually powerless before God. God could take your life or the life of your servants at any time. He could wipe you off the face of the earth. But He has a higher motive.'

"Pharaoh hated every word. Moses told him, 'God said for this purpose I have raised you up, that I may show you My power, and that My name may be declared in all the world. It is the God of Israel, not your gods, that has placed you in authority over Egypt.' You should have seen the look on his face!

"Then Moses warned of the next plague, but of course Pharaoh and his officials turned a deaf ear. And you know what happened. Moses stretched his rod out over the land. An east wind blew all day and night.

"The next day the sky blackened with swirling hordes of locusts. Descending upon the earth like advancing battalions in a well-disciplined army, they marched across Egypt. They crawled through pastures, hopped through farms, homes and palaces alike. Nothing could stop them. The ravenous grasshoppers devoured every ripening piece of fruit that had escaped the hail, the new shoots of wheat and spelt, every last living plant.

"This last judgment subjugated Osiris, the god of agriculture. By this time Pharaoh's officials were pleading with him, crying, 'Do you not know that Egypt is destroyed? We beg you, let the slaves go!' but he would have none of it.

"Well, of course Pharaoh called us before him. He conceded, 'I have sinned again.' But he quickly reasserted his posture of dictator, 'I order you to forgive me again and tell your god to take this plague away! Then I will let your people go!'

"Even though we knew that Pharaoh would not keep his word, Moses prayed, and God caused a west wind to carry every locust out over the Red Sea. With a single sweep of His hand, the Lord cleared the land of the insatiable insects. And can you believe that one more time Pharaoh turned cold and refused to let us go? Moreover, he accused us, 'Clearly you are bent on evil,' and had Moses and me driven from his presence.

"Looking back, can you see what God was doing? The plagues were specifically fashioned to confront all the main deities in Egyptian culture."

"No wonder the Egyptians are so afraid!" exclaimed Joshua.

You Will See My Face No More

By now the travelers had reached the edge of Goshen, where the boundary was marked by the Nile River. At the royal landing they met Tukoh. He was waiting to ferry them across in a large boat made of bound reeds.

While making the crossing, they ate the meal that Deborah had packed for them. Darkness concealed the land before them. Joshua could see for several miles to the east, but to the west an opaque tar-like cloud, through which no light could penetrate, obscured the land.

Chewing on a fig, Aaron said, "This ninth plague makes a statement designed for Pharaoh to take personally. He claims to be descended from the sun god, Amon-Ra. Neither he nor Amon-Ra can do anything about this present darkness. The ninth plague also shuts the eyes of the falcon Horus, the sky-god whose left eye is the moon and whose right eye is the sun.

"Their massive structures, built upon our own generations of sweat and blood, are but puny attempts to get closer to the great objects hanging in the sky, whose positions in the heavens supposedly give them authority over peoples' destinies. But now Egypt's very own destiny hangs in the balance. All external signs of light have been blotted out of sight. They have been hidden by He who made the heavens."

The boat glided into the darkness at the water's edge. They entered the outer limits of Egypt's untimely night and prepared to disembark. Joshua waited while Moses and Aaron bravely stepped forward out of the boat, then he followed. Glancing at Tukoh, Joshua wondered what impact Aaron's words had made upon their escort.

Entering the blackness was like stepping through a dense curtain into what Joshua imagined to be Hades itself. It was as if the darkness absorbed light. They could barely make their way. It was an unnatural, thick murk that, when inhaled, made one feel as if he was on the verge of smothering. He could sense it cling to his skin. The deep pall even muffled their footsteps.

Suddenly, the gloom shrank back from them to a distance of a few paces. Tukoh cried out in awe. All were astonished. God had placed them inside a pocket of light that forced the noxious fog to recede and enabled them to walk freely. Assuredly, this grace was not enjoyed by anyone else in this paralyzed land. Even the air they breathed was purged of oppression.

Their arrival at the palace was quiet, very quiet. Pharaoh's sentries, although stationed at their posts, were spooked at the very sight of anyone, for they could barely make out their own torches. The radiant cloud startled them. Tukoh announced to the ashen soldiers that Pharaoh had summoned them. The guards tucked in behind the visitors, following the safe glow of Moses and his party as they proceeded into Pharaoh's private chambers.

Surrounded by this cocoon of light, they approached the potentate. His face loomed out of the darkness, a mask of bitterness distorted by anger. The ruler was also shocked by their sudden appearance.

After a lifetime of picturing the mighty monarch reigning in all his intimidating mastery, Joshua was in for a surprise. Upon this first sighting, he observed that the King of Egypt was unnerved.

No one said anything for several moments. Finally, Aaron inquired, "You sent for us?"

Glaring at Moses, Pharaoh venomously spat out the words, "Go! Serve your God! You can take your families. But your livestock remains." A crooked smile betrayed a hidden agenda.

What arrogance, thought Joshua. Most of Egypt's animals have been ruined; now he wants us to leave our herds behind for them to appropriate.

Moses saw it another way. "Then we would have nothing to sacrifice to our God. Our herds must go with us. We will not leave a single hoof behind."

"No!" shouted Pharaoh, enraged. "Then you shall not leave at all!"

"Very well," said Moses calmly. "The Lord God of Israel has already told me what is to happen next. He has said to me, 'I will bring yet one more plague upon Pharaoh and upon Egypt. After that, Pharaoh will let you go.'

"Furthermore, the God of Israel has declared, 'At midnight a fortnight from now, I the Lord will go into the midst of Egypt. And all the first-born of the land of Egypt shall die, from the first-born of Pharaoh sitting upon his throne to the first-born of the woman working in the mill. Not only that, but the first-born of all the livestock will die.'"

Pharaoh tensed at the words, but Moses was not fazed.

"'There will be a great cry throughout the land of Egypt such as there has never been or ever will be. But the Children of Israel and their animals will not be harmed—that you might understand that the Lord God views the nations of Egypt and Israel differently.'"

Pharaoh said nothing. He simply sat there and glowered at them. Joshua was stymied at the news—it was beyond comprehension.

"Your own people, your own officials, will bow down to me," continued Moses softly. "They will beg me and my people to go. And then we shall leave Egypt. God also said that you, Supreme Pharaoh, would not listen to Him, so His wonders would be manifested in your kingdom."

Pharaoh could take no more. "Don't threaten me. I will not let you go. Get out of my sight!" he shouted. "I don't ever want to see your face. Don't come to me again or I will have you killed!"

"Very well, Great Pharaoh," said Moses defiantly. "Unless you ask me to come, you will see my face no more."

"I will not ask you here again!" screeched the tyrant. Pharaoh's servants were frightened. They had never seen the king distraught.

Moses and his party withdrew quickly. Joshua's last glimpse of Pharaoh's face was that of a hateful mask disappearing into opaque nothingness. Still angry with Pharaoh, Moses hastily departed the palace. Aaron and Joshua were at his heels.

On the way back, still protected by God from the blight, Moses told Aaron and Joshua, "The plague of darkness will lift now."

He fixed his eyes on Joshua. "We must go and prepare our people for the trial that is to come. Joshua, I have an assignment for you. As soon as we have crossed the river, you will run ahead. Be swift. Spread the word among the elders that the council meets at dusk. But don't repeat to anyone the words I spoke to Pharaoh. Oh, and tell your grandfather Elishama to put on his robe of authority."

Joshua was awed. The Lord was demonstrating absolute mastery over every event on earth, and using Moses and Aaron to bring it forth, right before his very eyes!

The Gathering of Elders

Joshua was contemplating God's miracles. The sky, which had been black over the empire for the past three days, had turned radiant and beautiful. The sun was going down when Joshua, Nun, and Elishama arrived at the lodge of meeting. The area surrounding it was packed with exhilarated people plus the donkeys and camels of those leaders who had come from Goshen's more distant villages.

Someone shouted, "Here come Moses and Aaron!" The crowd surged toward their leaders in anticipation of some great announcement. As the prophet and his brother arrived on foot to a hero's welcome, the masses parted into two groups.

A voice in the throng declared, "Moses! May the God of heaven and earth bless you and Aaron!" Many echoed in support:

A herdsman yelled, "Please rescue us from this loathsome land!"

God's chosen servant acknowledged each remark with a nod of his head.

Then the came the complaints:

"How long, Moses? How long?"

"Some of the plagues struck us too, you know!"

Moses closed his eyes and furrowed his brow. His sorrow was evident, but still he spoke not a word.

Joshua could see that Moses intended to say nothing until he had conferred with the leaders.

Emotions ran high. Some wept tears of joy, others, tears of sorrow.

"Is our ordeal at an end?" asked a merchant.

"After four hundred and thirty years, will we be free?" inquired an aged weaver.

Joshua wondered to himself, "Are the hopes and dreams of our nation about to be realized?"

While they made their way to the entrance of the lodge, hands stretched toward Moses and Aaron as if begging for the answers. Many of those who were celebrating the coming of Moses tossed bright ribbons in the air. Others presented honey cakes in gratitude. Moses slowly raised his palms, graciously refusing the treats.

When Aaron saw his brother turn down the delicious cakes, he made a comic face and licked his lips. He was hungry. Joshua couldn't help but laugh.

The setting sun threw luxurious beams of golden light over the shoulders of those gathered. By Hebrew standards, sundown marked the start of each Israelite day.

Joshua considered the irony—just as day was ending in Egypt, a new day was beginning for Israel.

Moses and Aaron entered the lodge, followed by an elder and a second in command from each tribe. Inside the tent made of tightly knit hangings, a fire burned brightly. Elishama and Nun represented the tribe of Ephraim. Jephunneh and Caleb, whom Joshua had seen at the bazaar earlier that day, were there on behalf of Judah. As Moses' newly appointed assistant, Joshua was also welcomed within.

On signal, the elders quieted down. Elishama brought the meeting to order and called upon Caleb to take the roll.

Moses beckoned Joshua to come close. He whispered in his ear. "This meeting is for leadership alone. I don't want anyone outside to listen in." Joshua immediately understood. His assignment was to watch the entryway. He went to his post at once, keeping an eye out for eavesdroppers.

The crowd was already dispersing. They had realized that there was nothing left for them to see or hear. It wasn't long before the only ones remaining outside were teenage boys watching over sleepy donkeys and camels. Joshua said hello to Iru, Caleb's son, who was tending the beasts. Many camels had assumed a kneeling posture to rest from their labors. Joshua observed Iru share a honey cake with one of the youngest camels and affectionately rub the creature's ears.

A warm gust of desert wind whipped past Joshua's face. Tent flaps fluttered in the breeze. Beyond the city a restless jackal yapped. In unison, the camels swiveled their heads toward the sound. The thinnest sliver of a new moon was barely peeking over the swells of sweeping desert sand dunes. Across the wadi, a chorus of jackals answered, their howls piercing the night air.

Joshua's keen eye scanned the area surrounding the tent of meeting. Seeing that all was well, he stepped back and stationed himself by the woven folds covering the entry. Here, he could watch over the perimeter, while still taking in the speeches of the elders. At key moments, he could pull back the cloth to get a firsthand view of the proceedings.

The elders were seated. Moses arose. A hush fell. All eyes fastened on the prophet.

Raising his hands, he prayed, "Lord, you have been our hiding place throughout all generations. Before the mountains were born, or even before you brought forth the earth, from everlasting to everlasting you are God."

There was a wave of "Amens."

Moses paused, then spoke softly, "When I was in the desert, the Lord showed me this very day."

At this prophetic utterance, a shudder ran through Joshua. His flesh was goose bumps from head to toe.

From his vantage point, he could see the faces of the council members illuminated by the yellow-white glow of smoldering embers and flickering flames. The men hung on Moses' every word.

Moses raised his rod. "Many have doubted. But now all Egypt is astounded by the awesome power of God's hand! I have told you how astonished I was when I stood at the bush that burned but was not consumed. I stood on holy ground. I was instructed in what I must do. I was given the rod of authority.

"God has used this miraculous piece of almond wood to demonstrate His absolute dominion to Pharaoh. He sent the plagues upon Egypt. We witnessed firsthand the incredible signs that God has given us. He has confirmed His intention to fulfill His covenant by doing the impossible—conquering Pharaoh himself! Egypt lies broken at our feet because of the incontestable power of our Mighty God!

"I am not a man worthy of God's favor," said Moses. "Yet, He selected me to work His wonders that the destiny of Israel might be fulfilled. You also have been chosen to take part in this sovereign move of God—an act so great that it will be spoken of by every generation to come!

"Who is this God we serve? I have told you, He is the One who says 'I AM THAT I AM!'" The words of the prophet washed over the men. Everyone was awestruck at this profound revelation of the eternal nature of the God of Israel.

Joshua joined the chorus of "Amens."

"The olive tree of Israel must be replanted and fed by fresh water in the sweet soil of our homeland!" exclaimed Moses.

What did this mean? The eyes of the elders divulged their searching to pick up every connotation of Moses' fervent message.

"Now we have come to a momentous turning point. Tomorrow we must begin preparations for a great sojourn. This is the journey the Lord has promised us. At the time of the next full moon we leave Egypt, never to return!"

There was a great stir in the room accompanied by several muffled shouts of surprise. Joshua was ecstatic. The nation of slaves was about to be freed. All had dreamed of leaving Egypt, now it was coming to pass. The elders broke into cheers. Suddenly they were on their feet, thanking God, dancing, clapping their hands, slapping each other on the back.

When the demonstration abated, Moses pressed on. "When we leave, we must move quickly. We will travel light. Any possessions that cannot be carried will be left behind. The hour has come when God will lead us to the Promised Land — a land flowing with milk and honey."

Somewhere within Joshua's youthful soul, a new vision was being born. For the first time in his life, there was a hope for the future welling up within him.

"The Lord instructed me while I was standing before the burning bush that we will not go out empty-handed. We are to plunder the Egyptians."

A nervous buzz ensued. When things quieted again, Moses proclaimed, "God has made our captors inclined to give us whatever we ask."

A sprinkling of laughter followed this last statement. "During the next ten days, every woman of Israel is to ask the women of Egypt for articles of silver and gold and fine clothing that you and your children may wear."

The elders gasped in wonder.

"Wherever our women have worked or served the Egyptians, they are to seek treasure and receive it," said Moses. "The men of Egypt will no doubt insist upon it." There was more laughter.

"You men of Israel will help our women bring the treasure home. We will leave Egypt with it in hand. See that our entire nation is notified of this task by morning. I have asked my sister Miriam to direct this work."

Moses gave them a few minutes to let everything sink in and discuss it among themselves. The council was delighted with the news. Not only were they leaving Egypt, they were taking the land's wealth with them.

Joshua noticed Dathan, of the tribe of Re'uven, stroking his beard. He could see the greed written across his face. He did not like the cut of this man. Dathan was a malcontent and needed to be watched carefully. Aaron also took note.

People Get Ready

Moses called them back to attention, "The Lord has ordained that henceforth this month shall be the first month of our year. On the tenth day of this month, every adult man of Israel shall select a lamb from his flock for a special offering. If your household is small, you may share a lamb with your neighbor. You must pick a lamb without blemish, a male yearling. You will keep your lamb in your homes, like a member of the family, until the fourteenth day of the month."

This statement was met with surprise and no small degree of curiosity. Animals and humans lived side-by-side in the community of Goshen, but there were limits. Livestock was never kept inside a house.

Moses continued, "Just before sunset of the fourteenth day, sacrifice your lamb. Take the life of your offering in the traditional manner. Drain the blood from it. Then dip a stalk of hyssop in the blood and strike it boldly on the two side posts and on the lintel of the doorway to your house."

There was a flurry of whispers. No one present knew what to make of this strange sacrifice and the unusual requirement of marking blood three times on their doorways.

Aaron explained on behalf of Moses, "You will roast the lamb whole, and eat it at home that night. You must not boil the lamb. You must roast it with fire, and eat it with unleavened bread and with bitter herbs. Don't keep any of it for the next day. Burn up every bit that you don't consume.

"You shall eat it with a belt on your waist, sandals on your feet, and your staff in your hand. Be aware at all times that you will be leaving hastily as soon as you receive my signal."

Moses took over from Aaron. "God has told me His plan. He said, 'I AM the Lord. During the night, I will pass through the land of Egypt and strike dead every first-born male, man or beast!'"

There were gasps throughout the assembly. Joshua saw the consternation on the face of the elders. This next plague would be the most frightening of all!

No one spoke. A log tumbled within the fire circle. The blaze snapped. Sparks danced around tongues of fire licking the air, brightening the room.

"The Lord said, 'I AM God. This is how I will execute My final judgment against all the so-called gods of Egypt,'" declared the prophet.

The assembly was in awe. Moses and Aaron gave them several moments to absorb the weight of this before Aaron continued. "God has told Moses, 'The blood on your doorways will be like a banner, signifying where My people live. When I see the blood, I will pass over you and the plague of death shall not affect your household.'"

Moses emphasized the words "pass over" with a sweeping gesture of his rod. Everyone was stunned. No one dared breathe.

"In the days to come, when your children ask you, what does this all mean, you will answer 'It is the sacrifice of the Lord's Passover, who passed over the houses of the Children of Israel in Egypt, when He punished the Egyptians and delivered us.

"You must eat only unleavened bread for the entire week of the Passover commemoration. You are required to keep this day as an annual feast from this time forth and forever."

The leaders of the tribes were overjoyed. Moses had prophesied the imminent release of the nation of Israel. Led by Elishama, the elders spontaneously bowed down, and then lay prostrate. Even the oldest among them assumed this posture of abject humility. Aaron led their worship. When he finished, he signaled them to rise to their feet. He then called Elishama to address the men.

Elishama spoke with a loud, clear voice. "Men of Israel, never forget these days. Remember them for the sake of your children and the sake of your children's children. Remember the signs God used to reveal his power over all creation. Remember that every prophecy and prediction that the Lord gave Moses has come true. Baruch Ha Shem Adonai! Blessed be the name of the Lord!"

Plundering Egypt

The family sat around the same table at which Moses and Aaron had been served their meal just a few days before. This unusual piece of furniture was a valued and rare possession among the Hebrew slaves. Moses had even remarked on its beauty. They had told him how the sizable and sturdy acacia-wood table had been carefully handcrafted by Elishama and given to Nun and Deborah as a wedding gift.

Deborah and Nun studied the heirloom while he told her of their impending departure from Egypt. "We have been instructed to take with us only what we can carry and nothing more."

Deborah's mind raced. She looked around forlornly at their scant possessions then back to their wedding gift. Seeing his daughter-in-law's plight, Elishama made the selection easier with a simple statement: "The table cannot go with us."

With that, her heart fell. She knew that once again, she was being called upon to sacrifice. She had so few precious things.

Deborah thought if she must give up her beloved furniture, then she had to be prepared to give up anything that would encumber them on the journey. "It is time to decide what to take and what to throw away," she declared.

Deborah got up and walked around the room, gazing briefly at everything of worth while fighting the impulse to be melancholy. Finally, she turned to Nun. "We will need mostly clothing, tenting, and cooking utensils." She added, "We can take the good memories with us and leave the bad ones behind."

Nun was sad that she had been deprived for most of her life, but happy that he had some good news for her.

"There's one more thing," he said. Her face fell, expecting to be disappointed. "Moses tells us that the Lord gave him a special instruction at the burning bush. We are commanded to collect the riches and the best clothing from the women of Egypt and wear them as our own."

Deborah's eyes grew wider. Instead of being pleased, there was a troubled look upon her face.

Nun had not expected this. Then he understood. Even though the prospect of receiving reparations from the Egyptians might be appealing to some, it was not in his wife's nature to take advantage of anybody.

"Are you sure they will relinquish their treasures?" she asked her husband.

"Moses says they will," said Nun.

"Then I will believe that when I am wearing these items of value, I am displaying God's kindness to me."

"You will look beautiful in them," said Nun.

Deborah gently put her hand to his mouth. "Enough already."

Early the next morning, everyone was out the door at first light. Joshua and Elishama dropped Rachel off at Caleb's home. Grandfather and grandson would spend the day with Moses. Deborah and Nun set off to meet with Miriam, Moses' sister, after which they would cross the Nile to appropriate Egyptian wealth. With all the activities to accomplish, the day passed quickly.

Night was falling when Elishama and Joshua picked up Rachel on their way home. The first thing they saw upon entering the house was a considerable pile of gold and silver jewelry along side excellent fabrics heaped on their table. Rachel's eyes grew large. She ran over and began to inspect the bounty. "I've never seen so many pretty things," she bubbled. Picking the articles up, she began to make a costume.

Deborah had dinner almost ready. "How was your day with Moses?"

"It was great," replied Joshua. "I worked as his assistant, helping to draw diagrams upon parchment."

Noticing his sister's antics, he pointed to the mound of precious goods on the table. "But tell us, what happened today in Zoan?"

They looked expectantly at Deborah and Nun to hear of their adventures. Deborah deferred to Nun.

"When we reached the river, we could see only fog, covering the far shore," said Nun softly. "Everything was shrouded in mystery even though the plague of darkness was gone. From our side of the river, nothing seemed out of place.

"It is hard to believe that up until a few months ago, a large fleet of boats took thousands of us daily from Goshen to our places of labor. Now, most of the barges sit idle, their owners dreaming of the day when the slaves might go back to work.

"While our boatman held out his hand for payment, we noticed great scars marring the man's arms and face, no doubt from the plague of boils.

"He asked us sarcastically, 'Going to work, are we?'

"'No,' I told him. 'We have come to receive tribute from your people to take with us when we leave this land.' He gave me a look of complete disbelief.

"The boatman said, 'Pharaoh says you can't leave Egypt.' While he spoke, I observed his son hurrying to unfurl the sail. There were large round scars on the boy's back as well.

"We cast off. The sun was burning off the morning mist as we drew near the far shore. The first thing to assault our senses was a revolting stench, the smell of death. Soon, we could distinguish rotting carcasses of cattle that died at the water's edge in their futile efforts to seek relief from the plague that finally killed them. It was a nightmare.

"The nearer we came, the more we could see: bones and flaps of hide, strings of putrid flesh. We covered our mouths with our wraps to filter the odor of uncleanness. Drawing closer, we noticed that the shore was lined with the spines of millions of fish that had died in the river of blood.

"We were horrified. When we stepped off the launch, there was a peculiar crunching sound beneath the soles of our sandals. I looked down and saw that we were walking on countless tiny bones, the skeletons of decayed frogs.

"Hungry swamp fowl skipped along the brown water looking in vain for any scrap of live food. On the roadside, scavenging birds fought one another for the dehydrated meat of dead domestic beasts. In the distance, once verdant grain fields were barren, even though it was the time of spring harvest. A few pitiful dried up stalks of flax were all that was left after the voracious locusts had devoured every living green thing.

"Mud huts along the way were battered from the great hail storm, some had even been partially knocked down. Only the massive columns of the royal city of Zoan were apparently unharmed."

Joshua interjected, "I had no idea what was all around me when we went to Zoan during the plague of darkness."

"Once inside the city," Nun continued, "it was plain to see that Egypt is in the midst of a depression. The streets are almost empty. The Egyptians are gripped with a profound sorrow. Their marketplace looks like a graveyard. There is a famine. I guess now they know what it is like to experience hunger.

"As you are aware, we went there to call specifically upon the Lady Neftiri, the wife of Sobek the royal surveyor, the woman for whom your mother had toiled for many years. Deborah, why don't you tell what happened?"

Deborah took over the narration. "Well, you know something is wrong when Lady Neftiri has to answer the door herself. You should have seen her face when she saw who had come. She covered her mouth with one hand because of an unsightly new scar on its left corner, spoiling her good looks about which she was famously vain.

"Your Father and I must have stood there for a couple of minutes watching the expressions race across her face before she realized that she was supposed to invite us in.

"Once the mistress discovered common courtesy, we went inside. There was fear in Lady Neftiri's eyes. She could not imagine why we had come. I must tell you, it was a moment I shall never forget when I told her, 'Our God has sent us. We have been commanded to ask of you gold and silver and fine garments.'

"Again, Lady Neftiri went through a multitude of emotions. She left us standing in her foyer and came back a few moments later with her husband. He was pale and nervous.

"'What is it you want?' he asked. I repeated our mission. Neftiri began to object. He turned to her and said sternly, 'If this will cause them to leave Egypt any sooner, we will do it gladly. Give them what they want.'

"Assisted by their oldest son, Get, a handsome young man, they presented us with much of what you see here. Neftiri started to take back that nice golden necklace you see there, but her husband Sobek became angry with her and said, 'Would you risk angering their God? Give it to them.'

"Then he told us, 'In truth, I believe that Pharaoh has needlessly antagonized your God and brought us to this ruin. Many have concluded you deserve to leave with a ransom.'

"And so we left with their things of value. Lady Neftiri was in tears. I told her, 'Thank you for honoring the great God of Israel with these riches.'

"When we came back to the dock, both of us loaded with valuables, the boatman and his son could hardly believe their eyes.

Nun reached for a particularly excellent dress and held it up in front of Deborah. "I think this one will be beautiful on you. I want you to adorn yourself with these golden earrings and the necklace Lady Neftiri so longed to keep. It is your right."

A Lamb Is Chosen

Joshua waited until he and his father were outside the house feeding their small flock of animals to ask him some questions that were troubling him. "If the first-born male of every family in Egypt is directly in the path of the Angel of Death, does that mean my own life is in danger?"

"Yes, it does," said Nun. "I don't think that the Lord would require the blood of a sacrifice to protect our home from the Death Angel if you weren't personally at risk."

Joshua responded, "I had not fully understood the seriousness of this sacrifice."

Nun elaborated. "It is not only a message for Egypt and our nation, to which the first-born heirs are everything, but it is a lesson for you."

"I am humbled that God values me so," said Joshua.

Nun nodded in agreement, impressed with the maturity of his son.

But Joshua had another pressing question. "Why do we have to keep the lamb inside the house for four days?"

Nun laughed. "I suppose we'll find out."

At dawn the next morning, Joshua and Nun stepped outside to choose a yearling lamb. "You know which one, don't you, son?" asked Nun. Joshua was genuinely disappointed. The entire family knew which lamb was the most popular member of their small flock. He was known as "Snowy." His coat gleamed in the sunlight. The little creature seemed pleased to be admired.

Although neither Nun nor any member of his family had ever seen snow, tales of mountains and their frosting of pure white flakes were often told. Joshua and his friends often imagined cold weather during the lengthy, dehydrating hours of labor under the scorching sun. If ever they were to see snow, they believed it would somehow resemble Snowy's coat.

Joshua looked at his father's eyes as he scooped up their lamb. Snowy would be an extraordinarily hard animal to sacrifice. But then, they had been commanded by God to select their best. It had to be Snowy.

As soon as they stepped inside with the lamb, Rachel was on her feet and running to them. "It's Snowy!" she bubbled. Obviously it was not the time to tell her that Snowy would soon be killed.

"Snowy is going to live in the house with us," said Nun. "Would you like to be in charge of him?"

Rachel could hardly believe her ears. This was too good to be true. "May I, Papa? May I please?" Nun nodded consent. Joshua set the lamb down for Rachel to fuss over.

Snowy was only too happy to move into the family's humble shelter. Soon he was thriving on the attention and acting as if he knew how cute he was. His favorite trick was to tug on the hem of Rachel's clothes, causing her to giggle. Inevitably this would lead to a game of chase around the kitchen table. When Rachel ran out of breath, the lamb would come over and lick her ears and face. This would restart the giggles and the chasing again.

That evening, while Rachel and Snowy played, Elishama, Nun, Deborah, and Joshua sat down at the table and discussed the inventory of their belongings. They now had to factor in the plunder and decide what else they would leave behind. Elishama and Nun told Deborah that they had also come to the conclusion that they must leave the cedar chest in which Elishama's robe of authority was kept. Deborah was relieved that the men had made the decision, for she had known it would be too heavy to carry.

When it was time for bed, Rachel snuggled up next to her fluffy friend and prayed, "God, please bless our family. Thank you for Snowy, too. Please watch over us while we sleep tonight."

Joshua listened to his sister pray. She was so young, playful, and innocent, like her lamb. True, there was much for which to be thankful. He was saddened, knowing that soon Snowy would have to die and that Rachel's feelings would be hurt.

In the morning, Rachel was joyful as Snowy bleated for his breakfast. Instead of slowly dragging herself away from her straw-stuffed cushion as usual, Rachel jumped out of bed to feed their lamb. For the first time, Rachel noticed that things were different in the house. "What's going on?" she asked.

Deborah realized that Rachel didn't know what was transpiring. "We're getting ready to leave Egypt for our new home," said Deborah. "Isn't that wonderful?"

Little Rachel became puzzled. She cocked her head to one side and squinted back at her mother. "I thought this was our home."

Her mother did her best to comfort Rachel. "We are going to a better home, and Moses is going to lead us there."

"Where are we going?" asked Rachel.

"God has promised us a land flowing with milk and honey," said Nun.

Not quite satisfied with these answers Rachel asked, "Can I take my doll?"

"Of course dear, you can take your doll," said Deborah.

"Oh," said Rachel. "Can Snowy and I go outside to play with the other lambs now?"

"Of course, precious," said Nun, relieved she had not asked to take Snowy to their new home.

Once she was out of the house, Nun and Deborah looked helplessly at each other. "She's going to be terribly upset," said Deborah. "We're going to have to tell her soon."

"I'm growing attached to the lamb myself," said Nun.

"I know how Rachel will feel," said Deborah.

Nun thought about it. "Let's not rob her of this special time," he said. "If God wants us to have a young lamb in our home, it most certainly must be to learn to love him and to be loved by him. I believe this is a thing to be cherished."

They were mindful that a protective covering of peace had settled over their home. They realized that this same spirit had come to abide in dwelling places across the land.

"You're right," said Deborah. "Laughter has come to Goshen in these last days here. We, too, should play with our lamb; it is a time to enjoy."

Joshua Suffers Silently

For the next three nights, Joshua was at the meeting lodge as the elders reconvened to discuss each day's activities and review plans for the journey ahead.

At last, the day of promise was upon them. This meant that the time had arrived when Hebrew families throughout Egypt must sacrifice their chosen lambs.

Nun's family gathered around the table. Snowy was quiet. He sensed that sadness had invaded the happy home. Nun prayed, "Father of Avraham, Yitzchak, and Ya'akov, we ask for your mercy and for your guidance. Give us courage for the days ahead. Help us to do your will." Rachel sat on her mother's lap, unaware that this meeting was mostly for her sake. Nun turned to his daughter. "Rachel, Snowy has to leave us in a few hours."

Dazed by her father's statement, Rachel asked, "He does? When is he coming back?"

Nun gently responded, "I am afraid he will not be coming back."

"No! I don't want him to go," she cried. "Where is he going?"

Nun spoke slowly, trying to calm her. "It is not so important that we know where he is going as it is for us to know that he must leave."

Rachel furrowed her forehead. She turned her head and looked to her mother, then around the room for help. Deborah lovingly stroked her daughter's hair, "It's all right dear. Everything is going to be fine." Nonetheless, Rachel was becoming disturbed.

Leaning against the kitchen wall, Joshua carefully observed his sister. Snowy rested peacefully at his feet. Joshua's stomach churned with emotion. Despite their age difference, his feelings were identical to his sister's. He wanted to say something to soothe her, but he knew that his sister would not give up their lamb without a struggle. Besides, nothing that he could say was going to change the outcome.

He heard everyone reassure Rachel, but she was old enough to know that this usually meant something unpleasant was about to happen—something beyond her control. He could see she didn't really understand.

Hoping to find a way to avoid losing her pet, Rachel asked, "Who's taking Snowy away from us?"

Everyone was quiet. No one had a ready answer. Then Nun said, "God wants Snowy."

Rachel was now completely distraught. She began to cry. She tried to think of anything she could do. She decided to offer another solution. Hoping aloud, she countered, "Can't we send another lamb in Snowy's place?"

Nun got down on his knees next to her and explained, "It is not that easy, dear. God wants our very best, and we all know that Snowy is our very best lamb."

Rachel was young but unafraid to speak her mind. She was fighting to save her lamb. Instinctively, she knew that Snowy was the very finest lamb she had ever seen, and that she must protect him. She looked squarely at her father. "But I want Snowy more than God does. This isn't fair." Rachel rubbed her bleary eyes. She did not know how to persuade her family to change their minds.

Joshua was overcome with emotion. He knew that he would have behaved much the same way at her age. The family waited patiently for Rachel to come around. It was crucial that she make up her own mind to go along with this decision. The lesson of Passover depended on it.

Seeing that her mother and father were not going to yield, Rachel turned to her grandfather, hoping he would overrule her parents. "I thought God loved us."

Although there was concern about the child's irreverent remark, everyone kept calm, determined to be patient. Elishama joined the conversation. Sitting next to Deborah, he cradled Rachel's chin in his palms and poured out his love. "God loves Snowy too, Rachel. We know it does not seem fair. But God is more important than anything in our lives. Everything we have belongs to Him."

Rachel choked, "Everything? Even Snowy?"

"Yes, even Snowy," said Elishama.

Rachel looked up and saw tears in her mother's eyes. "Mommy, are you sad, too?"

Deborah gently hugged her daughter as their tears mingled. "Yes, I am very sad. Snowy is also my friend. I will always love him." She added, "But we want to give Snowy back to God."

Just then Snowy arose and trotted across the room. He poked his head between Rachel and Deborah and licked away their tears. Deborah lifted the lamb's front legs. Rachel kissed the yearling on his forehead and said softly. "I love you, Snowy."

Joshua quietly slipped out of the room, motioning for his father to follow. Nun met him outside.

In a low voice, Joshua said, "I am deeply troubled by this. I don't understand why God wants us to get so attached to Snowy before we kill him."

Nun thought about it and replied, "Son, you have asked a question I don't know how to answer. We all have the same question."

Joshua still wanted an explanation. "Then I would like to ask Moses myself."

"You have his favor," said Nun. "Go see him. I believe he will tell you all that God wishes you to know."

Joshua ran all the way to Moses' shelter, conscious of the hour, for he wished to meet with Moses well in advance of the convening of the elders that afternoon. He knew that there would be no time to speak to Moses then, because the time to sacrifice the lambs would soon be upon them.

He found Moses outside his shelter playing with a lamb. It occurred to Joshua that Moses had been a shepherd for much of his life, and that he was accustomed to protecting sheep. Moses looked up, surprised to see that Joshua had come early.

"What brings you?" he asked.

"I am struggling with a question."

"I'll answer it if I can," said Moses.

"Everyone is deeply upset. Why does God want us to get so attached to our lamb before we kill him?"

Moses smiled broadly while stroking the lamb in his arms. "I don't understand it fully myself. The Lord did not tell me why."

Joshua was crestfallen. He thought that surely God had given His prophet a reason for this distressing ritual.

"We have to believe He has our best interests in mind and do what He has asked. We'll understand it better in days to come," said Moses. But he could see that Joshua was still not satisfied. He set the lamb down.

"I know that God is not cruel. In fact, He is showing us His mercy in the midst of our great suffering. The sacrifice of a beloved lamb is the price we must pay for deliverance."

Joshua began to appreciate Moses' words. "Perhaps it's because the loss is so difficult that we can never forget it," said Joshua.

Moses was pleased. "You may have answered your own question. God wants us to perform this sacrifice every year from now on, so it may have something to do with our future," he surmised.

Joshua was satisfied with this perspective, remembering that they were on the verge of a great adventure. He agreed enthusiastically, "I can't wait to see what God is going to do."

The Faith of Avraham

Joshua took his post at the entrance of the meeting lodge. The twenty-four elders representing the twelve tribes of Israel had gathered within the tented hall for their final instructions. The atmosphere was rife with anticipation. Moses blessed each man by name. He motioned to Aaron and passed the rod to him.

Aaron raised the rod and called upon the Lord. Each tribe was blessed according to the order of birth: Re'uven, Shim'on, Levi, Y'hudah, Dan, Naftali, Gad, Asher, Yissakhar, Z'vulun, Yosef, and Binyamin. As Aaron handed the rod of authority back to Moses, he placed his hand on his brother's shoulder. "Our God, we stand together as one to strengthen Moses and to ask You to give him wisdom for the great task before us. Amen."

All present echoed, "Amen."

Moses stood to speak. Before he could begin, Jepthah, one of the elders, asked a question without being acknowledged. "How can we be assured that yet one more plague, even as drastic as this, will force Pharaoh to let us go?"

Moses smiled sadly. Joshua could tell he had anticipated this question. "The greatest challenge we face is not Pharaoh," replied Moses. "God has sent nine plagues to prepare us for this hour. If we accept that the plagues and miraculous wonders are the works of His hand, then we must also obey his commands."

Jepthah was not satisfied. "Why must we each sacrifice a lamb? Is not God the protector of Israel? Will He not shield His chosen people as he has done during the last six plagues and punish the Egyptians anyway?"

Moses was exasperated. "You take too much for granted,"

Elishama signaled his desire to speak. Relieved, Moses yielded to the elder man.

"We must look to the tradition of our patriarchs for an example," said Elishama. "This we have learned since birth. Avraham was a man of great courage. No wonder the Lord chose him to be the seed bearer for Israel's future generations.

"God asked Avraham to sacrifice his only son Yitzchak on Mount Moriah. We can hardly imagine the heart-wrenching ordeal Avraham suffered upon this supreme test. Heaven forbid that a father should sacrifice his son!

"Avraham's blade was already in motion when the Lord stopped him. God honored Avraham's willingness to sacrifice his son and heir as an act of faith, and He accounted it to him for righteousness.

"The Lord miraculously supplied a ram to take the place of Yitzchak. Now, in the same tradition, is not God asking us each to place our son on the altar? Let us thank God that He also offers us a substitute to sacrifice, the lamb, just as He did to our Father Avraham. This we must do by faith."

Moses was obviously pleased with the elder's answer. The others were also satisfied. Joshua was thrilled with the words of Elishama. They could only have come from God, poured through this kindly, wise elder whom Joshua knew as Grandpapa.

The prophet signaled Caleb and Jephunneh to hold up a large diagram on sheepskin parchment for all to see. It was the chart upon which Joshua had worked so hard, under Moses direction. It displayed the location of each tribal unit on the plains of Goshen and its place in their departure.

Moses then issued instructions for the next day. He ordered each tribal leader and the families in his charge to take their prescribed places in the great assembly of all Israel. When he had finished, Joshua knew that the prophet had left nothing to chance.

Dathan, second in command of the Re'uvenim, raised his hand to be recognized. "This is all very well and good. But what if Pharaoh changes his mind again? We are not an army. We are but a nation of slave laborers and women and children. The Egyptians could slaughter us like sheep!"

This inflammatory statement prompted a restless disturbance in the assembly.

Moses raised his rod and squeezed it in anger. "Enough!"

His eyes blazed with fire. The elders hushed.

"Do not forget that the greatest judgment is yet to come. Do not forget that God has promised to loose us from the hand of Pharaoh. Do not make the sacrifice of your lamb a hollow act. Gird yourself for the Passover. Be prepared to move at a moment's notice. When the sun rises tomorrow morning, we will start on our journey to the Promised Land. The Lord will not fail us!"

"Amen," replied the council of elders.

But Joshua could hear in their tones that several were half-hearted. Moses eyed Dathan, but Dathan would not look back.

A Night To Be Remembered

Moses thundered, "Tonight is a night to be remembered! Tonight is our last night in bondage. Egypt will be brought to her knees. Pharaoh will not have Israelite slaves to rebuild his decimated and decaying kingdom. For all generations, your acts of faith will be remembered. From this time forward your children will know freedom!"

The Spirit of God swept through the room like a refreshing wind, removing all fear and doubt. Renewed and inspired, the elders began to clap and encourage Moses.

Moses was gratified by the turnabout and got down to details. "Each of you shall receive a small bunch of hyssop from Aaron. When you leave this tent, go directly to your homes. Do not tarry on the way. This afternoon you will sacrifice your lamb. You will sacrifice it in the doorway of your home. Collect the lamb's blood in the drainage basin at the entrance.

"You shall dip the hyssop in the blood from your sacrifice. With the hyssop, strike and smear the lintel and the two doorposts of your home as you have already been told. Then enter your homes. Do not step outside of your dwelling tonight. The blood upon the doorframe of your home is your family's protection from the Angel of Death."

"Recline when you partake of your sacrifice." This command was received with surprise. Reclining while eating was a custom forbidden to slaves, and reserved for the privileged.

"God wants us to enjoy this meal as free men," thought Joshua.

"Be sure to consume every morsel," instructed Moses. "Waste nothing. You are not to take any of your lamb with you on the journey tomorrow.

Savor each bite while you can. It is an offering of our faith in the power of God to liberate us from all that Egypt has done to enslave and exploit our people.

"When you have completed the meal, gather every scrap. Anything not eaten must be thrown into the fire and reduced to ashes."

Upon hearing this, the men stirred again. This requirement ran counter to their custom, one to which they had become conditioned after many generations of deprivation. If on some rare occasion an animal was eaten, all efforts were made to preserve the remaining meat for several subsequent meals. The idea of consuming an entire lamb at one sitting was mind-boggling. This kind of opulence was exclusively limited to the wealthy.

"This is to remind us that nothing must be left behind. We shall not look back with longing for Egypt. Remember Lot's wife."

The mention of that disobedient woman who had been changed into a pillar of salt while longing to return to her old way of life struck home. Everyone there realized that resistance to God's plan was to risk judgment.

"You will hear the wailing of those families who fail to apply the blood of a sacrificial lamb to their homes. The streets of Egypt will fill with the cries of parents who have lost their first-born to the Angel of Death. When you hear the mourning, pray to our God. Thank him for sparing our sons and that He is about to rescue us from the land of false gods.

"Remember, when you hear Egypt cry out for mercy, do not leave your homes. Under no circumstances must you leave your households until signaled to do so."

"For the sake of security, every man must have his weapon ready. We are leaving Egypt as an army. All Israel must leave as one. This is the Lord's command."

Moses halted. He turned and beckoned to Joshua's grandfather. "Elishama."

Elishama came to Moses' side. "You are a faithful and trusted servant. You, my friend, will walk with me. I will meet you on the ridge crest as the sun rises over the new morning that marks our release from bondage."

Joshua saw his grandfather's eyes widen, humbled by this honor. A chorus of approval ratified Moses' selection.

"Wear your robe," added Moses, confirming that Elishama's continuing presence alongside would reflect his official role as the presiding council elder. Joshua was bursting with delight that his grandfather would join him at the prophet's side.

"Now, make haste," the prophet directed. "See, the sun nears the end of its course for this day."

Quickly, the men filed out. Parting words were brief. Looking toward the west, they gauged the remaining hours of daylight. Much had been revealed. Much still needed to be accomplished.

Aaron stood by the door, handing out parcels of hyssop reed. Thanking him, the leaders carefully tucked the tall, slender stalks into their clothing and departed.

Joshua started home to tend to his duties. He detected a swift motion out of the corner of his eye. Swirling across the desert was a wispy cloud of dust caught in the updraft of an afternoon whirlwind. Turning his view westward, he could see the Nile river valley stretching to the north and south. The afternoon sky was darkening with clouds.

Joshua's mind echoed Moses' phrase, "Tonight is a night to be remembered!"

A shiver ran through him. He had witnessed the power of God displayed in Egypt through the plagues and the awesome destruction they had wrought. He dared not think about the inevitable horror of the night to come.

Glancing back, he saw a dove flutter down and light upon the crest of the meeting lodge. The white bird cooed softly as it watched Joshua stride down the path toward his home.

The Passover Lamb

Between the doorposts of Joshua's home, as before most residences in Goshen, was a narrow trough dug out of the ground. A long clay container was inserted inside the small ditch, designed to catch any excess runoff during the rainy season. This device kept the floor of the house dry. It was here, at the threshold, that the family assembled.

The Passover supper would indeed be unforgettable. Fresh meat always marked a rare and special occasion. However, there was not one person in any home who would not be willing to forego this supper that its lamb not die.

The family quietly gathered to say their farewells to Snowy. Although everyone had been prepared for this parting, it was terribly difficult. This was not just sentimentality. Each of them had spent personal time with the lamb. This was painful.

Elishama took the lamb in his arms. He moved deliberately from one member of the family to the next, giving each plenty of time to say farewell. Deborah and Rachel had tears streaming down their cheeks.

"Goodbye, little lamb," said Deborah.

"Bye-bye, Snowy. I love you," sobbed Rachel.

Joshua said nothing; he just scratched the little creature's ears and looked into its uncomprehending eyes.

Elishama handed the lamb to Nun and led Deborah and Rachel into the house. Once the women had been shown inside and the entrance shut, Elishama returned to supervise the sacrifice.

Nun instructed Joshua, "Place the basin to catch the blood."

Joshua carefully complied with his father's direction. Nun passed Snowy to Joshua, who gently cradled the lamb in his arms. Joshua whispered in his lamb's ear, "I will never forget you, Snowy."

Snowy responded with a quick lick of the young man's ear and a soft bleat. Snowy glanced back and forth between the men, unaware of what was happening. Nun motioned for Joshua to hold Snowy over the bowl. With a little coaxing by Joshua, Snowy obediently lay down upon the stones at the base of the doorway that would serve as the altar of his sacrifice. Joshua stroked Snowy, keeping the lamb quiet, so that his death would be fast and painless.

Elishama prayed, "God's will be done. May this lamb's blood protect us from the Death Angel and mark our emancipation. Blessed Lord, guide us in the days to come as we journey to the Land of Promise. We ask you to receive the life of our offering, Snowy—our Passover Lamb."

Inside their shelter, Rachel anxiously clenched her mother's hand. With her other arm she tightly hugged a straw doll. She could hear everything being said outside. Great streams of tears flowed down her cheeks.

Nun's hand rested on Snowy's forehead. The lamb was at peace. The end was swift and merciful. The incision was made. Snowy remained still. Joshua caught the scarlet flow of blood in the receptacle beneath the animal's throat. Life pulsed out of their sacrifice. The lamb appeared to fall asleep. His eyes dimmed. His breath left him. In moments, Snowy was dead.

Joshua had aided his father in the sacrifice of many animals throughout his lifetime, but this incident was altogether unique. Something was torn out of his bosom. He looked at his father and grandfather. They were affected the same way.

Elishama placed his hands upon the heads of his son and grandson and prayed for them. Nun and Joshua stood to join the elder man as the three of them encircled their holy gift.

For a short while, they comforted one another with a hug. All three men were overcome with emotion and could do little to conceal it. Their eyes were moist. A tear ran down Joshua's face, which he quickly brushed away.

When the moment subsided, they all blotted their eyes on their sleeves. Then, patting each other on their respective shoulders, they stepped back and silently considered the significance of the moment.

After a brief time, Joshua and Nun took the hyssop that Aaron had supplied. They took turns fulfilling the directions. First, Nun dipped the hyssop in the crimson pool at their feet before the door, then raised it up and struck the lintel beam above the door. He handed it to Joshua, who then marked both side posts at shoulder height with two quick smears.

Next. Nun instructed Joshua to pick up the body of their lamb. Doing so, Joshua continued to show tenderness to Snowy's body in death as he had in life. Joshua lifted the inanimate form gently, carrying it to a stone slab next to the hut used for preparing food. Nun swiftly and expertly skinned the animal. Joshua's emotions were jumbled. This was not just another meal that needed preparing.

Elishama arranged the limbs for roasting. A long, stout branch served as a spit. A second branch was used to stretch the front legs apart. Thus, the animal could be roasted whole.

As they completed the task, the sun sent shadows over the rooftops of neighboring mud huts. Late afternoon rays reflected in the puddle of fiery red liquid within the vessel lying at the threshold of their dwelling.

"The entryway is sealed," said Elishama.

Looking up and down the road, other men could be seen striking their doorways with blood in the prescribed manner. It was a spectacle. However peculiar it appeared, Joshua was pleased that God's command was being honored.

Suddenly, he was dismayed to notice a doorway, and then another, that was not being streaked with blood. "Papa. Grandpapa. Look!" He pointed for Elishama and Nun to see. "Is it possible that someone has not heard the instructions?"

Nun replied, "They heard the command but have chosen not to obey."

"Have they lost their minds?" asked Joshua.

"Or, heaven forbid, have they lost their faith?" added Elishama.

"Yes," said Nun. "Those are the homes of Lebo the sandal-maker and Hamran the leather worker. I know them well. What a shame."

"We must warn them," suggested Joshua earnestly.

"It is too late," said Nun. "They made their decision days ago."

Joshua was downcast.

Elishama was also grieved. "They endured a life of slavery, then were granted the privilege of witnessing mighty signs, proof of the power of God. And yet, they chose not to honor His command. How sad for someone to have come this far, then give up."

The three could only shake their heads in amazement as they finished their work and gathered up their implements.

A few of the family's belongings were placed next to the doorway, ready for their imminent departure. Their home looked strangely stark. Nothing hung from the walls. The shelves were bare. Only the hearth was warm and inviting. The relative happiness of the last few days seemed distant.

Outside, except for the sooty puffs from the fires of offerings, the air was cool and clear. Dark wisps of smoke curled up from almost every home in the valley, twirling and trailing across the sky toward an unknown destination to the east. In the west, the setting sun ignited the desert horizon with a firestorm of colors.

Joshua's thoughts returned to their lamb. He knew Snowy's death would be impressed on his mind forever. Throughout Goshen's dwelling places, prayers were being softly spoken. A deep sense of reverence enveloped the inhabitants.

Deborah and Rachel readied the unique meal. Rachel assisted her mother in preparing dough. This dough was unusual. "Why isn't there any yeast in this bread?" Rachel asked her mother.

"We have been commanded to eat bread without yeast," replied Deborah.

"Why?" asked Rachel.

Her mother thought it over before replying, "God has required it. The Egyptians are master bakers. Perhaps our bread must be different from theirs."

"It's funny bread. I wonder what it tastes like," said Rachel.

"I'm sure it tastes fine," said Deborah.

"What are those things for?" asked Rachel, referring to a bowl full of stocky white roots on the table.

"Those are for the Passover dinner too," said Deborah.

"What do they taste like?" asked Rachel. "May I try one?"

"No," said Deborah. "You wouldn't like it. Wait until the dinner."

"Why are we going to eat them if they don't taste good?" asked Rachel.

"You'll be told at dinner."

"I miss Snowy," said Rachel wistfully.

"Me too," said Deborah.

Meanwhile, the sweet fragrance from roasting lamb was beginning to fill the home. Wonderful warm aromas were caught up in the air and lifted to the skies.

Few words were uttered except for essential instructions. Everyone was engrossed in thought. Although it was only for four days, Snowy had become a beloved part of their home life and the family had just lost a member of their household.

Joshua was beginning to grasp the magnitude of what was unfolding. Freedom exacted a very high price indeed. Even if it meant death to tens of thousands of innocent lambs, Israel must submit to the Lord.

A strange combination of joy and sorrow filled his heart. The realization that this would be the last supper they would eat in captivity was beginning to sink in. Again, Joshua considered that Snowy had given his life for him, the first-born son of Nun and Deborah.

Nun looked through the window. Outside, all was serene as heaven held its breath. A full moon had just ascended over the horizon. The Passover night had begun. Nun drew the straw shutters closed and bowed his head. He silently thanked God for Divine protection over this, his family's home in Egypt.

After a few moments, he said, "Joshua, please recite the Passover directives."

Joshua did so, exactly as Moses had given them. When he finished, Nun said, "I am sure we all know that these commands must be followed to the letter."

Elishama took his place as head of the Feast. "Come," Elishama beckoned to Joshua, who sat down next to his grandfather. They all reclined around the low table.

"I have to say, this is a quite a luxury," said Deborah.

Elishama squeezed Joshua's forearm and appreciatively whispered, "You are the answer to a grandfather's prayers." Joshua acknowledged these words with a grin and firmly grasped Elishama's hand.

After he led prayer, Nun uncovered the unleavened bread. Its surface was baked to a crisp and could be easily broken into smaller pieces. Joshua tried the yeastless bread for the first time. It had a hearty, roasted flavor.

"This is good," he said. The others nodded in agreement.

"I helped make it," said Rachel.

"You did a fine job," said Nun.

The bitter herbs received a very different reaction. Before anyone could warn him, Joshua took a large bite of the bitter root. Immediately his eyes began to water and his nose started to run. He tried to cool his mouth with water, but to no avail.

Rachel laughed and pointed at him. "I didn't think anything could make you cry," she giggled.

Then Deborah said, "Rachel, why don't you try it?"

Rachel shrugged her shoulders. "Yes, Mother." She had decided to fool her mother by taking just a tiny nip off the root. Surely that wouldn't be all that bad. She bit off a little piece.

Rachel's eyes got big. "Yech! Mommy, what is that stuff?"

Before her mother could answer, the root began to work. Rachel grabbed her cup of water and took a big swallow. Her tongue and nose burned. Now it was Joshua's turn to snicker.

Rachel stuck out her tongue at Joshua to demonstrate her displeasure, while trying to cool her scorched mouth. Everyone was amused.

Nun ate his portion. Deborah laughed while he waved his hand in front of his mouth to cool the burning sensation. Then, Elishama and Deborah obediently took their portions. They both made comic faces. Before long, the whole family was in an uproar.

"Who would have thought that a small nibble of root could generate so much heat?" said Deborah.

Finally, the lamb was uncovered. It looked crispy-brown. The family members tried to avert their eyes while Nun took a knife and carved away those larger parts that were to be incinerated after the meal. He set them aside and covered them. He then carved off pieces of meat and placed portions before each of them.

The meal proceeded quietly. Emotions were mixed. Their enjoyment was tempered by the knowledge that they were consuming an animal that had been a part of their family circle. Even Rachel said nothing while they ate. In her own way, she appreciated it. The food was delicious, but its cost had been immeasurable.

When it was nearly over, Rachel turned to her father. "Papa, why are we eating this kind of food?"

Nun realized that this question was weightier than his child could know. He sat for several moments, deciding what to say. He directed the family's attention to the remnants of the meal before them and spoke. "This is a meal unlike any other we have eaten. God told us to do these things that we might not forget. We have dined like kings, but we have also been reminded of our tears of slavery in Egypt by eating the bitter herbs."

"And the unleavened bread?" asked Deborah.

"I think it must have something to do with the haste in which we are to depart."

"That reminds me, what am I going to do for yeast?"

"All I know is that Moses said to take no yeast with us," said Nun.

"I guess we'll have to do without until we get to the Promised Land," she said.

At the conclusion of the meal, Nun extended his arms to his family. They held hands and sang a song of thanksgiving.

Elishama sighed, "I will miss this home." His eyes traveled about the room as he surveyed the familiar surroundings. "But I will not miss Egypt."

As if on cue, a shofar sounded. "Hah-rooooooooot!"

It was midnight.

Elishama and Nun were startled. No one had been appointed to blow the horn of Israel. Who was it?

Suddenly, a great wind swept past their doorway shaking the house. It moved swiftly down the street.

They shuddered as they turned to one another. No one dare speak. They just listened.

Within moments the night was filled with cries of the bereaved in households near and far.

The wind picked up the discord of mournful wailing and carried it across the land. Desert jackals echoed the sound with their own forlorn crying.

The Angel of Death

The Slayer swooped down over Egypt swinging his scythe, cutting down the first-born behind every unstained doorway. Each dwelling not marked with the blood of a lamb was targeted for tragedy.

Down the broad avenues and up the narrow pathways of the once-thriving civilization the avenging Angel stole, hunting his victims. In his wake lay the wreckage of fractured and dismembered families. Not one neighborhood went unscathed.

The tenth plague swept over the land—an irresistible force, a towering avalanche of mortality. The Dispenser of Death sucked life out of the lungs of healthy children. Icy fingers snatched the living spirit from babes in their cribs.

Gone was the opportunity to grow up and take on the role of leadership, which a first-born son inherited. None of them would experience the joy of mastering a trade, taking a bride, being a father. Instead, an empty place was to be at the table of every Egyptian family.

In an instant, the Angel of Death finished his visitation of doom. The air was still.

Not long after, people were outside their homes looking for consolation, but there was no one who could comfort them. The cries of countless mothers pierced the air as they bemoaned their plight and lamented the horrifying loss of loved ones.

Even Egypt's domestic animals could not escape. They bellowed out their own tales of woe, for their offspring too had collapsed and died without warning.

Upon hearing the wailing of servants, Pharaoh ran to his son's bedroom. Stunned, he saw his child's limp, pale body. "My son. Does he not breathe? Quick! Get my physicians!"

The boy's attendants were deeply intimidated. It was plain the heir to the throne was dead. Pharaoh trembled with a mixture of grief and rage. Already the sounds of tragedy were wafting through the night air. "What is that noise?" he demanded, but the servants were too afraid to answer.

Doctors and priests arrived after some time. They were stricken with fright when they saw that even the crown prince was dead. Pharaoh was oblivious to what others were suffering. He wanted his son back.

The doctors pretended to examine him for signs of life. They whispered among themselves and appointed a spokesman. Finally, the priest-magician Jambres bowed and cautiously pronounced, "He is dead, my Pharaoh, like the others. He cannot be revived."

For a few moments, the Pharaoh was speechless. He fought the terror, seeking to keep control of his thoughts and emotions. Recovering his strength, he asked coldly, "What others?"

In the long pause that followed, he could hear the widespread lamenting of the bereaved. The night was full of shrill crying. As soon as Jambres thought it safe, he said, "I too have lost a son this night, my lord. All of us have."

The king was incredulous. Jambres added, "The first-born of every household has perished. The God of Moses is behind this, is He not?"

"Get out! All of you get away. Leave us alone." Pharaoh ordered.

After they left, and the doors had been closed, the tyrant cradled his son's cold breathless body in his arms. He buried his head upon the youthful chest that once held a beating heart and sobbed. His bitter crying was muffled by the child's bedclothes.

Back in Goshen, Aaron came to fetch Joshua. Elishama, Nun, and Deborah escorted the young man outside. A full moon cast well-defined shadows on the street. He could see no movement in the neighborhood, even though the glow of oil lamps seeping under closed doors and around shuttered windows proved that everyone was awake. They all awaited the signal to assemble and leave Egypt. Distant sounds of grief could be heard in the night, giving the moment a forbidding eeriness as they headed out.

"Be careful," said Deborah.

"Stay close to Moses," said Nun.

As Joshua and Aaron approached Moses' dwelling, they sensed the air was charged with excitement. The inconceivable had happened. Moses' prophecy was being fulfilled. The stage was set for Israel's departure. Moses greeted Joshua with a joyful embrace. The prophet shouted, "Our liberation is at hand!"

Before Joshua could ask what was next, they heard a clamor approaching. They wheeled around to behold an unexpected sight: Tukoh had arrived, accompanied by a crowd of dark-skinned strangers. Even more surprising, Tukoh was so elated he was practically dancing.

Joshua had figured Tukoh might be sent to summon Moses and Aaron. But he had not anticipated him to arrive at the head of a celebration.

"Tukoh must have brought nearly forty people with him," said Aaron, his jaw hanging open.

"Welcome, my friend," said Moses to Tukoh. "Who are these people?"

"They are friends and neighbors of Egypt, some of my relatives, my two wives, six daughters, and my first-born son, Thoth," he replied, his face beaming.

Moses, Aaron and Joshua were astonished. To their knowledge, all the first-born sons of Egypt had perished. "How is this possible?" asked Aaron.

Tukoh smiled broadly. "I obeyed the command of the God of Israel. When my clan and these others shared my roof at midnight, the doorway was marked with the blood of a lamb." There were "aahs" of understanding from the listeners.

Tukoh grabbed little Thoth and hefted him over his head. "The Death Angel passed over and my son is alive!"

"This is truly a cause for rejoicing," said Moses.

Tukoh continued, "We have noted the mighty signs, Moses, and know that your God is the One True God. We will no longer serve this wicked Pharaoh, who is no god, nor the gods of Egypt who cannot save us. We will follow you and your God. We have come to join your people. May we leave Egypt with you?"

"Your faith is righteous and pleasing to God. We welcome you," said Moses without hesitation, opening his arms to accept them. "Who are we to say you cannot leave the land of false gods with us?"

"We will honor the God of Israel from this day forward," said Tukoh earnestly. "We have brought our belongings and we are ready to go. But of course we must first attend to affairs of state. Pharaoh has called for you again, hopefully for the last time."

"I've been expecting it," said Moses. "Let us go at once and see him before dawn. We leave Goshen at first light."

This time when they reached Pharaoh's landing, there was no deep barrier of supernatural darkness to hide the destruction from view. Across the shining ribbon of water, the full moon illuminated the cloudless night to reveal the devastated landscape that Joshua's parents had so vividly described to him. Joshua gasped involuntarily.

When they entered the royal throne room, Pharaoh was perched upon his seat of power, grimacing and seething with hatred. Before they had taken three steps into the chamber, Pharaoh shrieked, "Your request is granted! You may take your flocks and herds. You and your people, go worship your God." Then, he angrily ordered them, "And also, you must bless me!"

Moses said, "As you wish." The trio withdrew.

Under his breath Joshua whispered, "The man continues to defy the living God."

Moses placed his hand on Joshua's shoulder. "All that remains of his kingdom is his pride. The victory is ours!"

Aaron and Joshua were elated.

They were barely outside Pharaoh's throne room when they were met by a highly aggravated group of men of evident stature. Surely, each of them had lost a son.

"Moses," called one of them, obviously a leader among leaders. "I am Apep, commander of the royal guard."

Moses and his company stopped in their tracks. Joshua put his hand on his sword. His heart was in his throat, fearing they would attack. He was prepared to fight to protect Moses and Aaron, even if it were at the cost of his own life.

Instead, the Egyptians went down on one knee and bowed their heads. Further surprising the Hebrews, Apep humbly spoke words that were obviously difficult for him: "We beg you. Have mercy on us. Hurry. Leave our country before the wrath of your God slays us all."

Joshua was stunned. He recalled the words Moses spoke to Pharaoh upon their departure from the royal chamber during the plague of darkness: "Your officials will bow down before me." Once again, Joshua marveled at the miracle of fulfilled prophecy.

"We desire only to go," said Moses softly.

"Then do so quickly, before Pharaoh changes his mind again," implored a distressed official.

While escorting them out, Apep added, "Sobek speaks for us all. Time is of the essence."

"Sobek." Joshua recognized that name. He realized the distressed official was the Royal Surveyor, the same man his parents had plundered just days before. Certainly many of the clothes on Elishama's table must have belonged to Sobek's family. Sobek's face revealed obvious despair. Joshua was sure he had suffered the loss of his son, Get.

The Hebrews emerged from the royal palace to find a throng of people. Almost ghostly by torchlight, some of the people were holding dead children in their arms, swaying, moaning, and crying aloud:

"Moses. Please go."

"May Pharaoh anger your God no more."

"Ask your God to have mercy on us."

Joshua was struck by the sight: people crowding the streets in the wee hours of the morning, crying bitterly over the loss of their first-born sons, sorry they had oppressed the Israelites, angry at their Pharaoh for his obstinacy, pleading with the prophets, hoping to placate their guilt, and anxious for Israel to make a hasty exit.

"We and our entire nation leave Egypt at dawn," announced Moses to the crowd. "Shalom. Peace be unto you."

Joshua realized that their lives were not in danger from the people of Egypt. They had been shattered by the plagues. Their way of life was destroyed. Their idols had been shown to be frauds. The death of the first-born was the last blow. They had been thoroughly humbled and were actually grateful that the Israelites were leaving.

Approaching the river, the three Israelites and their escort were followed by a large crowd. Few of the Egyptians spoke. They begged the Israelites to take some last-minute gifts. At Moses' direction, Joshua and Tukoh made arrangements for the plunder to be taken across the river to Goshen.

Once they had embarked, standing on the deck of Pharaoh's own river craft, Joshua looked back at Egypt. Despondent Egyptians lined the shore in silent vigil of their departure.

He thought about the testy boatman his parents had described encountering when they went across to plunder Egypt. His son was no doubt dead. Joshua wondered if the man was among those watching him leave.

The Exodus

Elishama stood in the doorway of his dwelling. His family was about to vacate the only home they had ever known. They looked around their hut for the last time. They were all self-consciously dressed in Egyptian finery received from their slavemasters. The clothes contrasted drastically with their humble surroundings.

"I feel so odd, dressed up like a queen," said Deborah. She thought about it for a moment and then cracked a smile. "But I could get used to it."

"How much of the unleavened dough do we have?" Nun asked her, happily adjusting his handsome new turban. He looked approvingly at Joshua, who was putting on an excellent new cloak and military leathers.

"A week's supply, as Moses commanded," she responded. "With our other foodstuffs, it is as much as we can carry anyway."

"That should be sufficient," said Nun. "The land of Canaan is but a few days journey from here."

Elishama interrupted them and spoke softly from the depths of his soul: "Our nation has waited more than twenty generations for this new day! The Lord has heard our cry. The inevitable night of judgment has come and passed. After ten plagues, culminating with the Angel of Death, Pharaoh has finally relinquished his grip. We are leaving the land of the Nile. We are free!"

Elishama looked toward the river. In the far distance, water sparkled in the last of the predawn moonlight. He recalled, "The first plague turned the Nile River into a river of blood. Tonight, blood has completed the cycle. Those lived who chose the blood of the lamb. Those who refused to submit to the God of Israel have lost the successor to their bloodline. Alas, this is the fate of those who doubt the Lord."

"It is harsh but fair," said Joshua sadly. "Any of them could have done what Tukoh did."

"No one will be left behind who has done what God required. It is tragic," added Elishama.

"May our people always stand firm in the God of Israel, lest we some day be judged harshly as well," concluded Nun.

Rachel had fallen asleep. She was dressed in the most beautiful little gown she had ever owned. She had frolicked in it much of the night. Deborah shook her awake.

"Can't I sleep some more?" asked Rachel, yawning.

"There will be time to sleep," said Nun.

Quietly, they filed out the door and walked away from their home. Each adult bore a pack containing only what he or she could carry. Joshua herded their domestic animals. Deborah spoke before they had gone twenty paces. "I'm not looking back. As Moses said, 'Remember Lot's wife.'"

They reached the plain of Goshen as the first signs of morning touched the eastern sky with a rosy blush. The family took their position at the head of the tribe of Ephraim. Elishama and Joshua helped Nun and Deborah get organized. Then it was time for grandfather and grandson to join Moses on the hilltop.

First, Elishama knelt and scooped a handful of sandy dust, purposefully letting it sift through his fingers. "The soil of Egypt no longer nourishes the branches of Israel. This era comes to an end." He paused for a moment and then added, "Our forebearers lived and died upon this ground with the hope of this day hidden in their hearts."

Elishama and Joshua climbed the ridge while the sun rose. Joshua spotted the prophet at his vantage point at the fore. He ran ahead to join him. When he turned and looked out to see what Moses beheld, it took his breath away.

Below, the nation of Israel was assembling in the ranks that had been assigned. It was a virtual sea of people, more in one place than Joshua had ever seen in his life. Their numbers reminded him of the Lord's promise to Avraham that his generations would be as numerous as the stars in the sky. This was the innumerable labor force that had built the pyramids and whose slavehood had made Egypt a land of leisure.

The gathering masses were as colorful as they were vast. The people were wearing their glorious new finery. Above their heads, each tribe carried a separate banner—a large flag to facilitate identification. Moreover, every family within each tribe was given a smaller flag to help leaders keep track of their own people.

Joshua noticed that Tukoh had climbed the hill and was bowing before Moses.

"Please don't bow," said Moses. "I am not a king. I am just a servant of God."

After an awkward moment during which he accepted this idea, Tukoh stood tall. "Venerable Moses, before this day I had only dreamed of freedom. Now I am free, and it still feels like I am dreaming." He searched for words. "Now I must plead before you." He seemed reluctant to continue until bade to do so.

"Go on, good Tukoh," said Moses.

Tukoh pointed to the distant southwest. "Look yonder and you will see many people forming up the rear. They're others like myself, slaves from foreign lands, as well as Egyptians. Like me, they put the blood over their doorways."

Joshua was alarmed but Moses remained unperturbed. "Yes?" asked Moses.

"There are thousands who have carried the burden of Egypt on their backs alongside you. They too wish to leave Egypt. They are sick of this dying land and its wicked Pharaoh. But they are afraid of your God. They fear that you will not welcome them. They also fear that Pharaoh will have them slain if you leave them behind. They have asked me to plead for them. Whatever you say, they will do. They will even be your slaves."

"They will not be our slaves," said Moses. "We have all been slaves long enough. You may join us in the Promised Land if you are willing to undertake a hard journey and obey the commands of the God of Avraham, Yitzchak, and Ya'akov. Our God honors the hearts of all those who long for freedom."

The look on Tukoh's face was one of astonishment. He jumped in the air and landed on his feet with a loud thud, startling Moses and Joshua. "Your God has a wise prophet indeed!"

They all laughed together. Then Tukoh took his leave, running down the slope to rejoin his comrades with the exciting news.

At last, the great moment arrived. Over two million Israelites stood alert, facing the sunrise, ready to leave Egypt. All men of military age had formed up in ranks of five, each carrying his weapon, prepared for action as Moses had ordered. It was an imposing sight.

The sun lay before them as Moses the Deliverer raised his rod and signaled the leaders of the Israelites. In response to this sign, the whole nation began to move in unison before him, tribe after tribe, clan after clan, wave after wave, an enormous creeping carpet of people and livestock.

A great cheer began to rise. Joshua could not believe his eyes or ears. The people were a magnificent sight to behold—dressed in the finest garments of Egypt, bedecked in gold and silver, singing and shouting.

Here and there in the swelling crowd, boisterous individuals began to call out.

"The weight of centuries is lifted off our backs!"

"The days of our oppression have come to an end!"

An old woman shouted, "God has saved us!"

A child yelled, "We are going to a land flowing with milk and honey!"

Soon millions of voices were one joyous song, thundering praises to God. Some people even danced as they went. Joshua felt the joy well up within him. He could not help himself. He joined in the cheering.

Moses was pleased.

Joshua looked along the procession. The flocks were endless. Herds of livestock guided by young shepherds moved forward. What few camels they had were heavily laden. Small children were bundled on their parents' backs.

They carried what they understood to be most important: the gold and silver of Egypt that they had been commanded to take; the dough without yeast, which they mounted on their shoulders in kneading troughs wrapped in clothing; and other foods such as dates, figs, and honey.

The wind trailed the pilgrims. At times, gusts would lift the powdery earth into the air, covering portions of the entourage, obscuring them from sight. Soon, scarves were drawn across faces to filter out the dust.

Just as waves at sea begin to mount and swell beneath a strong breeze, so this immense tide of people and creatures flowed toward their distant homeland. Joshua imagined the view was like that of a great migration of animals seeking water and greener pastures.

Down below at the head of their tribe, Deborah grasped Nun's hand. Looking side to side at the procession around them she declared, "Only our God could have accomplished this miracle."

Nun was practically speechless as he witnessed the massive march of humanity. Then he found the words: "Israel is leaving Egypt in triumph!"

An elaborate, prearranged system of communication began to operate. Moses had only to dictate orders to Joshua. Joshua would pass them to a dozen young couriers who would memorize them at once and set off to repeat them to the leaders of the tribes. The council elders passed these instructions on to additional messengers who transmitted assignments to family leaders.

The army of the Lord was marching out of the land of Egypt.

"Where are we going?" Joshua asked Moses.

"Succoth!" said Moses. Joshua was thrilled.

South to Succoth

A stop on the well-traveled way to Canaan, Succoth was an oasis with ample water. It was also the site of the grave of Yosef.

While Joshua was growing up, he often heard his father's stories about the patriarchs who had preceded them into Egypt. He particularly liked the story of Yosef, one of twelve sons of Ya'akov, who had been sold by his brothers into slavery. He was unjustly imprisoned in Egypt, but by the intervention of God, through the gift of interpreting dreams, Yosef rose to the pinnacle of power, second only to Pharaoh.

Yosef was a great man who not only forgave his brethren and invited them to remain in Egypt with him, he also saved Egypt from a great famine. It was because of Yosef that the Israelites initially dwelt in Egypt. He was revered as a great patriarch. Moreover, he was the father of Ephraim, Joshua's ancestor.

Joshua identified strongly with Yosef, who had known slavery, trusted God implicitly, and conquered adversity. Of all his ancestors, Yosef was Joshua's greatest hero.

Joshua remembered Elishama's words, "Yosef prophesied that we would one day leave Egypt. He said that God would come to our nation's aid and lead us to the Promised Land. Yosef's dying wish was that we would take his bones with us."

"All Israelites know the story of Yosef," Elishama reminded him. "In our world, which had little to offer for the future, no one should ever forget God's promise to Yosef that we would return to the land of our ancestors."

Joshua knew that transporting these bones was a sacred responsibility. Yosef's bones were buried in Succoth.

Despite its nearness, Joshua had never been there; life in slavery offered no such luxury. It was thrilling that they were now on their way to fulfill the patriarch's dying request.

"Joshua," said Moses, "You and your tribe will see to it that Yosef's bones reach the Promised Land. I want you to take personal charge of this task."

Joshua could hardly believe it. This was the greatest honor of them all. He couldn't wait to tell his relatives.

"You will watch over your ancestor's remains throughout our journey," continued Moses. "When we reach the Promised Land, you will see to his burial at Hebron. His bones will rest with Avraham, Yitzchak, and Ya'akov."

Joshua wondered why he, rather than Moses, would take charge of this great assignment. He supposed that it was because direct descendants of Yosef should do it.

At the end of the day's march, the nation encamped in the desert at Succoth. Moses turned to Joshua and said, "This is a milestone in our people's history. Let us have a time of rejoicing."

Joshua put the word out through his couriers. The festival began at sundown. The people danced and sang around bonfires, celebrating their first day of liberty. All were pleased that a time of celebration had been granted. They prepared fresh baked bread without leaven and set out dried fruit and honey. They sang songs of joy led by Miriam (the sister of Moses and Aaron), who danced and played the timbrel.

After telling his family the great news about his assignment to safeguard Yosef's bones, about which Nun and Elishama were particularly enthusiastic, Joshua surreptitiously made his way to town to meet with the local Ephraimite leaders. Mindful of their historic responsibility, a handful of them had stayed in Succoth while the rest had joined the exodus from Goshen the day before.

Joshua was beaming with joy because of this prestigious assignment from Moses. Well aware that he would meet with elders who might consider him a boy, he wanted to present himself with the dignity his task demanded.

At the city gates, he learned that the local Ephraimite leader was a gentle old man, Rehojemiah Ben-Bekher. In short order, they convened a meeting. "Shalom. I am Joshua Ben-Nun, of the Efrayim," said Joshua. "I have been sent by Moses to arrange for the carrying of the bones of Yosef, my great ancestor, to the Promised Land as was prophesied."

"Shalom, Joshua Ben-Nun. I know of you and your fathers, our great clansmen." He introduced the others with him. "We, like you, are all men of Efrayim and M'nasheh, descendants of Yosef," said Rehojemiah, tugging his whiskers. "We keep vigil over his grave. Our ancestors longed to see this day. This is a cause for rejoicing. Of course we will help you."

Joshua was pleased. Far from being condescending because of his youth, they had received him as a brother. They went to the burial site together, carrying torches and digging tools. "This is the place he lays," said Rehojemiah. "Let us disinter him now, and we will bear his coffin on our shoulders until we reach Hebron."

Yosef's bones were not secured in a crypt as was the custom of the Egyptians. Rather, they had been stored beneath an earthen mound for almost four centuries. The body was embalmed in the Egyptian manner and placed within a coffin, but then it was simply buried in dry ground to await future transport to Canaan. There was no monument. Pikes sporting bright strips of cloth were all that marked the site.

It occurred to Joshua this was a most humble burial site for such a noble person. That was probably for the best, so that the grave remained inconspicuous to the Egyptians. Joshua supervised while they dug into the grave by torchlight.

The occasion was a strange and solemn one. Although Joshua and these sons of Yosef had been unknown to one another, a deep sense of reverence was shared in this task. They all were keenly aware of the significance of their mission. In time, an Egyptian sarcophagus was uncovered, painted with gold and red and blue, bearing the likeness of a man upon its cover.

While they dusted it off, Joshua noticed how well preserved it was. He looked down at the image on the coffin, that of an elderly prince (for Yosef had lived many years). Joshua pondered the likeness of the godly ancestor who had requested this very moment to come. Another prophecy fulfilled.

The next morning on their way to join Moses, Joshua and Elishama talked.

"The messengers have all been telling me the same thing," said Joshua. "The nation is ready to fight. In fact, there is great enthusiasm. Our men can't wait to fight the Philistines and take the land that God has promised us."

Elishama frowned, "They have only seen victory chariots on parade. They have never seen the gore and horror of a battlefield. They do not understand war. It is the most terrible experience known to humankind. However, I suppose it is a good thing that our men are ready and willing.

"The main trade route is not far away from here; it is a well-traveled highway. We'll be in Canaan in a few days. We will face the military might of the Philistines soon enough. Let us hope that we remain committed and brave."

The Children of Israel moved north. Word spread quickly that Yosef's bones were also headed toward the patriarch's ancestral home in the Promised Land. The sun beat down on the sojourners all along the dusty way, but the land of promise was just over the horizon. After a long day, Moses called a halt and the people rested.

Joshua overheard someone say jokingly, "I will celebrate the mercy of God. He has allowed me to stop walking in this horrible heat for a day."

Someone else added, "I would keep walking if God required it. Every step away from Egypt is fine with me. I want as much distance between me and Pharaoh as I can get."

The evening was warm. Many saw no need to put up tents. The women busied themselves fetching water for the livestock. The children frolicked in the gathering dusk. Soon, campfires twinkled as the evening's ration of unleavened bread was baking, which had a pleasant fragrance, inviting to the senses, wafting through the expansive camp.

The following morning, the nation of newly freed people continued toward Etham, a thriving trade community on the way to Canaan. The weather was sweltering. Water was rationed. Joshua was kept busy with the details of coordinating the movements of the tribes. Arriving at Etham late in the day, they set up camp in the valley to the east of the trade route. All seemed to be going well enough.

While the people rested, the local Egyptians called upon Moses. Appearing quite nervous, they bowed before him.

"We have seen the wonders of your God," said their spokesman, a thin fellow who traded in oil and honey. "Please, do not slay us," he begged.

Moses looked to Aaron, Elishama, and Joshua for their reactions. Moses probed the man incisively and learned that news of Israel's departure from Goshen had preceded them.

"You have nothing to fear from us," said Moses. "Rise. Tell me, how did you learn of this?"

The Egyptians got to their feet. "It is not wise for your servant to report Pharaoh's business to you, Lord Moses," said the man, still quaking.

"Are there many Egyptian soldiers operating in this vicinity?" asked Moses calmly.

The trader settled down, realizing that Moses was not threatening him. Yet, he chose his words carefully. "Pharaoh's eyes and ears are everywhere."

Moses thanked him and gently dismissed the delegation. After the visitors were gone, Moses turned to Aaron and said, "Pharaoh's soldiers intend not to be seen." Aaron, who had spent so much time scouting for them without detecting a sign, could only agree.

The Fiery Pillar

Joshua felt the light on his face and stirred. He always awoke before dawn. He would never have slept until first light. His eyes shot open. Alarmed, he jumped to his feet to discover that the illumination was not from the sun.

Around him, thousands of people were rising, equally startled by the unusual glare in the night. There were gasps and utterances of fear and awe. A brilliant billowy column of fire stood suspended in the air not far outside the camp.

The intense, magnificent phenomenon lit up the terrain for miles. It appeared to be a roaring flame, burning without any visible supply of fuel. What could it be?

"It is a natural disaster that will kill us all!" shouted someone in terror.

"No! It is standing still!" cried another.

"Look! It doesn't diminish!" exclaimed others.

"It is a fire that burns without being exhausted!" said Joshua, astounded. "Could this be the fire that Moses saw at the burning bush?"

"It is the Glory of God!" breathed Nun in amazed reverence.

Joshua raced to Moses' camp, where the messengers were already gathering for instructions. Tukoh arrived at the same time. As soon as Joshua took his place before Moses and Aaron, Moses told Joshua what to say to the messengers before dispersing them throughout the frightened peoples.

"Do not be afraid!" commanded Moses. "Be comforted instead. It is the very Presence of the Lord. It is a sign that He is with us. He will be our beacon in the night!"

The messengers ran off to inform the leaders. Before long, the sounds of alarm ceased. Not surprisingly, no one was able to sleep. The vast millions stood in awe, staring at the pillar of fire in the sky, transfixed by this breathtaking manifestation of God. Speculation soon arose as to what would happen when sunlight returned.

When first light crept into the sky, the luminous column began to change. The glory gradually transmuted into a glowing pillar of swirling cloud, rising toward heaven. It was as if a towering storm had surrounded a roaring furnace. It was no less magnificent than the pillar of fire by night. It continued to declare the Glory of God Almighty.

When Elishama and Joshua returned to Moses that morning, they found the prophet flat on his face, deep in prayer. They stood by quietly until Moses finished. He arose with an odd look upon his face.

Moses spoke. "The challenges before us are formidable. Thus, the Lord has told me that I am to lead our people away from the northern road that runs near the seacoast. That route leads to the armies of the Philistines. For the time being, the God of Israel does not want us to face such a foe. We will continue to move southeast."

Joshua was shocked. "Surely God can deliver the Philistines into our hands," he said.

Moses shrugged his shoulders. "We are not ready," he said. "God has willed that we go into the wilderness. After all, that is what God told us to tell Pharaoh, is it not? God wants us to go into the wilderness to worship Him."

Elishama and Joshua were completely bewildered. Elishama finally said, "Amen. So be it." The elder looked up at Moses and said, "Moses, this is going to take a lot of people by surprise."

"Yes, it will," said Moses.

Joshua's messengers arrived for their morning briefing. He repeated Moses' instruction that they were to change direction and march southeast. He could read the troubled look on their faces as he sent them off to notify the tribal elders. Within minutes, Joshua could hear the clamor of raised voices. Soon the entire nation was consumed with controversy.

A delegation of militia leaders arrived. There was a man from each tribe—every one of them well known to Joshua. Joshua was in fact a member of this group, with which he often met and drilled as captain of the Ephraimite company. He was also conspicuously the youngest.

Present were Shammua of the tribe of Re'uven, Shaphat of the tribe of Shim'on, Caleb of the tribe of Y'hudah, Igal of the tribe of Yissakhar, Palti of the tribe of Binyamin, Gaddiel of the tribe of Z'vulun, Gaddi of the tribe of M'nasheh, Ammiel of the tribe of Dan, Sethur of the tribe of Asher, Nahbi of the tribe of Naftali, and Geuel of the tribe of Gad.

Joshua presented them to Moses, who crossed his arms and listened.

"Why are we turning away?" asked Ammiel on behalf of the others.

Moses shook his head. "God has commanded it," he replied.

"We are moving into the Sinai desert," said Gaddi. "What good will that do?"

"Is there some military strategy here that we are unaware of?" asked Geuel.

Moses smiled. "No." He could see their disappointment. "It will not be long before you have the opportunity to fight," said Moses. "But for now, young men of Israel, you must be good soldiers and follow orders." Moses paused. He was done speaking.

The fervent militiamen reluctantly accepted his order. As they were leaving, Igal said to Caleb, "The Sinai is under Egyptian military control. Perhaps God would have us engage them in the desert first." Caleb shrugged.

Moses instructed Joshua and Elishama, "Summon the council."

After the twenty-four elders had assembled before him, Moses announced, "God has indeed provided for us. He has given us a sign."

Everyone agreed that this was most certainly true, but worry was written on their faces. How could they continue marching in the beastly heat?

"I understand His purpose now," said Moses. "Prepare the people. The glory of God will lead us. From now on, we will follow the light of the pillar of fire by night, and by day we will follow the pillar of smoke. Whenever the pillar moves, we will move. Whenever the pillar stops, we will stop."

The council buzzed with this news. Then Dathan asked, "Does this mean we will be walking longer hours?"

"Where are we going?" asked someone else. "We will be moving away from the Promised Land."

"I will tell you once more," said Moses. "We are going where God leads us." He pointed at the smoldering column. "There! That is the sign that God is with us!"

"Now, go tell your people that it is time to march!" commanded Moses.

Aaron spoke out, "If Moses says 'It's time to march', it's time to march!"

Jephunneh exclaimed, "The tribe of Y'hudah is ready! We will walk and the Lamp will guide our footsteps!"

Within moments, everyone was in agreement. Aaron dismissed the council. The column of smoke demanded their attention, dominating the sky.

Then they saw a further sign that confirmed Moses' directive. The fiery phenomenon began to slowly move away from them. Its direction was unmistakable: South, as Moses had dictated.

"Behold! The beacon leads us!" cried the lookouts.

Climbing upon a ridge, Moses raised his rod and Israel marched into the wilderness. The pillar led on.

They walked well into the morning until the heat began to rise. "Will we march forever?" some asked.

As they moved inexorably away from both Goshen and the Promised Land, the controversy over their destination continued, with people divided over the issue. Joshua overheard many heated debates.

"Moses takes his orders directly from God. We must obey," said one man.

"The farther we go into the Sinai, the hotter it gets," said another.

"We could call this progress if we knew where we were going," was often said.

"There's no milk and honey in this direction."

Complaints about the heat became the talk of the day. It occurred to Joshua that walking under the blazing desert sun, even slowly, was exhausting work. Skins heavy with water were a burden in addition to everything else the people carried on their shoulders. Harder still, there were reports of elderly people who had difficulty walking or keeping pace with their families.

The Fiery Pillar

Moreover, it took far more water to walk in the sun. They weren't sure which was worse, carrying the water skins or running out of the precious liquid. It seemed that their problems were mounting with every step they took into the wilderness.

As the column proceeded, Moses assumed high ground so he could supervise its movement. Joshua hated to interrupt the prophet with the all-too-obvious report. "Moses, the people grow weary. They are wilting in the heat. They're afraid that soon they will not be able to continue."

Moses nodded. "I know." Joshua could see the burden of responsibility upon Moses' face and prayed silently that God would soon provide an answer to their dilemma.

Joshua perceived Aaron lost deep in thought, staring off to the far west. Finally, Joshua, in his youthful candor, asked, "What troubles you, Aaron?" Moses and Elishama perked up their ears.

Aaron dropped his gaze to look at Joshua while he spoke. "With our people on foot driving so much livestock, our progress is slow. I am thankful that there are no signs we are being pursued.

"We are moving parallel to the king's road. We have undoubtedly passed close to Egyptian military outposts. They are probably tracking our movement and know exactly where we are."

"Ah, you are worrying about Pharaoh," said Elishama. "I share that concern."

"The tyrant is fully capable of changing his mind again and coming after us with an army," said Aaron. "If he does, he may find us tired and weak."

They all looked to Moses for a response. Moses grimaced. "Yes, Pharaoh could send an army seeking to destroy us," he conceded.

Aaron pressed the point. "What will we do if he does?"

Moses' reply was curt. "The Lord will instruct what we must do if that should happen. God did not bring us this far to abandon us."

"Just the same, we must keep an eye out," said Aaron anxiously.

"Go ahead," said Moses. "Let me know if you see anything unusual."

Aaron nodded his head and resumed his watch.

Without warning the pillar turned toward the east.

Not surprisingly, the elders requested a meeting with Moses. When they had gathered, Moses kept walking, following the smoky column, without breaking his stride. This forced the leaders to attempt to hold a meeting while on the move.

Dathan darted up to Moses and spoke first, without seeking recognition from Elishama. "Our peril increases with each step we take!"

Moses' face turned dark with anger. This Dathan dared to speak for the elders.

"I knew nothing of this," said Elishama to Moses, glaring at Dathan.

"Nor did I," said Jephunneh on behalf of the tribe of Judah.

"Well then, let me explain," sneered Dathan, breathlessly. "There are some of us that know the geography of this province. We are greatly alarmed. We are now headed toward Pi Hahiroth, a place hemmed in by rugged terrain and the desert. We will have our backs to the Red Sea!"

"So what?" challenged Nun. "If that is where the Presence of God is leading us, that is where we must go!"

"But why is He leading us to a place where we can be cornered by Pharaoh's troops?" Dathan snapped.

Several worried leaders concurred. "Yes. Tell us why."

Moses, Aaron, Elishama, and Joshua, among others, realized that discontent was beginning to boil over. Word that the Egyptians might know of their whereabouts had spread quickly throughout the camp when they were at Etham. Now, panic was setting in.

More questions came:

"We are moving into a blind alley!"

"Is the Egyptian army near?"

"If the royal troops come, they will show us no mercy!"

Moses spoke to Dathan and his supporters hotly. "Would you turn back and risk God's wrath? Or would you have the Pillar go on without us?"

Neither Dathan nor his cronies had an answer.

"Then we will follow the Lord to wherever He goes!" thundered Moses.

"Yes, but Canaan is in the other direction!" countered Dathan, seeking to ignite the controversy again.

Moses held his rod over his head. "Enough!"

At that instant the smoky pillar stopped moving.

Joshua looked ahead. The Red Sea lay before them.

The smoldering tower had halted at the water's edge.

Revenge!

Hidden within his palace, Pharaoh sulked. He had been brooding for days. His eyes burned with bitterness. He'd had enough of mourning.

At last he could ponder other things. His thoughts turned to his prestige. The king realized, "I am being blamed for the disasters that have befallen Egypt, but no one dares tell me so!" This was an unfamiliar situation for a crafty ruler of an ancient realm at the apex of his might.

"It is as if I have no power. This is the fault of Moses and the Hebrew slaves!"

He reverted to his longstanding resentment of Israel. Molten rage flowed through his veins, feeding his inherent arrogance. He demanded of his personal servants, "Speak the truth, or forfeit your lives!"

Trembling, they told their master, "Your officials bowed down before Moses and begged Israel to leave."

"The Israelites made us give them our treasures. It seemed like the thing to do at the time."

"Tukoh and thousands more have fled."

"The destruction of the plagues and the absence of slave labor have left the kingdom teetering on the brink of collapse."

Pharaoh erupted. "I should have killed them all! Why did I let them go?" he hissed through clenched teeth.

He summoned his officials so that he could hold court and resume the affairs of state before it was too late. He would reassert his reign of terror and recover control.Shortly, the officials came cowering into his court. The king was pleased to see from their flushed faces that they were too intimidated to speak. They could feel the heat of his wrath. He was particularly upset with Apep, the captain of the royal guard, for his presumed role in the desertions.

Pharaoh fumed while he stood upon the porch of his palace. From here, he could see the land of Goshen. He pointed across the river and growled, "There used to be more than two million Israelite slaves over there!"

As the ruler became more agitated, the veins on his forehead surfaced and pulsed. "What do our runners say? Why haven't I been kept informed of my slaves' movements? I want to know where they are going!"

"We have been watching them, my Lord," said the frightened Apep. He chose his words carefully. "They started out headed for their ancestral homeland."

Pharaoh leaped from his throne sputtering, "Of course they did, you idiot! In fact, you begged them to go!"

Apep bowed and slipped back a few paces, afraid for his life.

"But why then do we not hear from our allies that they are watering the land of Canaan with their blood?" demanded Pharaoh.

"Because, for no apparent reason, they started south before turning toward Canaan. They went up to Etham where they are presently camped." Apep replied humbly.

"Be gone from my presence!" he thundered. "Do not come again unless you have something of value to say."

Apep, a cunning man nearly as ruthless as Pharaoh, privately summoned the rest of the leading officials, including the high priests of Egypt. He hoped that together, they could find a way to placate the king.

Because of the contempt with which Pharaoh now held them, Apep proposed flattering their leader. They would encourage him to retaliate against the slaves whose god had slain their sons.

Jannes and Jambres agreed, knowing that this plot could lead to their return to the monarch's good graces and possibly provide revenge for them all.

The officials entered Pharaoh's throne room together and bowed. Before they could propose their scheme, Pharaoh began thinking aloud in his usual fashion.

"Is it not enough that we have been plundered by our slaves? As if losing our sons was not enough. There is no way we can dismiss this final and greatest offense!"

Pharaoh was now fully his former self. Sinister thoughts flashed through the despot's malevolent mind. He ranted, "I still have my chariots! I still control the military might of this land! And the fools are completely vulnerable!"

Apep was about to suggest his plan when Pharaoh protested, "What have we done? We have lost our workers! We have let them go!" He vowed, "Someone must pay. We must take back our wealth. Israel must be stopped!"

Apep saw that the moment was ripe. He used information he had learned that very hour. "Great Pharaoh, I have just received reports that the Hebrews have broken their camp and turned south from Etham. They have since traveled some distance into the desert."

"What can Moses possibly be thinking?" asked Pharaoh. "How stupid! They will never be able to survive there. They will return to the security of Mother Egypt and beg to be taken back."

Apep smiled. He knew he had Pharaoh just where he wanted him. "Great Pharaoh, they are headed to Pi Hahiroth, a place from which there is no escape. We can trap and destroy them there!"

Pharaoh laughed harshly, "That proves that they are confused and ripe for the crushing. One charge of my chariots will trample these renegades under the pounding hooves and spinning axles of my war machinery. I will annihilate them in the desert! Who will stand with me?"

Relieved as well as inspired, Apep, Sobek, and the others stepped forward and shouted as one, "We will!"

Pharaoh sprang into action. "Where is my army? Get me my generals! Ready my chariots! Assemble the troops! Mount up!"

At once palace guards rushed toward the armory.

Pharaoh shrieked, "I will not permit them to get away with it! I will have my revenge on Israel!

"Attack! Attack! Attack!"

Walls of Water

It was midafternoon when the pillar of cloud stopped near Pi Hahiroth and hovered by the shore of the Red Sea. The Israelites made camp with sea cliffs on two sides and water on the third. The children of Israel were anxious. These natural barriers hemmed them in, preventing an exit from any direction except the one from which they came. The camp was in an uproar. There was a lot of ugly talk, much of which sounded to Joshua like the words of Dathan and his cohorts:

"You can't get to Canaan from here."

"We're trapped against the sea."

"What if the Egyptians find us?"

"Why, after all this effort to escape, should we place ourselves in such danger?"

"How can we possibly defend ourselves against the swift, fierce chariots of the Egyptians?"

"Why have we have put our trust in this so-called prophet and his brother?"

Joshua dutifully reported it all to Moses, who scowled but said nothing.

"Joshua, I want you to send several of the young men to high ground where they can watch the rear." Aaron nodded approvingly.

Joshua recruited six of his friends, including Caleb's son Iru, and sent them to find an outlook. It was not long before their greatest fears were confirmed. Iru returned, running breathlessly. Joshua intercepted him as the scout scurried up the rise toward Moses' camp.

Obviously greatly alarmed, Iru was pointing behind him. "Egyptians!"

Joshua wasted no time. Before Iru could catch his breath, he was ushered before Moses and Aaron.

"There's a huge cloud of dust growing on the horizon," reported Iru.

Joshua could see the concern written on Moses' face. "Instruct the nation to get ready," he ordered.

"What are we going to do?" asked Joshua.

"I don't know." Moses looked toward the swirling cylinder that continued to float above the beach. "I will ask the Lord."

"Should I send the militiamen to the rear to fend against attack?"

"No," said Moses.

This puzzled Joshua, but he instructed the runners as told.

"Go get Elishama and report back to me," said Moses.

Joshua ran all the way to where his family was camped near the sea. Elishama keenly assessed the situation. "We are boxed in against the seashore. I wonder what we will do."

"I had hoped that Pharaoh would let us go without a battle," said Nun.

"You would think the plagues had dampened their zeal," offered Joshua.

"They want their slaves back," Deborah surmised.

"They want blood," said Elishama.

"We are ready for whatever God wills," said Nun.

Not wanting to upset Deborah and Rachel, Joshua did not make a big fuss out of this farewell. He and his grandfather kissed them each good-bye as if they were just leaving for the day. There was no hint that this might be the last time they saw each other alive. With great haste the two men were off.

By the time they reached Moses, the shadows were growing long. Some council members arrived at the same moment. Their mood was less than friendly.

"What have you done to us by bringing us out of Egypt?"

"How can we defend ourselves?"

"When the Egyptians attack, how will we protect our women and children?"

"Is it because there are no graves in Egypt you have brought us into the desert to die?"

"Didn't we say to you in Egypt 'Leave us alone. Let us serve the Egyptians'?"

Then Dathan uttered the ultimate insult, "Moses, have you truly talked with God?"

The prophet's eyes flashed and his knuckles whitened as he clenched the rod of authority. Moses exchanged glances with Aaron. Joshua was shocked at Dathan's insolence when the very Presence of God in the form of the magnificent pillar of fire hovered over the seacoast in front of the nation of Israel.

Nudging Joshua to distract him from the conversation, Elishama pointed at the shoreline, "They are not keeping their eyes on God's glory."

Just as Joshua turned to witness the manifest glory of the Lord, a chilling blare from Egyptian war trumpets cut short the conversation. They all swung their heads toward the sound. They could distinguish horse-drawn battle chariots, looming on the horizon.

At that moment, several runners reported in:

"There are hundreds of chariots!"

"Pharaoh himself is leading the troops!"

"They have thousands of archers deployed!"

"Foot soldiers are moving up!"

"Moses, the archers are within two bow shots!"

"They are about to attack!"

"Their trumpets have sounded the call to battle!"

"Their chariots are preparing to charge!"

"Do not be afraid!" shouted Moses. "Hold your peace, and see the salvation of the Lord which He will accomplish for you today!" It struck Joshua that it was as if the man of God was breathing words of fire.

"He has no answers!" bellowed Dathan. "We should go defend our families!"

"No! The Egyptians whom you see now, you shall see again no more! The Lord will fight for you!" announced Moses.

Dathan could stand the pressure no longer, "Wait? Wait while our nation is destroyed? You have all lost your minds." Throwing his hands in the air, he left abruptly.

The remaining elders nervously watched Moses step away and lower himself onto one knee, leaning on his shepherd's staff for support. Gravely, he looked up at the pillar of fire, which was increasing in brightness as daylight faded. Joshua could hear him speaking to God, but he could not decipher his words. For just a brief moment, Moses was quiet, listening.

Unexpectedly, Moses smiled and stood up. He quickly walked out upon an adjacent point overlooking the Red Sea. Then an amazing thing happened. The pillar of light moved quickly from the seashore to the rear of the Hebrew camp and came to a halt. It positioned itself directly in the middle of the open ground separating the Israelites and the Egyptian army. The sky was now ablaze with the glory of God.

Suddenly, as if a curtain had fallen, implacable darkness engulfed the Egyptians. Joshua gasped. On the far side of the pillar, the land had turned dense pitch black, just as Egypt had during the ninth plague. In an instant, Joshua lost sight of the Egyptian army. The entire force disappeared from view, apparently stopped in their tracks.

Elishama and Joshua stood side by side. They looked at each other, then back at the blazing pillar. Nobody spoke. Elishama's jaw hung open. He scratched his head. On the near side of the wondrous column, the side facing the Israelites, brilliant light flooded the entire Hebrew encampment.

Moses shouted. "Behold the glory of the Lord!" Joshua felt as if lightning had struck his body. He was witnessing a supernatural intervention by God.

Out on the promontory, Moses extended his arm and thrust his rod out before him. Immediately the winds shifted in the opposite direction. What had been a west wind was now roaring in from the east. As it whooshed back past the prophet at gale force, he swung his rod toward the water. Powerful gusts swept down upon the now illuminated Red Sea, whipping the waves higher and higher. Everyone gulped involuntarily. The wind was driving the surface of the sea backwards, causing it to divide!

Joshua stared with wonderment as the sea floor became visible. Hurricane drafts pummeled the ocean like a precision tool in God's unseen hand. Waters were pushed back into walls of churning foam. Soon a broad unobstructed passageway opened through the sea! The ocean floor was sandy and firm, looking unmistakably like a roadway. Within minutes the newly exposed seabed was blasted dry by hot desert air.

With the wind tearing at his clothes, Moses commanded the Children of Israel: "Step now into the midst of the sea, on dry land!"

The heretofore paralyzed nation lurched forward. In the forefront were Nun and Caleb, their tribes immediately behind them. They were in clear view of multitudes, moving down the slope and onto the beach. Many were concerned about what would happen when these men came to the edge of the sea. Would they dare step into the ominous canyon that had opened into the waters?

The Divine Pillar was now two-faceted. On one side, impenetrable darkness held the Egyptians at bay. The opposite side of the column shimmered with fiery light, the glow of God's glory, highlighting the corridor between massive embankments of raging seawater.

Nun and Caleb strode forward unhesitatingly, beaming with pride that they had been honored with the opportunity to lead the procession. Demonstrating their faith and inspiring obedience, they went gladly into the gorge. Their respective tribes of Ephraim and Judah came obediently behind them. By the time they were a hundred yards out, it was obvious that the roiling walls of water would stay restrained. The tribes of Ephraim and Judah began to cheer and praise God.

Thus, the entire nation of Israel began to move through the trough. As they marched, millions of eyes fixed upon safety on the far shore. Soon all Israel was singing and chanting. The sound of their voices could be heard over the rushing wind and surging waters. Rejoicing filled the air as they moved forward. "Hallelujah! Hallelujah! Hallelujah!"

Within a short time, tens of thousands were traversing the breach. Cheers broke out again as Nun, Caleb, and their tribe arrived on the far side with Yosef's coffin, escorted by Rehojemiah Ben-Bekher.

Moving millions of souls with all their possessions and livestock through the chasm was a monumental undertaking. All night long the Hebrews crossed the Red Sea while the Lord kept back the waters.

A New Dawn

Shortly before dawn, the last of the tribes and their herds, as well as the peoples led by Tukoh, were completing the journey. Moses stepped down from the promontory from which he had pointed the way. Moses and Aaron, along with Joshua and Elishama, brought up the rear.

While they walked briskly through the passageway, Moses told them, "We are going to the Mountain of God. The Lord told me at the burning bush that I would bring the entire nation of Israel to worship Him there."

Joshua and Elishama were dumbfounded. Moses had known their destination all along. Aaron laughed.

"You both knew?" Joshua asked.

"Of course," said Aaron. "Remember, I joined Moses at the mountain before his return to Egypt."

"Why were we not told this?" asked Elishama.

"Because God did not wish it known," said Moses. "I could never have imagined that this was how He would make it possible." He smiled broadly. "Until the waters parted, I was as worried as anyone."

By the time they reached the far shore, Joshua was shedding tears of joy for the means God had used to allow His people to escape safely and completely across the watery strait. He thanked God that he was chosen to serve at this moment in time. Few people had ever witnessed so much of God's power, grace, and His compassion for His people.

At the break of day, Moses climbed upon an outcropping of rock on the eastern shore. The column of fire had followed the nation of Israel through the sea, lighting the huge trench from above.

As Moses looked back down and through the divided waters, he beheld a terrifying sight. The Egyptian army was no longer restrained by darkness. Chasing after the pillar of light, war chariots had already driven deep into the corridor. Behind them were charging archers and infantry.

Joshua shuddered. Riding in a general's chariot at the head of the first wave of war wagons, he recognized the man Apep, who had for a brief time submitted to Moses. Riding alongside in their own chariots were two other unmistakable figures, the evil magician-priests Jannes and Jambres.

Joshua realized that Pharaoh was now more than likely upon the very point of land from which the prophet had directed the crossing of the Israelites. The enraged dictator undoubtedly hoped to use the miracle God had provided for the Hebrews to overtake his former slaves.

Moses began to pray aloud for divine protection.

Aaron whispered, "Surely God will not allow Egypt to thwart His plan for our people."

To Joshua, it was as if God was instantly answering their prayers. Moses stretched out his hand over the sea and proclaimed, "The Lord God told me, 'Behold! I will harden the hearts of the Egyptians and they will go in after you; and I will gain glory through Pharaoh and all his army and his chariots and his horsemen. And the Egyptians will know that I AM the Lord!'"

Joshua moved closer to the prophet, allowing him to see things from Moses' perspective. He found himself beholding the most dreadful spectacle imaginable.

Inexplicably, chariot wheels began breaking. Axles snapped. The ground beneath Pharaoh's minions suddenly became unstable and they began to sink into soggy soil. Only about a hundred yards from the eastern shore, the two horses pulling Apep's chariot lurched in opposite directions, causing them to stumble, breaking the momentum of the charge. A charioteer screamed, "Turn back!"

It was no use. The disoriented horses reared and pawed the air as if desperately flailing at some unseen force. Other horses struggled as they tried to pull their loads on broken rims and missing wheels. The chariots behind them collided into one another. Joshua saw Jannes and Jambres tossed from their chariots and dozens of horsemen thrown from their steeds. Men cursed and yelled. Apep grappled with horses gone mad, as his chariot broke apart beneath his feet.

The unnerved Egyptians pleaded to their gods. Then they cried to one another, "Let us flee from these Israelites, for The Lord fights for them against us!"

Meanwhile, a regiment of archers tried to push forward ferociously, fighting to regain their pace. They found themselves blocked by the jam of disabled vehicles, horses, and cavalry.

Unaware of the chaos well in front of them, the last wave of Pharaoh's army advanced into the channel. Now the entire Egyptian force was inside the liquid gorge.

Moses stretched his hand over the sea.

The tempestuous east wind suddenly stalled. For a breathless moment, time stood still. The fierce storm ceased. Then, with a thunderous crash, the walls of water buckled and fell. Like twin tidal waves, the two massive torrents collapsed upon the hapless hordes of Pharaoh with a frightening roar.

There was no way for anyone below to get away. The only sound was the horrendous noise of thousands of tons of tumultuous onrushing sea. Joshua watched in fearful fascination as soldiers, horses, and chariots were swallowed in an instant.

In a few moments, the Red Sea returned to a seamless ocean. The enemies of Israel had completely vanished — submerged and drowned, buried in the deep.

It was several minutes before anyone spoke.

Finally, Aaron broke the silence, proclaiming, "The Lord has overthrown the greatest army on earth with one gesture of His prophet's hand!"

Finding his voice, Elishama shouted, "Behold the miraculous authority God has given His faithful servant!"

"Even the waters are subject to His command," said Joshua in awe.

A cloud of mist had risen from the implosion. Drops of dew began to settle gently upon the nation of Israel, refreshing the people.

The brisk eastern wind that had split the waters in two throughout the night changed into a quiet breeze gently nudging waves across a peaceful pond. The only sign that the waters had ever been disturbed was a wide band of foam floating over the now-submerged highway through the sea. Gentle waves began to slowly disperse the debris. A few lifeless bodies washed up along the shore.

"Our God has claimed His vengeance for His honor's sake," said Joshua solemnly.

From their lofty perch, the prophet and his chosen leadership surveyed their new surroundings. The waters' bubbly froth was highlighted by luminous hues of golden light shed by the awakening rays of a new dawn. To the east, the sun was rising over the nation of Israel.

The pillar of God had transformed itself once again from fire to smoke as it moved inexorably to the lead. The Children of God were leaving their past behind them and moving forward into another wilderness.

Moses began to sing praises to God, accompanied by his sister Miriam and the rest of his family. Others, who had climbed to higher ground, joined him:

> *I will sing unto the Lord,*
> *For He has triumphed gloriously!*
> *The horse and its rider*
> *He has thrown into the sea!*
> *The Lord is my strength and song.*
> *And He has become my salvation;*
> *He is my God and I will praise Him;*
> *My father's God, and I will exalt Him!*

A holiday was declared. All Israel rejoiced with their prophet in celebration of their deliverance. At Moses' invitation, Nun's family joined those of Moses and Aaron for the festivities. They could scarcely stop hugging one another.

"Last night, when I saw the Egyptians breathing down our necks, I was sure we were dead," said Elishama.

"I thought I would never see the light of day again," agreed Joshua.

"But our God is faithful, and He kept His word," said Moses.

Forming a large circle, Joshua, Nun, Deborah, Rachel, and Elishama linked raised hands with Moses, Aaron, and their families.

They all sang and danced for joy.

PART II

The Last Supper

Every valley shall be raised up,
Every mountain and hill made low;
The rough ground shall become level,
The rugged places a plain,
And the glory of the Lord
Will be revealed,
And all humankind together will see it.
For the mouth of the Lord has spoken.

ISAIAH (YESHA 'YAHU) 40: 4-5
(a. 700 B.C.E.)

Jerusalem
Passover (Pesach) 30 C.E.

Noonday. The sun had just reached its zenith. Abruptly, the heavens blackened. Light was vanquished from the skies over Jerusalem. Gloom draped its streets.

Opaque, swirling, sable clouds mounted on violent updrafts. Thunderheads collided. Ominous, foreboding vapors mushroomed their threats overhead. Electricity snapped back and forth inside the mysterious haze. Lightning bolts crackled down supercharged channels of jagged light.

Next came the wind—heaving and howling across rooftops, rushing over the city of King David, ripping at tree limbs, tearing at tent flaps, yanking at awnings. Flimsy garments hung out to dry were snatched away by angry gusts, vanishing into thin air. Anything not tied down was tossed about with reckless abandon.

Particles of sandy soil were swept up in the gale. Small pebbles struck against stony walls as they were sucked into the buffeting attack. Their staccato rhythm resembled that of a spring rainstorm when its first drops smatter upon a dry and dusty loam. It sounded like hail. But there was no hail, nor was there any sign of rain. All moisture had been extracted from the air. The windstorm propelled itself through vacant city streets, emptied of occupants, sequestered inside due to the eerie absence of light.

Just outside the confines of the city walls, watching mournfully upon a hilltop, stood a small cluster of forlorn friends. They had come to honor their leader while he was dying, hanging on a wooden instrument of execution. The life of the condemned man was nearing an end. Those friends unwilling to witness the cruel Roman judgment stayed away. Not surprisingly, the hope of the faithful had failed with the light, matching the mood of dreary, downcast skies. The sudden squall added to the confusion and deepening despair of the bereaved.

Unexpectedly, a young man separated himself from the rest of the mourners. Greatly agitated, he could wait no longer. A meeting on the Temple Mount summoned him away. Knowing that his father awaited him there, and would be concerned because of the threatening changes in the climate as well as the ugly political atmosphere, the young man forced himself to leave. With every fiber of his being he wished he had not promised to join his father, but duty called. He was deserting his dearest friend at the hour of his greatest need.

With the wind tugging at his clothing, struggling with extremely limited visibility, the lad felt his way back down the rocky slope of Golgotha, the Mount of the Skull. Wisely, he pulled a protective wrap over his face. Crossing the road at the foot of the mountain, he reentered Jerusalem through the Damascus Gate, the northernmost of the city's gates. Passing by King Shlomo's quarry, he steadied himself against the shifting air currents by leaning on the large blocks of limestone bordering the grotto. Wind-driven dust stung his eyes.

Once inside the city walls, inviting structures offered some shelter. He ducked behind buildings for protection and quickened his pace. After half a kilometer, the way became more familiar. He found some cover in the gully along the narrow road leading toward the eastern entrance to the Temple. Finally, he reached the Temple Sanctuary on Mount Zion. He entered at the Gate called Beautiful.

John Mark (whose first name was according to his Hebrew heritage, Yochanan, and whose second name, Markon, came from the Greek language) crossed the first portico of the Temple. His father could barely make him out in the diminished light. Benjamin was relieved to see his son was not hindered by the storm. Embracing him, he asked, "What is the news from Golgotha?"

"Yeshua is dying, Father," replied John Mark. "It's gruesome."

Sadness furrowed Benjamin's face. "This is indeed a day of horrors. Have you heard the news about Judas who betrayed him? He has hanged himself."

John Mark could hardly believe his ears, but there were more pressing matters with which to deal.

Benjamin asked, "How are your mother and grandmother holding up?"

"All things considered, they're doing well," said John Mark.

"We must be moving along if we are going to view the priest's sacrifice," said Benjamin. John Mark followed his father into the restricted area surrounding the Temple. Crossing the Women's Court, the two men climbed the Temple steps to enter the Court of the Israelites. Here they would be able to observe the annual sacred sacrificial ceremony about to take place near the Brass Altar of burnt offering. This was the location where animal sacrifices were presented to God Almighty.

As a Levite and a man of stature in the community, Benjamin was required to assist in the Temple sacrifice preparations. Not being a member of the priesthood, he was not allowed inside the Temple itself. However, he was chosen to serve in the area around the Brass Altar within the Temple courtyard. Before meeting his son, he had spent the morning completing the numerous tasks under his supervision to prepare for the offering of the Passover lambs.

A long line of pilgrims from lands far and near was moving slowly toward the slaughterhouse next to the altar. As good people of Israel in submission to Torah, it was their responsibility to pay tribute to God with their Pesach sacrifice.

The holy offering was of such importance that John Mark had been compelled to leave the execution of his esteemed friend and rabbi—who that very morning had been treacherously condemned and brutalized. However, John Mark knew he must honor his Jewish religion and his God first, for this was the way he had been taught to attain redemption. As directed by his father, he had come to the Temple.

Temple guards kept the many thousands of pilgrims in line as they pushed forward toward the altar at the center of the courtyard. Benjamin and John Mark edged their way around the walls. Silently, they made their way past the ramp to the Brass Altar and crossed in front of the Water Gate on the southern wall. The two approached a side entrance to the Court of the Cohanim (priests); they had to squeeze between the

Cohanim's Washing Basin and the foundation wall of the Sanctuary. Finally, they reached the foot of the stairs, which led to the Porch of the Sanctuary.

At the third hour, the cohanim had just finished the ritual washing that prepared them for the Temple's own sacrificial offering for the Pesach. They moved to the top of the stairs. The crowd parted as they made their way down the steps from the porch.

Hurtling the Temple's walls without warning, the angry tempest blustered and billowed, causing the cohanim to secure their garments. They were fully outfitted in fine robes and their best prayer shawls. John Mark and his father could even see the detailed workmanship on the priestly clothing. He marveled at the pageantry of it all, the traditions of his people for over a thousand years.

The young lad could not help but think of Yeshua, who at that very moment was hanging from a wooden limb, slowly dying as the blood from his wounds dripped to the ground. He could not shake this image from his mind. "How could these same cohanim condemn a rabbi to death, then go about rituals that honor God?"

The priests passed in front of the two men, leaving the stairway to the porch unoccupied. With such great masses of people present, these stairs provided a better overlook of the ceremony. The pair quickly moved up the steps. John Mark told his father he felt the need to pray. Benjamin approved, for prayer was a way of life to these devout Hebrews. If ever there was an appropriate occasion for prayer, this was it.

Facing the direction of the Most Holy Place, John Mark lifted his hands above his head in the traditional manner, and then lay face down upon the cool limestone landing at the top of the stairway to humbly beseech the Lord's mercy. Benjamin, despite his own distress watched his son with empathy, joined in the prayer. There, before the Holy Place, they sought God with heavy hearts.

As when King Shlomo (Solomon) consecrated the First Temple, tens of thousands of animals were to be slain today as a peace offering. Their blood was to be presented to God. What an awesome spectacle. What a price to pay for sin. It was commonly accepted that these sacrifices would continue forever. Despite the fact that animal sacrifices were a part of life, John Mark was repulsed by the carnage. He wondered aloud, "When will this sacrificial bloodbath come to an end? How many animals will die? How much blood will be spilled?"

John Mark ached with tormenting questions. "If Yeshua is the Messiah, why did God allow him to be crucified as a criminal between two outlaws? What had he done to deserve such a death sentence?" The young man faced the front of the entrance to the Holy Place. Fervently, he attempted to pray, but to little avail. He felt spiritually parched.

Instead, his thoughts drifted back over the last week. He recalled the day of Yeshua's triumphant entry. So much had occurred. John Mark's life had been totally transformed. And to think that only a few days earlier . . .

The Triumphal Entry

It was Monday. After admiring the brilliant blue sky over Jerusalem's western wall, John Mark headed home. Preoccupied with an important assignment, he took no notice of the unusual quiet in the normally bustling streets. His mind was upon his new companion—a lamb that had just been washed in the Sheep Pool.

John Mark's newly chosen pet playfully tugged on its short tether. He reached down to stroke the yearling's soft ears. It was now just four days before Pesach. A sacrificial offering of atonement was required annually of each family. John Mark knew that once his new playmate was declared fit, it would be his family's offering for the feast at the end of the week. This fact filled him with mixed emotions. Why should this innocent, friendly creature die for his family's sins? At least he would be able to care for his cute little woolly follower for a few days.

Suddenly, he was alerted by an uproar from below the wall. He heard the sound of the shofar: "Hah-rooot. Hah-roooooot. Hah-rooot." The trumpeting of the ram's horn made the hair on the back of his neck stand on end. Was this an alarm? What was happening?

John Mark ran to a nearby archer's turret in the city's protective wall overlooking the road to the Sheep Gate. Below he beheld an awesome sight. The route that climbed along the base of the fortification was crowded with pilgrims who had made their way up to Jerusalem to celebrate the Feast of Pesach. They were shouting something. John Mark listened carefully to discover what the ruckus was all about.

Voices carried up and over the embankment: "Hosheanu! Hosanna! Save us now! Hosanna! Save us now! Baruch haba b'shem

The Triumphal Entry

Adonai! Blessed is he who comes in the name of the Lord! Hosheanu! Hosanna!"

The pilgrims were heralding the approach of Yeshua, the controversial rabbi from Nazareth. John Mark was dumbfounded. He knew that such words of tribute to a mere man were blasphemy. Drawn from the Psalms of David, their praise was only fitting for the Messiah himself. The participants were, in effect, calling for Yeshua to become their king and overthrow the Romans.

He recalled remarks made by his father earlier that month as they studied the Scroll of Dani'el. "In light of Dani'el's prophecies and current events," Benjamin had exclaimed, "It appears the time of Messiah's arrival is nigh! Many of our brethren expect it will bring the overthrow of Roman rule and the beginning of a golden era for our people. The streets are awash with rumors that Messiah is near, and that the revolution could begin at any moment."

John Mark was mindful that Yeshua was a name of a great hero of the Tanakh, who led the nation of Israel into the Promised Land. Although he had never laid eyes on Yeshua, John Mark was well aware of him, as were all throughout Israel. Enthusiasm swirled about as thousands ran outside the city gates to greet him. Cheering Israelites straddled the road as far as the eye could see.

John Mark imagined how, in days gone by, the city had saluted great Hebrew heroes in like manner, but he had never expected to witness such an event himself. Cries rang out. "Yeshua of Nazareth! Savior! Son of David! Our King! Hosanna! Hallelujah! Our Messiah has finally come!" People jumped ecstatically in the air. It seemed the city of David had literally erupted with praise.

The return of Yeshua was beginning to look like the city's most momentous event since the Maccabees had delivered Jerusalem from the hands of the Syrians more than a century-and-a-half before. All Jerusalem buzzed with excitement. What would Yeshua's latest visit to Jerusalem reveal, or perhaps provoke? A peculiar blend of apprehension and premonition hung in the air.

John Mark's eyes focused on Yeshua. He saw the figure of a solitary man sitting upon a donkey's foal. His head was covered with a prayer shawl. All around, admirers cast their garments on the road in front of him. Some were cutting palm branches from nearby trees and spreading them on the road before the rider, a high honor reserved only for a king.

For the past three years the miracles of Yeshua had been the subject of great public debate. Events in recent weeks had further intensified the controversy. The purported resurrection of Lazarus was on everyone's lips. John Mark had heard reports from many spectators:

A mason had said, "Right before our very eyes, Yeshua raised Lazarus from the dead, just like the prophets of old."

A horse trader exclaimed, "Yeshua the Nazarene called Lazarus out of the tomb where he had lain for four days!"

An elder woman added, "No one wanted to see his body; we expected him to have begun to putrefy."

John Mark was astounded by what he had heard. At the time, he had thought, "Only the Messiah himself could have achieved such a miracle." Now he understood Yeshua's marvelous popularity. But the outpouring of praise was far beyond anything he could have imagined. He asked himself, "Could this Yeshua be the Promised One?"

John Mark knew it was not wise to express such ideas openly. This might spell trouble for his household and jeopardize their standing in the Jewish community. Benjamin and his mother Naomi had become discreet followers of this rabbi. John Mark had heard great things, but had never met the man or seen his works firsthand. He had yet to be completely convinced. Even so, the rallying cries for the man of God astride a donkey sparked John Mark's greatest desire — the deliverance of his people from oppression. Could it be that the time had come?

Benjamin had warned him about the Judean hierarchy, or Sanhedrin, comprised of the Tz'dukim (Sadducees) and P'rushim (Pharisees). The Tz'dukim were the dominant party of cohanim—priests. And they had taken their name from Tzadok, the high priest just prior to the time of the First Temple.

"They are highly influential," Benjamin had warned him. "They manipulate politics and control events at the Temple. Despite numerous Scriptures to the contrary, they do not believe in even the possibility of someone rising from the dead. Indeed, the news of Lazarus' resurrection threatens their priestly authority.

"On the other hand, the P'rushim are the party of the rabbis—teachers. They believe in resurrection, but it is a political position more than an article of faith. They wield power and maneuver public opinion by making themselves spokesmen for the Law and the traditions of the elders. They are noted for their strict, legalistic approach to Torah.

"Although Palestine is completely under the authority of Rome, the leaders of these competing sects meet regularly on the Temple grounds to deliberate public policy. Even though we need to be united as a nation, they often neglect important matters due to their bickering.

"It is rumored that they all agree on one thing—their fear that the story of Lazarus' resurrection might ignite fires of discontent among the people and provoke a popular uprising that would unseat them. They are said to have placed a price upon the head of the once-dead man Lazarus! Inconceivable. How could it be that a man who died and received life again should once again be marked for death?

"But the Tz'dukim refuse to accept the miracle, even though responsible eyewitnesses swear to it. Furthermore, the P'rushim could not accept the possibility that this young upstart rabbi knew more about Torah than they themselves, as Yeshua repeatedly demonstrated—much to their embarrassment. How dare he teach them authoritatively!

"In their fear and selfishness, they cursed this outspoken fellow Jew who so wonderfully mirrored the acts of Israel's greatest prophets with healings and resurrections."

"I wonder what they think of him being hailed as a king?" thought John Mark. From his vantage point on the wall, the young Israelite watched as the foal carried its celebrated burden down the slope of the Mount of Olives, across the Brook Kidron, and up Mount Zion, into the very heart of Jerusalem. What a sight.

Just that morning, on the way to fetch his lamb, John Mark had seen two of Yeshua's talmidim, or disciples, leading a young donkey out of the city in the direction of Bethany. It appeared to be the same beast upon which Yeshua was now sitting.

Yeshua halted. Despite the cheers of the people, something was amiss. By the way in which he cupped his hands about his face, it was clear that Yeshua was wiping away tears. He was crying. How strange. John Mark found himself staring in disbelief. If this was such a mighty man, why was he weeping? Perhaps these were tears of joy?

John Mark looked more closely. The passion of the crowd was so overwhelming that only those nearby seemed aware of Yeshua's deep sadness. Most were so caught up in the celebration that they were oblivious to the sorrow of the person they praised.

After a brief pause, the humble rider urged the young beast forward. John Mark thought, "This could hardly be the type of man to lead a rebellion."

John Mark turned heel and set out through the ancient streets of Jerusalem to tell his family the news. As he ran, he noticed that his lamb was having trouble keeping pace. He picked up the young creature and cradled him safely under his arm. He dare not let harm come to his four-legged friend, for this would render the lamb unsuitable for sacrifice. His family's offering must remain without blemish.

Unexpectedly, a group of Roman soldiers attired in imperial crimson and leather came around the corner. John Mark gasped. He slowed to a walk. They were drunk. Fortunately, they paid no attention to him. His father had warned him to steer clear of the authorities. These intoxicated troops would not hesitate to harass anyone they thought was in a hurry. Then, too, they might decide they wanted the lamb for themselves. Thankfully, the lamb remained quiet until they were well out of earshot.

After a quick sprint, John Mark entered his own neighborhood. There he encountered two Essene priests dressed in their traditional white garb. The Essenes were a sect of devout ascetic Jews that frequented this quarter of the city.

Recognizing their young neighbor as he hustled by, they asked if he had any news concerning the coming of Yeshua. John Mark excitedly shared what he had seen. Pointing behind, he said, "Yeshua is approaching the Eastern Gate now!"

Abandoning their usually pious demeanor, the Essenes ran eagerly toward the north wall of the Temple Mount, shouting for their brothers to join them. A dozen others poured out of nearby quarters and scurried along the way to catch up with their friends. John Mark slowed down his pace and watched with amusement. They disappeared around the corner. He had never seen Essenes so excited.

The Triumphal Entry

Running again, John Mark soon reached the end of the row of shops that bordered the narrow street where he resided. Turning to his left, he entered through the tall wooden gate to his home. He carefully closed the portal behind him. Crossing a small garden area, he gingerly set the lamb down. His mother was wiping off the table. He was panting, but could hardly contain himself. "Mother, Yeshua has arrived! I saw him!"

Miriam stood straight up and turned around. "I thought I heard a shofar. Was that why?" She blessed the Lord out loud, "Oh, faithful God, You are answering our prayers." John Mark had often heard his father speak favorably of Yeshua, but this was the first time his mother had openly referred to the rabbi with such reverence.

"At this very moment, he's riding a young donkey through the Eastern Gate!" declared John Mark. "Do you remember what we read last week in our study of the Scroll of Z'kharyah? That the Messiah will come to Jerusalem riding upon a donkey foal? And to think Z'kharyah lived five hundred years ago. Mother, I may have seen it with my own eyes! Where is Father? I can't wait to tell him. Is Grandmother home? She will want to know."

Miriam replied, "They are in the upper room discussing preparations for the Pesach." She saw John Mark start toward the stairs. "Wait just a minute. You must give our lamb some milk."

Bending down to caress the yearling sheep, Miriam added, "Your Father is expecting the lamb. We need to welcome the newest member of our family and prepare a place for him. You and your sister will have plenty to keep you busy."

John Mark could scarcely contain himself. Quickly, he tied the lamb to a table leg and fetched a bowl. The lamb smelled the milk and bleated. He was thirsty. Glancing in the direction of the hearth, he saw his little sister Rebekah come into the room. The six-year-old had been out back tending the hens. Gingerly, she put some fresh eggs in a basket. Humming to herself as she played, she had taken little notice of her brother's entry. She did not realize that John Mark had brought a lamb into the house.

Hearing voices, she looked up the stairs. Benjamin and Naomi, John Mark's father and grandmother, were descending. Seeing the lamb, Benjamin came over and kneeled, speaking gentle, loving words. "This is such a precious animal."

John Mark was dying to give his father the news, but he was held in check—Miriam was extending the palm of her hand in his direction. Blessing the Pesach lamb was customary when it first entered the home. This lovingkindness was a genuine reflection of her husband's character.

Hearing her father's voice, Rebekah became curious about the object of his affection. It was only then that she saw the animal. "A lamb!" she laughed. Jumping forward, she skipped over to join her father in petting the furry creature.

John Mark was about to burst with excitement. He interrupted, "Father, aren't you going out to see Yeshua? The whole city is buzzing."

Benjamin raised his hand and placed a finger in front of his mouth to quiet his son. He reached out with his arms to either side and around his wife and son. The other members followed suit and completed the circle. Rebekah was wide-eyed over her new pet. Both brother and sister were eager to speak, but they submitted to their father's wishes. Benjamin lifted his hands, as did the members of his family, and prayed over their little lamb.

When Benjamin finished he looked about. "I can hear a great throng welcoming Yeshua to Jerusalem. Come. We must join the festivities. Come on, Mother!"

John Mark breathed a sigh of relief. By this time, Miriam was already helping Naomi adjust her shawl over her head and shoulders. Naomi suggested to her daughter, "Miriam, make sure our new family member is secured." A broad smile covered Miriam's face. She double-checked the rope around the lamb's neck. Then she grabbed Rebekah's hand and headed for the door.

Rebekah looked longingly after her new friend. "Mama, I want to stay here with the lamb."

Miriam reminded her, "Our lamb will be here when we return." Rebekah frowned.

With that settled, John Mark shouted joyfully, "Let's go!" Excitedly, he coaxed them down the avenue, "Come on. We don't want to miss him."

The Temple

John Mark loved going to the Temple. His earliest childhood memories were of visits there. Its construction had begun before his father was born and even today was not yet completed. John Mark remembered going to the site and watching huge limestone rocks being gently and precisely placed to form its massive walls. Hurrying to see Yeshua, the young man still could clearly recall his father teaching him the history of the Temple during his youth …

"It began with the Hebrews in the wilderness," said Benjamin. "While on the Mountain of God, the Lord had instructed Moshe (Moses) to construct a Tabernacle. As our ancestors journeyed through the desert, a pillar of cloud and fire led them. At God's command, the pillar would begin to move. All Israel would obediently follow. Thus, the Tabernacle was designed to be portable and would be disassembled for each leg of their passage. When the pillar stopped, the Tabernacle was reassembled, no small task indeed.

"The Tabernacle was an enclosure made of ten curtains woven out of blue, purple, and scarlet yarn and finely twisted linen, magnificently portraying winged angelic figures, or cherubim. At the center of the structure was the Holy Place containing a candlestand with seven candles, incense burner, and table for the unleavened bread—all meticulously crafted by inspired artisans and diligently maintained by Levite priests. The sacred objects occupied specific positions in front of a hidden room, the most sacred place of all—the Holy of Holies.

"Concealed behind the folds of a majestic tapestry, this innermost sanctuary was strictly off limits to everyone, even the priests. Its drapes were perpetually closed, symbolizing no access—except for one day each year, the Day of Atonement.

"Inside the Holy of Holies stood the Ark of the Covenant. This most sacred chest was entirely covered with gold, both inside and out. From opposite ends of the cover, two golden cherubim faced one another, holding their wings outstretched, silent sentinels guarding the earthly throne of God.

"It held the consecrated items that God commanded must be entirely set apart for Himself: the tablets inscribed by God's hand with the Ten Commandments outlining the Covenant between God and Israel; the bowl of manna, or heavenly food, that God sent to earth to sustain the Children of Israel for their entire wilderness experience; and Aaron's rod, the sign of his authority as High Priest, used by Moshe to part the waters of the Red Sea (and which had miraculously sprouted when his priestly authority was questioned). No person, under any circumstances, was allowed direct contact with the Ark. By God's command, the slightest touch would result in instantaneous death.

"The cover of the Ark of the Covenant was also fashioned of gold. This was the Mercy Seat or Throne of God. Here was the place where the pillar of cloud and fire came to rest. In those days, a shaft of resplendent light from the heavens bathed this most hallowed site with the overwhelming brilliance of God's glory. Our sacrificial system focused all its attention upon this place of mercy and atonement.

"It was inside the Tabernacle in front of the Ark during those forty years in the desert that Moshe was given the entire Torah. Whenever Moshe entered the Tabernacle he would encounter the Presence of God and behold His glory. Each time Moshe emerged from the Most Holy Place, his face was shining as the sun.

"Over a thousand years ago, King David prepared the way for the Temple by unifying Israel. David's son, King Shlomo, built the First Temple upon this permanent site. It was modeled after the Tabernacle in the wilderness. When the fabulous Temple was completed, it was consecrated as a Tabernacle to house the Ark of the Covenant. On that day, King Shlomo acknowledged God's covenant: 'There has not failed one word of all His good promise, which He promised through His servant Moshe.'

"What a sight that must have been when Shlomo beheld the Temple filling with the glowing majesty of God's Presence!

"In time, when the people of Israel turned away from the One True God and worshipped the gods of the pagans, the original Ark of the Covenant was mysteriously removed, and no one knows what became of it. Shortly thereafter, the Temple was destroyed by the Babylonians, who took its remaining contents and our people to Chaldea. Upon our nation's return some 70 years later, the Temple was rebuilt. Although it followed the blueprint of the ancient Tabernacle, it never attained the glory of its predecessor.

"The long, laborious process of renewing the Second Temple was initiated at great cost by Herod the Great several decades ago, during my youth. Its beauty bears eloquent witness to the gifting of its designers and builders. They have labored for forty-six years in an effort to recapture the magnificence of Shlomo's Temple, and still the work continues even though Herod is long dead.

"This is the great representation of the spiritual heritage of our nation. Therefore, you and every good Jewish youth shall remember by rote all that you have been taught and you shall teach this to your children."

On Top of Mount Zion

John Mark and his family hastened down the street toward the center of activity. It appeared that the whole city, whose numbers were swollen by many thousands of devout pilgrims, had turned out to greet Yeshua. Two young men dashed in front of them carrying a banner declaring, "We Proclaim Our King." The crowds were jubilant and boisterous. Rejoicing and dancing filled the streets.

"Everything seems to be building toward a coronation!" exclaimed Benjamin. "Such a rousing demonstration will inflame many factions, not to mention the Romans."

As John Mark and his family neared the procession, the throng that had earlier entered the Eastern Gate with Yeshua was now moving up toward the Temple Mount. John Mark glanced up ahead. There, standing high upon Mount Zion, towering over the landscape, was that magnificent edifice, the Second Temple.

As they neared the structure, Benjamin pointed, "Look at the pilgrims. They are sincere worshipers who have come here from many lands in obedience to the Scriptures. Yet sadly they have no choice but to exchange their Roman currency for shekels to pay the Temple tax. On top of that, the cohanim have turned God's House into a marketplace. Those traveling great distances must buy sacrificial animals and doves within the Temple Court, where they are charged exorbitant prices. And to add insult to injury, the scales are crooked!

"It's robbery! It's an affront to everything Torah teaches! Any of the prophets from Moshe to Mal'akhi, 'Amos or Yirmeyahu, and especially King Shlomo would be outraged to see this scandalous abuse of the faithful's offerings. One can only imagine what the Lord thinks about it!"

Yeshua's bustling company neared the expansive Temple area. Many families had their newly selected young lambs with them. Having heard the tumult, they had decided to turn aside to have a firsthand look at this so-called prophet from Galilee. Yeshua watched his admirers and smiled at the children while they sang and leaped with joy. Despite the zealous reception and the blessings of the people, Yeshua still seemed troubled. It could be seen upon his face. Most of the time he looked straight ahead toward the Temple. It was evident that the focus of his attention was upon something of far greater significance. John Mark wondered what it could be.

Yeshua slipped off the foal and stepped into the sea of onlookers, moving out of the view of the cohanim above. This caused the cohanim to crane their necks in search of his whereabouts. The next thing John Mark knew, the man of God was standing directly in front of his father Benjamin. Yeshua stepped toward him with a smile and they embraced. They obviously knew each other. Miriam hesitated at the edge of the crowd. Benjamin beckoned her to come closer. When she did, he humbly introduced her to Yeshua. The rabbi took her arm and whispered something in her ear. She smiled and nodded. A friendship had begun.

Then, as if summoned, Yeshua pivoted and mounted the Temple steps. With an even, steady stride, he appeared at the head of the crowd. Dreading his every move, several of the Sanhedrin banded together at the entrance, not quite blocking it, but hoping to discourage his visit. The visitor paid them no heed.

Yeshua entered the House of God. His visit did not last long. He surveyed the commerce and trading inside the sanctuary. Shaking his head in anger, he spun about and abruptly left. The moneychangers breathed a sigh of relief. They had feared a confrontation. There was no question that Yeshua was displeased with what he had seen, but he had taken no action. Without comment, he walked down the stairs and headed out of the city toward Bethany. Many of the faithful followed him down the road.

No overt disturbance had taken place, but it was certain that something ominous was pending. After Yeshua had departed, John Mark's grandmother, mother, and sister left for home. All were relieved that there had been no public dispute.

John Mark sat down on the Temple steps. His father was nearby, discussing the day's events with several men from Galilee. Also present were a few Essenes. Their hooded white clothing made them easy to identify.

Hundreds of Israelites lingered on the broad stairway to debate the significance of Yeshua's turbulent reception in the city, including many pilgrims in town for the annual Pesach celebration. The diversity of economic and social backgrounds provided an unusual mixture of Jewish sub-cultures and practices. Every one of them held strong opinions about Yeshua. Passionately, they raised their voices: "Perhaps Yeshua was afraid to do anything."

"He didn't look scared."

"Do you think he's planning something?"

"I wouldn't be surprised."

"This is going to be an eventful week in Jerusalem."

A young student noticed the seething hostility of the Sanhedrin leaders on the steps and pointed to them, "It looks like trouble to me."

All eyes shifted to the dark figures at the top of the stairs scowling from beneath their prayer shawls. While the crowd disassembled, the cohanim retreated into the Temple.

As soon as the bystanders were gone, John Mark couldn't wait to ask his father, "What did Yeshua say to you?"

Benjamin could only shake his head, as if to say he could not reveal the rabbi's private words.

How Will We Know the Messiah?

In recent weeks, Benjamin and other elders in the community had discussed matters concerning the Messiah with the Essenes. "Tell us why you think Yeshua is the Messiah?" they asked of them. In the wake of Yeshua's notoriety, the Essenes discarded their normal reserve and openly shared carefully researched evaluations of key passages in the written Word of God. In so doing, they revealed numerous reasons for their expectations of the imminent coming of the Messiah, the Anointed One.

The previous month, Benjamin had been invited to study the scroll of the prophet Yesha 'Yahu (Isaiah) with the Essenes. The Essenes liked to discuss the more obvious messianic passages in Yesha 'Yahu's prophecies.

The Essene scribes were direct. "The Holy Scriptures clearly prophesy many signs. They tell us the blind will see, the deaf will hear, and the lame will walk. We have all witnessed these things being done by Yeshua. Many have previously claimed to be the Messiah, but never performed such miracles."

Benjamin soon shared these Scriptures with John Mark. Looking up from the family scroll, Benjamin told John Mark, "The Essenes say that Yeshua was claiming that he fulfilled Yesha 'Yahu's description of the Messiah when he read his famous prophecy in the synagogue in Nazareth:

> The Spirit of the Lord God is upon me,
> Because the Lord has anointed me
> To preach good tidings to the poor;
> He has sent me to heal the brokenhearted,

> To proclaim liberty to the captives,
> And the opening of the prison
> To those who are bound;
> To proclaim the acceptable year of the Lord."

"Doesn't he quote Yesha 'Yahu often?" asked John Mark.

"Yes," replied Benjamin. "Yeshua also quoted Yesha 'Yahu the last time he purged the Temple. He drove the moneychangers from the Temple while he said: 'Is it not written, My house shall be called a house of prayer for all nations?' And he added from the words of the prophet Yirmeyahu, 'but you have made it a den of thieves.'

"I have not heard anyone speak with such fervor since the early days of Yochanan the Immerser," said Benjamin. "I remember when he proclaimed Yeshua to be the Messiah."

Benjamin enjoyed reminiscing about the remarkable Prophet Yochanan...

"He stood at the river's edge. He came out of the desert. His hair was windblown. His eyes flashed with fire. His gaze was steady, his face resolute. A leather strap served as his belt. His body was covered with the skins of wild animals.

"Over one shoulder, a bow was slung; and over the other was a shofar. This man was suited to desert life. His diet was locusts and wild honey. His roof was the firmament of heaven. His form was rugged and powerful. His movements deliberate. He was a man, but nothing human could tame him.

"He continually called upon God, lifting praises to His Holy Name. Yochanan's voice carried on the wind. No one who heard him speak could ever forget his words. 'Repent! For the Kingdom of Heaven is at hand!'

"He immersed souls in the waters of the Jordan, the river Joshua had crossed to enter the Promised Land. Word spread quickly that a great prophet had come.

"Just as Israel had waited for four centuries before they were led out of Egypt by the Prophet Moses, it has been some four hundred years of silence since the voice of a true prophet has been heard in the land of Zion.

"The Spirit of God was upon Yochanan, just as God's Spirit had been upon all the prophets who were summoned by Him to instruct His

Children. Some said Yochanan was Eliyahu (Elijah); others said he was the Messiah. But he denied being either."

Benjamin relished mimicking this exceptional prophet. He loved to loudly proclaim, "I am just a voice crying in the wilderness! Prepare ye the way of the Lord!"

Benjamin continued, "I believe he was the herald of the Messiah found in the Scroll of Mal'akhi. He said he knew not the day nor the hour of the Anointed One's coming. He simply promised us, 'The Messiah is coming soon!'"

"Yochanan was imprisoned shortly after that. Some months later, he was beheaded through the connivance of Queen Herodias and the cowardice of King Herod Antipas. This sent shock waves throughout our nation. Even so, the Immerser's unwavering witness encouraged many of us to prepare our hearts for the Messiah's imminent appearance."

Benjamin lowered his voice in reverence. "When Yeshua began his public career, multitudes believed he was the one of whom Yochanan spoke. Reports of healing miracles flowed like wine from the mouths of Yeshua's admirers. Curious travelers sought him out upon hearing of his wondrous curative touch and astounding deeds of exorcism. Once they had been exposed to his feats first-hand, they could not stop praising Yeshua. Taken together, their accounts along with the Holy Scriptures, I am wholly persuaded that Yeshua is of God and that as he proclaims, the Kingdom of God is at hand."

John Mark could clearly see into Benjamin's heart. His father was a believer!

Cleansing the House of God

The day after Yeshua's entry into Jerusalem, John Mark sat at the doorway to his home. He puzzled over the previous day's happenings. Particularly, what was he to make of Yeshua? His behavior was certainly unpredictable. Suddenly, John Mark heard a commotion up the road. Several people ran by shouting, "Yeshua is returning to the Temple!"

Benjamin poked his head out the window. He needed only to nod in his son's direction. Neither wanted to miss the next appearance of the man from Nazareth. Calling to the women to let them know they were going to the Temple, they were off in the blink of an eye.

Shortly after their arrival at the foot of the Temple Mount, they saw Yeshua emerge from a group of spectators. Once again, he had returned to the base of the massive staircase leading to the main entrance. The crowd was already swollen and anxious. What would happen next?

Without notice, the man of God lifted his hands. Everyone fell silent. He gestured for all to remain calm; he did not want the people to become unruly. He turned and started slowly upward. As before, at the top of the steps a dozen Tz'dukim (Sadducees) glared at the ascending figure. Jealousy and rage contorted their faces.

Just the previous week, as Benjamin was laboring near the Temple's Porch of Shlomo, he had overheard a debate between members of the Sanhedrin. Because he often supervised the cleaning and maintenance of the brass work around the altar, he was privy to many happenings on the Temple grounds.

He later told his family of the things he had seen and heard. "The cohanim have dismissed Yeshua's teachings over and over again. They choose to ignore Yeshua's appeal from Tanakh, our Hebrew Scriptures, or his explanation of the intent of these texts. They claim that they have an exclusive understanding of the Holy Scrolls and that he is deceiving the people.

"Hence they seek to discredit Yeshua. They have sent a steady stream of spies to entrap him with trick questions and riddles. But Yeshua has a superlative answer for each and every challenge. This has only intensified their hatred. Let me tell you what they said about him."

"Yeshua has not been formally schooled."

"But his knowledge of Torah surpasses that of our scribes."

"He's intruding on our domain and causing dissension within the congregation."

"But he has escaped every one of our traps with ease."

"And the truth is," said Benjamin, "their dogged efforts to trip Yeshua have failed repeatedly. I had to turn away from the cohanim so they would not be able to see the joy written on my face. Yet, it is a matter for grave concern. Who knows what plots they may be forming against him? And I heard more."

"How can we keep him out of the Temple?"

"We can't. There are too many witnesses."

"This desire for Yeshua has turned the people into an unpredictable mob."

"We must be careful. He's a rebel, and very powerful."

"Is there no way to stop him?"

The memory of these words echoed in Benjamin's ears as he observed the cohanim eyeing Yeshua from the top of the main stairway to the Temple.

It was clear to him that, on this day, Yeshua had business inside. Perhaps he was going to disrupt the House of God again. The authorities were afraid; they drew back upon his approach. Yeshua deliberately kept climbing the steps. In his wake, a swarm of energetic followers streamed up the stairway crying out.

"Hosanna, Son of David!"

"Save us, Yeshua!"

Again the expressions of the crowd infuriated the chief cohanim. They snapped at Yeshua, "Do you hear what they are saying? Why don't you renounce them?"

Yeshua brushed by the fuming cohanim. John Mark knew the time for debates was over. In past times Yeshua frequently heard such criticisms and repudiated them masterfully. He had told about the coming Kingdom of God. The rabbis had witnessed dozens of miracles but were unwilling to open their minds! Now the cohanim were livid.

John Mark sensed the tension. Anticipating Yeshua's next move, he whispered to his father that he wanted a closer look. Benjamin, also preoccupied with the drama on the stairs, offhandedly approved John Mark's request, but cautioned restraint. "Watch yourself, son."

John Mark had a secret viewing place in mind. He was fully familiar with the Temple grounds from the days when he studied for his Bar Mitzvah. He knew a quick way inside through a seldom-used entrance. Taking full advantage of his youth, he ran all the way to the western wall, skirted the crowd, and circled back to the far side of the Temple. Entering the courtyard just seconds before Yeshua, he found an ideal hidden position behind a pillar from which to observe Yeshua's entry. He expected this to be exciting, but he was hardly prepared for what happened next.

Yeshua, the presumed archrival of the Sanhedrin, adjusted his prayer shawl and strode directly into the Temple compound, ignoring the autocrats. Entering the Court of the Israelites, he ascended the stairs and halted in front of the Holy Place. After a brief prayer, he returned to the outer enclave, the Court of the Gentiles.

Yeshua's eyes fastened upon the tables of the moneychangers. John Mark could tell things were going to turn ugly. Just then, he noticed that the man of God was holding the small riding crop that he had used to goad the young donkey the previous day. Discreetly, Yeshua flipped the crop in his hand, allowing the flexible end of it to point back toward his body.

The onlookers stayed close on Yeshua's heels as he swept into the Court of the Gentiles and approached the booths of the traders. They nervously watched his every move in anticipation of what was to come. John Mark could hear their complaints:

"Oh, no, it's Yeshua!"

"Not again!"

"That rabbi is asking for trouble!"

Undeterred, Yeshua took the butt end of the crop and inserted it beneath the balance beam of a moneylender's scale. A quick jerk sent the pair of weighing trays tumbling across the floor with a loud clang. Exchangers scrambled to retrieve their scattered coins. But one look from Yeshua checked them in mid-stride and sent them fleeing for cover. Retreating into the recesses of the Temple, they trembled in fear. Yet the instant Yeshua turned his back on them, they resumed their cowardly ranting and insults. Tempers flared. Men yelled:

"That's my property!"

"Leave my shekels alone!"

"Call the Temple guards!"

Yeshua was aflame. As once before, when he had cleansed the Temple, he shouted and quoted the prophets. He cleared the Lord's House of illicit commerce and interfered with its illegitimate exchange. He threw open the cages containing doves, releasing them into the air. At each stall, the attendants cowered and turned tail at his approach. No one could face him.

Once the offenders had all left, things quieted quickly. Yeshua sat down peacefully in the courtyard. His followers flocked before him.

From his hiding place, John Mark soon saw a group of blind and broken people being brought to Yeshua, assisted by his talmidim. Among those who came for his healing touch were many with twisted limbs and grotesque physical deformities. Others were covered with oozing sores and chronic skin conditions. These unsightly beggars would normally be denied entry into the Temple courts as unclean. Yeshua received them like family, talking and laughing with them.

As the ill and infirm approached him, Yeshua prayed for each in turn. With most, he gently laid hands on them. Others required only eye contact. Every needy person who ventured into Yeshua's presence was restored. None were overlooked or rejected. No malady was too severe. Before healing each individual, he looked up to heaven and thanked God for His tender mercies. John Mark was awestruck. The healing was real and he was seeing it first-hand.

This did not set well with Yeshua's critics, who held that Torah commended healing ministry to the cohanim. The enraged Tz'dukim were too afraid of Yeshua to challenge these indisputable healings in front of the masses. From his hidden vantage point, John Mark heard their grumblings:

"Yeshua claims to be a teacher of Tanakh, but he consorts with the diseased!"

"Horror of horrors! He actually touches the bodies of the afflicted!"

The P'rushim and Tz'dukim joined together with angry shouts: "Unclean! Unclean!"

Conversely, their outcry was drowned out by, "Hosanna! Heal now! Hosanna! Save us now! Hosanna to the Son of David! Hallelujah! Glory to God in the highest!" Shouts of praise echoed throughout the Temple. It was grand. Yeshua's followers danced for joy. Tears flowed in celebration of God's goodness.

With this, the people were beginning to hope that rebellion would now come. "Surely, if Yeshua can restore the sick to full health, then he can restore our country!"

John Mark again wondered how this gentle rabbi could lead such an uprising. He had cleansed the temple, but taking over the nation? How could Yeshua conquer Rome?

Evil Plans Are Laid

The tumultuous praise on the Temple grounds became too much for the cohanim to ignore. They had not given the crowds permission for such informal worship. They demanded, "These indignities must stop!"

Turning to one another they complained, "This kind of praise is only appropriate for God or His Messiah, the heir to the throne of King David! This man is an impostor! Does he wish to usurp our authority?"

Yeshua heard the challenges, but gave them no mind.

Bristling with envy, the cohanim attempted to pressure him, "Do you hear what they are saying? They are calling you Messiah. How dare you accept the praises of these people!"

John Mark could clearly discern the voice of Caiaphas, Cohen Hagadol (The High Priest) of the Temple. He spoke loudly as he lectured his fellow cohanim, wanting Yeshua to overhear his words. "When the Messiah appears, he will be easy to identify. We seek a prophet like Moshe, who will exalt our Temple and bring Israel to prominence among the nations. Only then will we be sure we have seen the real Messiah!"

Nervously, the cohanim nodded their heads in agreement. Several of them glared furtively at Yeshua. One shot out a question, "Do you seriously think that this illegitimately-born, rogue magician and self-appointed rabbi from the hinterlands is the Anointed One, our Savior? I see nothing in Torah that points to one such as this."

Yeshua raised himself up. "You diligently study the Scriptures because you think that by them you possess eternal life. These are the Scriptures that testify about me, yet you refuse to come to me to have life."

John Mark saw the leaders stiffen with resentment. Before they could say anything more, Yeshua responded to their objections about his supporters. He identified their tributes to God with a quotation from the Hebrew Psalms: "Out of the mouth of babes and nursing infants You have perfected praise."

Caiaphas turned to his cohanim and sneered, "To think that an uncouth Galilean declares the voices of the ignorant and uneducated to be more acceptable to God than our own! Yeshua is saying that his followers have 'perfected praise' by honoring him. How dare he accept these accolades that belong to God alone. This is blasphemy!" With that, the Cohen Hagadol stalked away in a huff, followed by his entourage.

Cautiously, John Mark retreated from the inner court. He was uneasy. All this spelled real trouble for Yeshua. He knew that most of the cohanim cared primarily about their prestige. Their authority had been openly challenged and rebuked.

After Yeshua had left the temple, the frenzy subsided and the crowd began to disperse. John Mark came to his father's side. Together, they began to review the extraordinary events that surrounded Yeshua's life. It was no accident that wherever he went, miracles took place.

Now, John Mark had witnessed some of them with his own eyes. He marveled at Yeshua's seemingly unlimited power. His frequent signs and wonders were performed so graciously. And they were so compelling. However, Yeshua's every step was punctuated with controversy. While they descended the Temple stairs, it was clear to both father and son that the mounting conflict between Yeshua and the authorities was not likely to be peacefully resolved.

Looking over his shoulder, John Mark could see shadows against the Temple walls of sulking cohanim brewing their deadly broth of revenge. He suspected by their behavior that their frustration was reaching the boiling point.

John Mark was deeply distressed. One moment Yeshua had been riding into Jerusalem and the throngs were ablaze with desire to crown him king over all Israel. The very next moment, Yeshua was walking into a spiteful swarm of vindictive opponents and intentionally infuriating them.

John Mark could not shake himself free of a strange sense of impending doom. He said to his father, "Won't Yeshua need the backing of the cohanim if he is to overthrow the Romans? If he really wants to be king, why does he intentionally stir up the hostility of the Sanhedrin?"

Benjamin scratched his forehead, "Now that you mention it, Yeshua does not call for the overthrow of the Romans. He only exposes religious hypocrisy." He paused to think, "Fear and hatred of this great man may unify the divided religious establishment. If they were to join forces, heaven only knows what might happen. It appears they have decided the time has come to stop Yeshua — no matter the cost."

* * *

As predicted, the cohanim had begun to entertain ideas that violated Torah itself. Diabolical plots were taking shape. Evil thoughts flooded their minds. They cared not that a conspiracy against Yeshua violated the sacred honor of the Hebrew Priesthood.

"As cohanim, we cannot ourselves take anyone's life."

"He embarrasses us publicly. Something must be done."

"The P'rushim will join us against him."

"Perhaps the Romans could be enticed to offer some assistance?"

"They can do the unspeakable."

Late into the night, united in hatred, the embittered hierarchy laid out their unholy schemes. They huddled together between the limestone pillars that upheld God's house of glory. Caiaphas spoke for all: "Yeshua must be made an example before the nation. Only this will discourage such traitors from challenging us."

He added, "We must act quickly before the Pesach is upon us. If not, our official duties will interfere. If we wait too long, Yeshua will leave the city. We must strike while he is accessible and vulnerable."

Stroking his chin as his eyes scanned the rooftops of the Temple, Caiaphas said coolly, "Why don't we bribe one of his friends?"

By now, their feud with Yeshua had escalated to the point that the cohanim gave no thought that such horrible words had come from a priest — especially one as exalted as Cohen Hagadol. Thus Caiaphas openly revealed the depths to which the Judean priesthood had fallen as his bitter words exposed his twisted soul.

* * *

That same night Yeshua returned to Bethany to rejoin his friends Mary and Martha and their brother Lazarus, the one whom he had raised from the dead. While he returned to the eastern slope of the Mount of Olives, his mind dwelled on the Pesach. He knew that soon he would be giving his final words to his talmidim.

He also knew, as he had told them many times before, that he was going to die.

A Test of Faith

Late that afternoon, Benjamin called a family gathering to welcome their new lamb into the household and assign duties for its care. As in previous years, John Mark and Rebekah were delighted with their traditional roles in the Pesach celebration for the supervision, feeding, and grooming of the family's lamb.

A special place was prepared at the foot of Rebekah's bed for their fuzzy guest. Rebekah begged John Mark for permission to feed the lamb. He gladly agreed, knowing how much pleasure she would gain from tending the animal. Besides, at her age it would have been useless trying to dissuade her.

Benjamin began his annual review of the wonderful story of Israel's liberation from Egypt. He started with Moshe and the first Pesach. He reminded them, "It is said that our forefathers began the practice of naming their Pesach lambs in Egypt. Early this morning, as I prayed, I was impressed to give our new lamb the name 'Moriah.'"

Looking toward the Temple mount, Benjamin stated, "'Moriah' was the name of the land—a place of worship—where God instructed Avraham to take his son Yitz'chak to be sacrificed. It is this same land, this same mountain that is now the heart of Jerusalem, on which the Temple of Shlomo was built and where we offer sacrifices to this day. Now it is called Mount Zion."

Benjamin was emphatic: "What kind of man would have enough faith to be willing to sacrifice his own son to God? This was the greatest test of faith anyone can imagine, one that I would never have wanted to face myself. Yet Avraham was obedient, as was Yitz'chak, who submitted to being placed upon the altar. He was willing to do what his father asked, even to the point of facing his own death."

While Benjamin related the familiar story, John Mark's mind drifted back to ancient days. He put himself in Yitz'chak's place. He considered how Yitz'chak would have felt. Fearful? Confused? How relieved Yitz'chak must have been to see the ram caught in the nearby thicket. Miraculously, God Himself provided a substitute sacrifice.

It struck John Mark that, although he had witnessed many previous Pesach celebrations, he was now experiencing something that affected him on a profoundly personal level. It was as if John Mark could hear Moshe's voice transcending the ages, instructing Israel to prepare for the very first Pesach. God had called each family to select a lamb, a substitute whose blood would protect them from the coming judgment on all Egypt's first-born. This too was a great test of faith.

He asked himself, "What If I had been living back then in Egypt, and I was the eldest son in my family? That would mean that I was the one marked for death. Had it not been for the sacrifice of a lamb, I might have died." Like other young Hebrew men before him, John Mark grasped how deeply serious God is when it comes to matters of life and death.

John Mark sensed an analogy that spanned the centuries. "Just as Avraham offered his son and God provided a sacrifice, and just as the ancient Israelite families were commanded by Moshe to offer a lamb, a temporary member of their family as a substitutionary sacrifice, so too Moriah fulfills the need for my family this Pesach."

John Mark was sure his emotions concerning the impending loss of Moriah at this Pesach must be very much the same as were those of his ancestors. "Moriah" was a suitable name—worthy of the sacrifice.

Late that night, thinking that all had retired in the household, John Mark rose to spend a few minutes with Moriah. When he reached the foot of his sister's bed he discovered the lamb was not there. Then he noticed soft humming coming from the kitchen area. Putting on his sandals, he tiptoed into the next room. The house was still warm from a few remaining embers in the hearth. There, by the fireside, was his mother. She was holding Moriah in her arms, gently rocking back and forth. John Mark stood there observing the scene of love and affection.

He marveled at what a wonderful woman of God his mother was. She had deliberately taken this time to build her attachment to the lamb as God required, even though her heart would be all the more grieved when the animal was slain. But indeed, this was the whole purpose of having the lamb.

Without turning her head Miriam whispered, "Is that you John Mark?"

"Yes," he replied, moving to her side.

John Mark tousled Moriah's ears. Miriam looked up at him and smiled. Both knew exactly what the other was thinking: Although parting with something you truly love is not easy, each was confident that blessings would surely result from their obedience.

Benjamin's Surprise Announcement

The next morning, Benjamin hastily summoned his family. He could hardly suppress his joy as they came together. He then made a momentous announcement — one that would change the course of John Mark's life. Benjamin took Naomi's arm. They had John Mark's rapt attention.

Carefully addressing his family, Benjamin said. "Yeshua the Nazarene brings us great honor. He has asked us to prepare the upper room of our home to serve him and his talmidim the Pesach Feast!"

John Mark and his mother turned to each other. "Simultaneously they exclaimed, "Yeshua?" Their eyes returned to Benjamin.

"Yeshua knows our home will be a safe place for the Pesach celebration. He knows he is genuinely welcome here. But before God, we must not breathe a word of this to anyone."

The family sat stunned. Benjamin addressed his wife, "Miriam, everything must be prepared with the strictest care. All leaven must be removed from the house at once, as required for the week of unleavened bread.

"Everything must be spotless. Our upper room must be fit for a king. There will be no special decorations. Yeshua will want no ostentatious display. The table shall be set for fourteen guests. Yeshua is bringing all twelve of his talmidim, and as always, we must provide a place for Eliyahu, the harbinger of the Messiah. Most of these men are Galileans and are accustomed to simple surroundings. Our home will reflect its humble best, but as for our important guest, we will treat him as royalty, for such he is."

Looking around, Miriam contemplated how she would prepare a meal for fourteen men. No small task, but this upper room was often the gathering place for special occasions. This would be a grand celebration of Israel's deliverance.

John Mark noted that his father had once again implied that Yeshua was the Chosen One. Benjamin stopped talking while his words sank in. He was grinning from ear to ear. John Mark was overjoyed. Yeshua was coming to their house. He would meet the man of God in person!

Arm-in-arm, father and son, grandmother and mother danced together then switched partners. Rebekah and Moriah joined in the fun without an inkling of its reason. Following the jubilation everyone collapsed laughing and breathless. Naomi took Rebekah's hand and led her back to the kitchen. Moriah was all too happy to tag along.

After a couple of moments, Benjamin instructed John Mark, "Son, empty the large water jug and thoroughly rinse it. We will need it before the meal. Also gather several pitchers for water and wine.

"On the Day of Preparation you will station yourself near the Sheep Gate with the jug of water. I know this may seem odd, but it has been arranged as a signal. When you see two of Yeshua's followers enter the city, you will lift the jug onto your shoulder as a sign. Say nothing to them. Simply return to our home. They will follow you. When you arrive here, show them to the upper room. If they request any kind of help, you are to offer it without any hesitation or question. Is that clear?"

"Yes, Father." John Mark rapidly nodded his head.

Benjamin looked at his son with great pride. "A reading of the traditional Exodus passage for the Pesach will be required. Son, this is your opportunity to use the skills that God has given you. Study the Scriptures and prepare yourself."

"You can count on me, father," said John Mark.

All of the family members were elated as they went downstairs. John Mark stayed alone in the upper room. Falling on his face, he thanked God for blessing him and his family with this singular distinction. He loved God so much.

Jumping up with youthful enthusiasm, John Mark set forth to complete his assignments. His feet barely touched the floor.

The Upper Room

At the break of day, the whole family climbed the narrow stairs to the upper room to pray. Moriah dutifully bounced along behind the party. The room was comfortable and inviting. Several windows supplied daylight, adding to its warmth. Grabbing Moriah, John Mark cushioned their lamb securely under his arm as he stroked its woolly head.

Most homes in Jerusalem were single-storied with a deck on the roof. A few years earlier, Naomi had a second floor added. The upper room was designed to be a banquet or meeting place. It was not unusual for several families to use this room together. It was a popular gathering spot for those who shared the owner's deep faith. During the three major annual convocations held at the Temple on Mount Zion, this particular upper room was often pressed into service as a banquet hall or guest quarters for visitors.

Normally, the room served the family as a place to study Torah and pray. A long, low, wooden table occupied the middle of the room. When guests gathered around, its broad surface was ideal for either feasting or displaying scrolls as they were examined or publicly read. Numerous oil lamps hung overhead and were set on the table to illuminate the room with soft, warm, rich tones.

On the far wall, safely set apart in a private area, was a small wooden ark holding the Torah, the family's most precious possession. The scrolls upon which the Word of God had been painstakingly copied by hand, and checked and rechecked to assure their accuracy, had passed to Benjamin from his late father, a scribe. A lamp fueled by olive oil burned above the ark. John Mark's most important daily chore was to maintain this light.

It required inspecting the level of the oil and keeping the wick properly trimmed. Just as the Israelites were instructed in the Scroll of Leviticus: "The fire must be kept burning on the altar continuously." The flame representing the presence of God over the ark containing the Torah was never allowed to be extinguished.

Every night without fail, when the day's activities ceased, John Mark quietly climbed the stairs to the upper room. As usual, he examined the lamp hanging over the ark to assess the condition of the wick, oil, and flame. He always prayed before opening the ark. Then, he carefully lifted the Torah from within the ark and gently placed it upon the table. Next, he removed the cover over the Holy Text, revealing two cylindrical rolls of specially treated animal hide. Finally, he untied the cord securing the scrolls, providing access to their contents.

Benjamin had taught his son how to handle the scrolls and study Torah. John Mark learned to grasp the handles firmly at the base of the two columns of coiled parchment, and to unwind the sacred record. As the scroll unrolled from one large wooden dowel held by one hand, it was collected around a matching holder by means of the careful rotation of the second turning handle in his other hand. By placing the two handles approximately one-half meter apart, a full page of Hebrew text was revealed.

It was in this room John Mark was taught Tanakh under the guidance of his father's discerning eye. Here he learned what it meant to be a man—that he needed to follow the Law as God had given it to Moshe on the Mountain of God after the Red Sea crossing.

He learned that Torah, or Law, constituted the first five books of Tanakh. Tanakh also included the complete record of the Neviim (Prophets) and the Ketuvim (Writings). This total collection of laws, prophecies, genealogies, wisdom of the ancients, and hymns of worship had often been used to enrich and correct the Israelites throughout their long and tragic history. Due to their length, many of the books required an entire scroll of their own.

John Mark often marveled at the fact that the words he read in Tanakh were identical in every respect to the original texts, and were the very words of Moshe, Dani'el, Sh'mu'el, Yesha'Yahu, Yirmeyahu, Yechezk'el, 'Ezra, King David, King Shlomo, and a host of others. These authors ranged from kings to priests to common men, all called to remarkable service. In every case, their words were inspired, literally "breathed into them" by God.

Benjamin said, "Yeshua teaches that Tanakh is altogether the written Word of God. Even though the Prophets and the Writings are not as well known as the five books of Moshe, their words are equally inspired by the same Almighty God and therefore hold the same authority. Yeshua quotes from Neviim and Ketuvim just as he does from Torah."

John Mark studied Tanakh daily and sought to write its truths on his heart. It was a pleasure to the young scholar. He hungered for knowledge of God and to know His ways. John Mark also knew that if he remained a faithful son, one day he would inherit this precious possession, a family treasure of immeasurable value.

Yeshua's Miraculous Works

Early the next day, two of Yeshua's talmidim located John Mark waiting at the prearranged meeting place. As instructed, he held a heavy jug of water upon his shoulder. John Mark was tense. Since men seldom carried water, he felt conspicuous. However, this sign was a simple, effective way to attract the talmidim's attention.

Knowing that the authorities sought their master, the two men covertly signaled the young man, then furtively followed him as he made his way up and down the avenues into the Essene quarter of the city to his house and its gathering place.

John Mark was relieved as he delivered the earthen vessel home. Leaning against the door jam, he wiped his brow. A few minutes later the talmidim softly tapped on the wood. John Mark opened the door and the two slipped inside. Each man extended his hand to the doorframe, as was the custom, to touch the mezuzah—a small capsule containing a Hebrew scripture. Each offered a silent prayer.

Benjamin stepped forward, greeting them at the entryway, "Welcome brethren. Please come in."

Peter, the leader of the talmidim, looked at Benjamin, "The teacher asks, 'Where is the guest room where I may eat the Pesach with my talmidim?'"

Benjamin responded, "You have found it."

Reassured, Peter turned to John Mark and slapped him on the shoulder approvingly. "Well done!"

His mission accomplished, John Mark beamed with satisfaction.

After pulling their prayer shawls back over their shoulders, John and Peter thanked Benjamin for his hospitality. Peter offered to help with the jug. The fresh water was intended for use that evening in the ceremonial hand washing that was part of the Pesach Feast. John Mark bid the visitors to follow him.

Having climbed the steps to the upper room, Peter eyed a sturdy side table holding a large clay bowl. His compatriot John quickly moved the empty basin, making room for the water. Much to the guests' delight, they found the banquet room thoroughly cleansed in preparation for the Seder, as the traditional order of the Pesach Feast was called. The rest of the family eagerly greeted them.

The disciple John spoke first. He was young and alert. His hair was curly and his eyes sparkled with joy. He complimented Benjamin's wife. "Miriam, your home is beautiful. We can see the work that you have done to prepare for the master. He will be greatly pleased."

Miriam smiled at John's kind words. Rebekah was holding onto her mother's apron and peeking at the strangers around the folds of her skirt. Moriah was busy licking Rebekah's fingers, having found the hint of a sweet dessert.

"This is marvelous," added Peter. He was rough looking, broad chested, and solidly built. "You have outdone yourselves."

Both men commanded respect. Their arms and hands displayed scars and calluses from years of fishing the Sea of Galilee. One could see from their dark skin that they had spent much time under the sun.

While they attended to details for the evening Pesach Feast, John Mark was determined to make the most of their time together. Surely they could share with him all sorts of stories about Yeshua. He had so many questions to ask.

But first, he had to help them locate and organize all the necessary utensils and dishes for the feast. While this was being accomplished, the talmidim were inspired to comment on the first Pesach and the Hebrew exodus from Egypt.

The conversation shifted, and the talmidim began to recall details of their travels with Yeshua. Whenever miracles were mentioned, John Mark was hardly able to control his curiosity. He pressed for more details about Yeshua.

"Do you know about the prophet Micah's prediction?" asked Peter. "Our master showed us in the scroll of Micah that the Messiah's birthplace would be Bethlehem, where King David was born. And you know what? Yeshua was born in Bethlehem."

John noted, "Yesha 'Yahu the prophet said over 700 hundred years ago that the Messiah would be a Son of David. Both of Yeshua's parents are descended from the House of David."

Peter said, "Are you aware that Yeshua's parents fled to Egypt to preserve their baby's life? King Herod the Great, who ruled Israel at the time of Yeshua's birth, ordered all the male children of Bethlehem two years and under massacred, just as Pharaoh had called for the slaughter of all male Hebrew children born at the beginning of Moshe's life. Herod feared his throne might be usurped. He took seriously the accounts of visiting wise men who had come by caravan seeking the King of the Jews."

"All Israel has heard about that atrocity," said John Mark, who was unusually impressed with Peter. He was so plainspoken and earnest.

"It is not as widely known that the wise men went to Bethlehem where they recognized the child Yeshua as the Anointed One," said Peter.

He continued, "There are so many things that are singular about Yeshua. He was conceived without his mother Miriam being intimate with Joseph, or any other man. She was a virgin. If ever there was a miracle, that had to top the list. It was even greater than the miracle of Sarah and Avraham conceiving Yitz'chak when she was ninety years old and Avraham had reached one hundred."

John Mark had heard this sensational story many times, but never from those who knew Yeshua personally. If this were true, it meant that Yeshua was a gift from God Himself!

After the preparations for the supper were completed, Peter, overcome by his zeal for Yeshua, blurted, "We were eyewitnesses to his shekinah you know!"

John Mark was instantly alerted because Yeshua was being linked with God's glory.

John quickly cautioned him, "Peter, we cannot tell our friend everything." He turned to John Mark. "Our master has instructed us not to disclose certain things for the time being."

John Mark was frustrated. He sought more knowledge. Just as something marvelous was about to be revealed, it was interrupted.

He was about to ask more questions when John wisely turned to another subject. "On a certain Sabbath day, while Yeshua was being scrutinized by the P'rushim, it happened that he saw a blind man everyone knew. One of our brethren asked, 'Rabbi, who sinned, this man or his parents, that he was born blind?'

"Yeshua answered, 'Neither this man nor his parents sinned, but that the works of God should be revealed in him.' Then he added: 'I must work the works of Him who sent me while it is day; the night is coming when no one can work. As long as I am in the world, I am the light of the world.'

"I cannot tell you who was more amazed by this proclamation, our fellow talmidim or the cohanim. Yeshua had shown us that he is lighting the path that we should follow. He is the One who will lead us out of darkness."

Now Peter picked up the story. "When he had said this, he spat on the ground, made paste with his saliva, and used it to anoint the eyes of the blind man. Then he said: 'Go, wash in the pool of Siloam.' So the blind man went and washed, and came back seeing!

"Naturally, the friends of the one with new vision insisted that he should go tell the priests. Now it was no accident that this miracle took place on the Sabbath. When the P'rushim asked him how he had received his sight, he told them: 'He put clay on my eyes, and I washed, and I see.' But some of the P'rushim said, 'Yeshua is not from God, because he does not keep the Sabbath. You can't heal on the Sabbath!'"

Peter paused. "Can you believe it?" he remarked. "Performing a miracle on the Sabbath is a bad thing?"

John jumped back into the conversation, "They did not believe that the one who had received sight had been blind in the first place. So they called his parents. But even his parents' testimony was not enough to convince the P'rushim. The men further inquired of the one who had been blind. He answered and said, 'Now we know that God does not hear sinners; but if anyone worships God and does His will, He hears him. Since the world began, who has ever heard that anyone opened the eyes of one who was born blind? If this man were not from God, he could do nothing.'"

"You should have seen the look on the faces of the P'rushim," said John. "They were filled with contempt and told him, 'You were completely born in sins, and are you teaching us?' And they denied him further access to the local synagogue. What gall."

When John finished his account, John Mark sat back. He was appalled by the bigotry of the religious authorities. He said, "Here is a man who has received a miraculous healing touch, yet he has been rejected by those who claim to represent the only God that heals."

Peter said, "That is a very astute observation for a young lad such as yourself."

Then Peter related another story: "I remember when Yeshua stilled the waters in the midst of a wild storm on the Sea of Galilee. We were on our fishing boat in the middle of the sea. A wicked squall swooped down upon us. Our ship was foundering, and we feared for our lives. Unaffected by the threat, Yeshua was sleeping like a baby in the ship's stern. Imagine that. When we thought the boat would capsize and there was no hope, we awakened him. He arose, rebuked the wind, and said to the raging sea, 'Peace! Be Still!' Instantly the wind died down and all was completely calm. I have spent my entire life fishing the Sea of Galilee, as have the others, but never have any of us seen anything remotely like this. Only one sent from God can do such miracles."

John took hold of John Mark's elbow. "Then came Chanukah in Jerusalem. It was winter, and Yeshua was walking inside the Temple, in Shlomo's Porch. Inevitably, some cohanim surrounded Him. They said, 'How long will you keep us in suspense? If you are the Messiah, tell us plainly.'

"Yeshua answered, 'I did tell you, but you do not believe me. The miracles I do in my Father's name speak for me, but you do not believe because you are not my sheep. My sheep listen to my voice. I know them, and they follow me. I give them eternal life, and they shall never perish. No one can snatch them out of my hand. My Father, who has given them to me, is greater than all; no one can snatch them out of my Father's hand. I and my Father are one.'" John Mark knew this was a most powerful claim. To Jewish understanding, if this claim was not true, it was blasphemy.

"They became incensed," said John. "Many of the cohanim took up stones to kill him. But Yeshua had the last word: 'If I do not do the works of my Father, do not believe me. But if I do, though you do not believe me, believe the works, that you may know and believe that the Father is in me, and I in Him.' Then he left them abruptly before they could do him harm. So you see, instead of accepting his love, they only got angry and threatened to kill him."

John Mark was pondering this when Peter brought up another controversial issue. "They acted the same way when we told them about Lazarus."

At the mention of this name, John Mark moved closer to the talmidim. Since both of these men had witnessed this widely publicized event, John Mark implored them to describe it. "Please go on."

Appreciating their young host's curiosity, Peter tilted his head toward John Mark and gave his personal account. "We regard this as the most vivid proof of our rabbi's authority." The young man was all ears.

"It was just a few weeks ago that Lazarus' body was placed in a crypt and the opening sealed with a huge stone. Four days later, standing before the tomb, Yeshua called for Lazarus by name. Neither the decay of the corpse, nor the great rock discouraged Yeshua. He knew, even before the dead man had started to stir in his grave, that Lazarus would appear.

"When Lazarus walked out into the daylight, still wrapped in his funeral dressings, we were stunned at first, then beside ourselves with joy. Yeshua called for his friend to be loosed from his burial linens. Before we had recovered from the shock, there stood Lazarus in front of us, restored to life! What could we say? Everyone had to agree that Yeshua was master over death itself."

John Mark was sitting on the edge of his seat. Peter added, "I must confess, sometimes he says things that I do not understand. For example, he keeps talking about dying and 'laying down his life'. His exact words were, 'I am the good shepherd. The good shepherd gives his life for the sheep. And other sheep I have which are not of this fold. Them also I must bring, and they will hear my voice. And there will be one flock and one shepherd. Therefore my Father loves me, because I lay down my life that I may take it again. No one takes it from me, but I lay it down of myself. I have power to lay it down, and I have power to take it again. This command I have received from my Father.'"

Peter drew a deep breath. "Frankly, I don't know what to make of that." John Mark was speechless.

John Mark spent several hours in the upper room with these two men. They studied Torah, they prayed together, and they worshipped God. It was early afternoon when Peter and John left to rejoin their group. Indeed, it had been a great day of discovery for John Mark.

Farewell to Moriah

Later that same afternoon, as the hour of the sacrifice approached, Benjamin called his family together again. This was the last time Moriah would be a part of the family circle. Miriam picked up Rebekah and held her in her lap. Naomi took off her apron and hung it on the wooden hook by the hearth. John Mark carried Moriah into the center of the room and carefully set him down.

Benjamin sat quietly as the family gathered in a ring with Moriah in the center. He spoke softly. "Rebekah, my dear, the time has come to say good-bye to Moriah."

"Papa, he can stay with us. I promise I will take good care of him."

Benjamin smiled, "That is so sweet of you. But what I mean is that we need to give Moriah back to God."

Rebekah looked up at her mother quizzically. "Mama, I thought you said God gave us Moriah."

Miriam stroked her daughter's hair and added, "Yes I did, Rebekah. God did give us Moriah. But now is the time for us to give him back to God."

Rebekah turned to her father. She was perplexed. "Give him back? We just got him. He's my best friend. Oh, Mama, please let me keep him."

Sensing that her parents were not responding as she had hoped, Rebekah tried a different approach. "Can't we give God another lamb?"

Sympathetically, Benjamin interjected, "Rebekah, God needs Moriah."

Rebekah countered, "But we need Moriah too." Tears ran down her cheeks.

Naomi signaled Benjamin that she wanted to say something. Reaching out to hold her granddaughter's hand, and knowing her heart, Naomi did her best to put things in terms the child could understand.

"Rebekah, do you remember that we told you this is the time of Pesach?" asked Naomi. Rebekah agreed with a nod. "This means that all our friends in Jerusalem are giving their lambs to God. It is our way of expressing gratitude to Him for protecting us and delivering us from Egypt. This is because long ago, long before any of us were born, our people were in cruel bondage. There was no way out of our trouble until God sent Moshe to deliver us from slavery. Moshe told our ancestors God wanted everyone to give Him their best lamb as a sign of faith in Him."

Rebekah listened restlessly, bunching the fabric of her grandmother's dress.

Naomi continued to help her. "God wants to be sure that we are putting our faith in Him. One way that we do this is by loving our lamb and keeping him safe until it is time to return him to God. We must obey God and give Moriah back to Him."

In earlier years, Rebekah had been too young to bond with a lamb. Of course she had always enjoyed their Pesach lamb, but now she was old enough to get attached to their guest, and she didn't want to let him go.

Rebekah wrestled within herself. She was beginning to realize that she had to release her hold on her pet, but it was still deeply disturbing. She whimpered, "I thought Moriah was mine." More tears flowed.

Naomi held Rebekah close and said, "Moriah belongs to all of us. We feel the same way that you do. We don't want him to go, but we know God wants us to give Him our most cherished possession as a sacrifice. Do you understand?"

Rebekah nodded, but she was still trying to figure a way out. Naomi continued, "If we did not love Moriah, we would not remember him. But God wants us to remember Moriah forever. Will you ever forget Moriah?"

Rebekah was ready for this question. "Of course not. I love Moriah."

Miriam joined in, "By loving our lamb Moriah and remembering him forever, we will never forget God's Pesach release of our people from horrible slavery in Egypt. They had lambs in Egypt and they took them into their households, just the same way we do. It was very hard for the slaves in Egypt to give up their lambs. And it is very hard for us too. Does that make sense to you?"

"Yes," said Rebekah. Bravely she told her mother: "When I think of how much I love Moriah, I will remember that God helped our people." Miriam dabbed her daughter's wet eyes with her apron and gently brushed the hair off her forehead. She had made a great step of faith, and her mother and grandmother were proud.

Believing that Rebekah was finally willing to loose her hold on Moriah, Benjamin offered a suggestion. "Moriah looks hungry. Would you like to feed him his last meal?"

Resigned at last, Rebekah looked toward her brother. "John Mark, will you help me?"

John Mark picked up the lamb. "Rebekah, you get the food. I'll pour the water."

Rebekah seemed satisfied with this and grabbed her brother, who had tucked Moriah under his arm. "Come on, John Mark. We need to make the best meal ever."

John Mark gratefully tagged along. Somehow helping Rebekah come to grips with the impending loss of the lamb was helping John Mark and the rest of the family to adjust to their own feelings as well.

On that peaceful note, the discussion ended. The grown-ups sighed with relief. Their hearts went out to Rebekah. While the younger two went about feeding the lamb, the adults wrapped their arms around each other. With heartfelt tears, they thanked God for His care for their family and for blessing them with Moriah.

Outside, Rebekah sat next to her brother as they watched Moriah. Rebekah sniffled as she held John Mark's strong arm. John Mark had a tough time maintaining his composure. Moriah came over and spun into a small circle as he lay down at their feet. He yawned and licked his face, cleaning the last traces of food. With a gentle exhalation he settled down for an afternoon nap. Seeing the lamb was at peace helped to ease their sadness.

Sacrifice of the Lamb

A short time later, the family gathered at the front door to bid farewell to Moriah. The yearling did not bleat or whimper. Each family member sat with the Pesach sacrifice for a time. Many tears were shed. Then Benjamin and John Mark set off for the Temple with the family's live offering. According to Torah, the Pesach sacrifice was to be made at the brass altar before the Temple.

While they walked, John Mark thought of the unique requirements that God had placed upon the sacrifice. "Every household must choose a yearling lamb. Second, it must be a male lamb. Third, it must be without blemish or fault. Fourth, the lamb must be killed in the traditional manner, cutting its throat. Fifth, all blood must be drained from its body. Sixth, the blood was to be cast upon the base of the sacrificial altar. The result was that God would use their lamb to substitute for the sins of Benjamin's family and they would be pardoned from punishment for their transgressions. This was a remarkable feat for God to accomplish through only the blood of a yearling lamb."

When the time arrived for the sacrifice, the lamb was placed upon the altar. Benjamin put his hand on the head of their friend. He thanked God for His willingness to forgive him and his family for their many wrongdoings. Moriah lay still for the blessing. It was difficult to determine if the lamb knew that his life was about to conclude.

The end came quickly and without struggle. John Mark stood by courageously. He held a silver basin to catch the lamb's blood. Benjamin carried a razor-sharp knife in the folds of his robe. He pulled it out and put his other hand on Moriah's head. Using a swift arching movement, with practiced accuracy, he deftly severed the artery in the lamb's neck.

The lamb did not flinch. Moriah simply accepted his fate without a sound. Slowly, he went limp. His blood filled the basin. As the last drops fell, Benjamin quoted from Leviticus: "The life of a creature is in the blood, and I have given it to you to make atonement for yourselves on the altar; it is the blood that makes atonement for one's life."

Benjamin took the bowl containing the blood from John Mark, carried it to the altar, and splashed its contents upon the base. Benjamin carefully wrapped the area of the open wound with linen to keep the flies off, then helped lift the dead lamb up onto John Mark's shoulders. Together, father and son descended the Temple steps with the body.

John Mark was overcome by sorrow. Benjamin looked at him, "Don't be sad. Moriah has served his purpose on earth for the glory of our God in heaven, as surely as each of us must answer His calling on our own lives."

The two made their way home in silence. Torah verses, spoken as Moriah's life was offered, continued to ring in John Mark's ears. Many centuries before, God gave the words to Moshe in the Scroll of Leviticus, "It is the blood that makes atonement for one's life."

The lifeless animal weighed heavily, like a yoke on the young man's neck. Soon, thousands of other such sacrifices would be carried to homes throughout Jerusalem. John Mark could not stop thinking about this lamb that had brought so much joy to his family. He was touched by the way it had died so sweetly and peacefully.

Benjamin watched him carefully. He sensed the emotion his son was experiencing. He recalled the same feelings during the Pesach season when he was growing up; when the pet lambs in his home were slain, and year after year, he too had to deal with the issue of the atoning blood.

"You seem very quiet, son. Is there anything you would like to talk about?" As Benjamin expected, the questioning began.

"Killing a lamb is so cruel," said John Mark. "Why not some other kind of sacrifice? And please don't tell me about tradition."

Benjamin thought for some moments before answering. "It is what God requires."

"How come?"

"So that an innocent creature receives the penalty that we deserve for our sins."

"Why would God want that?" asked John Mark.

Benjamin realized that he had to provide a substantive answer. "We find in Torah that the punishment for sin is death."

"That's awfully severe."

"It is because sin is the destroyer of life," continued Benjamin. "God created life and said it was good. God hates sin because He is holy, pure, and good. When we sin, it separates us from Him, just as it did Adam and Eve. It is only because of God's great love for us that He accepts a substitute death in payment for our sins."

John Mark was disturbed. "Is all this really necessary?"

"Yes. It is important that we appreciate the devastating results of our sins. Sin is always costly," explained Benjamin. "It can cost us everything that God intends for us."

"I think I understand. But what happens to our sin?"

"Do you remember," asked Benjamin, "That I placed my hand on Moriah's head at the time we prayed? I stood there as the representative of our family, the priest of our household." John Mark nodded. "Placing my hand on his head represents the transfer of our family's sins to the lamb."

"Is that really possible?" John Mark asked.

"Yes. By faith we believe this to be so," Benjamin replied, then added, "My prayers were offered to God that the sacrifice of our lamb might serve as a protective covering for the members of our family."

"How can a lamb equal a human life?"

"It can't," said Benjamin. "The life of an animal, or even thousands of animals, can never equal the value of a single human life."

John Mark was completely amazed by his father's words. But then he became annoyed. "Father, I haven't done anything wrong. Or at least I have not done anything for which I deserve to be killed. Is God so angry with me?"

"God is not angry with you, son. But you must take a careful look at your heart. Are you saying that you do not have thoughts that are unpleasing to God? Are you saying that everything you do is good?"

"No, I can't say that."

"Of course not," said Benjamin. "Sin is when we do not honor God's standards."

"So who can measure up to them?" asked John Mark.

"Nobody," Benjamin stated firmly. "But sin can't just be ignored. This has been a fundamental principle of life throughout our history. For example, when the Pesach story is recounted this evening, we will find that God did not release the Israelites from Egypt until their sin had been paid for. All Egypt came under God's judgment. It cost the Egyptians the lives of their first-born sons. They had no substitute sacrifice. But because of God's great mercy, a lamb atoned for each family in Goshen."

"That was a long time ago. What about the people today who don't care if they sin?" asked John Mark. "It seems as if they get away with doing anything they want."

"Good question," exclaimed Benjamin, "Many people act as though God is neither present nor interested in the details of their lives. Nothing could be further from the truth. Since judgment for sin seldom strikes immediately, it is easy to be deceived into believing there are no consequences for sin.

"Thank God that He is more intent on offering us His mercy than in punishing us. He does not force us to follow Him. He allows us to choose for ourselves. His greatest desire for us is that we recognize our faults, and repent, and then decide to do His will."

"How do we know," asked John Mark, "If we are not doing God's will?"

Benjamin wanted John Mark to know that he was not the victim of some plot conjured up by a cruel Creator to shame him. "Rabbi Yeshua teaches us that when we choose to put anything above God or between ourselves and God, we are not doing God's will."

John Mark thought long and hard about this as they drew near to their home. Then he abruptly broke the silence and asked, "Father, is it possible to live without sin?"

Benjamin rejoiced that he had been blessed with such a wise and inquiring son. He stopped walking and faced John Mark. Placing his hands on the young man's shoulders on either side of the slain lamb, he said, "Son, none of us knows how to live a sinless life. We need forgiveness.

That is why we have to make atonement. That is why we need God's help. That is why we had to sacrifice Moriah."

"You mean the lamb really does takes away our sin?"

"Absolutely! Were this not so, it would be you and me on the altar, not a lamb." replied Benjamin.

John Mark laughed. He knew his father was right. He shifted the weight of their lamb with special tenderness as Benjamin opened the garden gate. There, waiting for them in the doorway of their dwelling place, were the three women of the household.

Rebekah frowned. She was still not prepared for this. "Mama, Moriah is dead." A flood of tears streamed down her face.

Miriam knelt by her, "Rebekah, everything's all right."

Rebekah was too choked up to respond. John Mark could offer no solace. He viewed her with understanding and compassion. The older women took Rebekah into the house. Benjamin directed John Mark to a flat rock alongside the house. There the animal would be dressed for cooking.

Choosing Sides

Naomi had the fire blazing. As soon as the body of the lamb was brought inside, the family assembled for prayer over their offering. Rebekah's tears flowed freely as she helped her grandmother. After the blessing, Naomi continued readying the side dishes for the Seder. But her thoughts were elsewhere. As her skilled hands went about final preparations for this special meal, she felt an intimate connection to God.

John Mark enjoyed listening to her hum and watching her sway back and forth to the melody. Indeed, Naomi was at her best when she was cooking. The simple act of fixing dinner was her favorite way of blessing her family. As she poured her love into the items that she was preparing, a lovely serenity settled over the house. Rebekah settled down and was soon playing with her dolls.

Naomi spent the late afternoon in silent reverence as she roasted the sacrifice. Somehow the turmoil of this current Pesach season released pent-up emotions. She started to shed tears for an assortment of reasons. Tears for the loss of their defenseless lamb. Tears of gratitude that Yeshua would be their guest. Tears of joy, because, in spite of the anger and torment rampant in an all-too-wicked world, God had always been faithful. His protection and provision had never faltered.

After amusing herself with her playthings, Rebekah gave a hand with the details. She ran up and down the stairs, hauling plates, cups, and pillows to the upper room.

Miriam was engrossed in private thoughts. She sensed the mounting spiritual confrontation—and she knew that battle lines had been drawn.

Yes, bringing Yeshua to their home could expose all the members of her household to danger. But she was sure it was the right thing to do.

Knowing the evil forces at work outside, Miriam began to pray: "Once again Lord, our great and gracious God, Israel is in need of Your help. Roman troops have taken over our land and ransacked our treasuries. Our religious leaders have exploited our people. As in the past, we are in bondage. I beseech You Lord to make this Pesach a time of spiritual renewal and liberation for Your people. Hear our prayers as You heard the prayers of our ancestors in Egypt. Please send a deliverer to rescue Your Children!"

Miriam heard her son coming down from the upper room. He entered the kitchen and sat beside her. John Mark had been thinking about the Pesach lamb. He was getting dejected. "I hope Yeshua appreciates how much Moriah meant to us."

Unexpectedly, Naomi stood up. She had been resting by the fireside. Both John Mark and Miriam thought she had been napping. Naomi leaned across the table and spoke with quiet authority. "We must be willing to share this sacrifice. We could have no more important guest than Yeshua. He may be the deliverer that your mother has been praying for."

Naomi moved around the table to face her grandson. "What is happening here tonight is far more important than any of us can fully realize. There is much at stake. Yeshua has risked his life by returning to Jerusalem. Do you understand this?"

"Yes Grandmother," said John Mark with a fresh appreciation of the seriousness of the situation that was gathering momentum and ferocity in their city.

Just then Benjamin entered the room and joined the conversation. "Those who accuse Yeshua would have us believe that he is not following Torah, when his teachings, his behavior, in fact, his entire life are expressions of his love and respect for our Heavenly Father's Law."

Benjamin pulled his prayer shawl over his head and shoulders, and then turned to Miriam, allowing her to drape it over his arms. As if the shawl further empowered him, Benjamin's words now became even more forceful.

"Yeshua is a teacher of the Covenant, that is why he is welcome here. He keeps the Pesach, as do we, because we honor Torah. We study Torah.

We live by Torah's commandments and its precepts. It is God's design for our lives. In our home we serve the God of Avraham, Yitz'chak, and Ya'akov, according to Torah. We cannot forget God's Eternal Covenant with our people that He gave to Moshe."

Naomi added, "This is all true. Choosing to support Yeshua is a dangerous thing. It places us in opposition to both seats of power—in Rome and in Jerusalem! But this is the right choice for us to make. We must be strong and of good courage!"

John Mark had never heard his grandmother speak like this, but he had to agree that what she said was true. He offered, "My heart is filled with joy that God has given me a family that stands for what is right."

"I am so proud of you John Mark," said Miriam. "You are the kind of son every mother prays to have."

She glanced out the window. "Look at the hour!" instructing John Mark to get ready, "Our guests will arrive any moment. Wash your hands and face. And don't forget to brush your hair."

Locating the water-filled basin on the kitchen table, John Mark rinsed his face and hands. Toweling himself dry, he looked up and noticed his mother's tear-stained face. "Mother, are you all right?"

Miriam smiled sweetly. She reached over and took Naomi's hand, then looked back to John Mark. The women interlocked arms, in support of one another. "My son," she said, "I have never been better."

There was a gentle knock on the front door. Miriam removed her apron using the hem to dry her bleary eyes. John Mark looked at Naomi. She beckoned him to open the door. He ducked into the front vestibule adjoining the kitchen at the bottom of the stairs. Using his fingers as a comb, he swept the hair away from his eyes. Taking a deep breath, he reached for the door handle.

Yeshua Arrives

A company of men stood huddled outside, having arrived shortly before twilight. Peter spoke first: "Let us come inside quickly before someone sees us."

Quietly, John Mark showed them in. Yeshua stepped to one side to allow the talmidim to enter first. He kissed his fingertips and then touched the mezuzah. The others followed suit, quickly passing by, whispering hushed tones of greeting. Within moments, the last of them quietly went up to the upper room. Turning about, John Mark found himself facing Yeshua, the man of God!

Yeshua reached forward, took his hand, and smiled cheerfully. "Shalom, John Mark. We are honored to be guests in your home."

John Mark wanted to speak, but he was at a loss for words.

Yeshua continued, "I saw you at the Temple. You were watching me when I went into the inner court. You saw me purge my Father's House."

John Mark blushed. "Shalom. Rabbi, come in." Embarrassed by this encounter and still searching for the proper words. "I didn't know you saw me. There was so much confusion. You were very brave."

"Thank you," Yeshua responded. "However, I believe you are the brave one. You have witnessed many things that others have only dreamed about. And you have not turned to the side. God can use a man such as you."

John Mark was stunned. He had not expected praise from one so illustrious.

Sniffing the fragrance of the meal, Yeshua remarked, "Truly, this home is blessed. You have made us feel welcome."

John Mark looked down and realized that he was still holding the hand of his celebrated guest. It was an awkward moment. Before he could withdraw his hand, Yeshua laughed and squeezed it tighter. John Mark had to laugh too. The family noticed what was happening, and all had a good chuckle.

Then Yeshua placed both of his hands on John Mark's head and prayed blessings upon him. As the family members looked on, they could see from the expression on John Mark's face that he was in heaven.

Yeshua's eyes searched the kitchen and settled on John Mark's mother. Miriam stepped forward and bowed. Moving into the kitchen Yeshua returned her bow with his own. "We are deeply honored by your hospitality."

Miriam returned the compliment. "Master, the honor is ours."

They stood quietly. Yeshua smiled. Miriam responded in kind. Something very special passed between them, even though no other words were spoken.

Benjamin came down the stairs and entered the kitchen. "Ah, my Lord, I see you've greeted Miriam. All that I am, I owe to her."

Yeshua looked at him. "You have found a man's greatest complement, a loving, faithful wife." Yeshua then handed both mother and daughter pomegranates. The child clutched hers, not knowing what to say.

"Thank you, rabbi," said Miriam.

With that, he ascended the stairs. Miriam's face was radiant with adoration. Her glow would last throughout the evening. Pomegranate in hand, Rebekah raced ahead and up the stairs.

Benjamin and John Mark followed reverently with the Seder dinner platter. They would not be eating with those in the upper room this night. Their call was to serve. Fortunately, this allowed them to observe and listen as Yeshua spoke to his talmidim. They were deeply pleased.

Naomi welcomed each guest at the top of the stairs, took their cloaks, and carefully folded them. She was the perfect picture of hospitality. Rebekah huddled shyly at her feet.

When Yeshua reached the top step, he gently brushed Rebekah's head with one hand and lifted Naomi's bowed head with his other. Naomi blinked back tears of joy and Rebekah beamed at the attention.

Yeshua became somber as he softly said, "Tomorrow, you will meet my mother. You two are very much alike. She will need friends such as you for the days ahead."

Naomi wondered what the coming days would bring. She replied, "I shall try to be her good friend. She, too, is welcome in our home." Pausing, Naomi carefully studied Yeshua's serene face. A contentment she had never known surged through her. Quietly, she returned to the kitchen.

"Oh, can't we stay?" pleaded Rebekah, but her grandmother gently led her away despite her protests.

Yeshua moved to the center of the room and surveyed his surroundings. All could see his great pleasure. His talmidim drew close to him. He prayed for John Mark's family, for the household, for the room, and for the food set before them.

Benjamin removed the Torah from its ark. Yeshua and his talmidim stood respectfully. As tradition dictated, the Passover reading was from the Exodus portion of Torah. The passage concerned God's initiation of the Pesach celebration in Egypt. The men encircled the ark. Benjamin signaled John Mark to begin.

John Mark summarized before he read: "This portion of Torah includes the selection of the sacrificial lamb; the method for preparing the Pesach meal; the judgment by the Angel of Death; the ordinances for eating only unleavened bread; and the instructions for marking the doorframes of the households with the blood of the Pesach lamb."

Although John Mark had memorized the verses, he used the silver pointer and followed the Torah writings carefully, not wanting to misstate the Word of God.

When he was finished, Yeshua looked at John Mark and said, "Tov meod." The young reader silently rejoiced that he had been praised for doing well.

The talmidim spread themselves around the banquet table on top of the cushions, assuming the reclining posture of free men. The Seder Feast was set simply. Even though there were thirteen at the table, a white cloth rested beneath fourteen place settings. The extra place was the traditional setting for Eliyahu, the prophet whose return the prophet Mal'akhi had said would precede the coming of the Messiah. Each setting had a linen napkin and goblet. All the serving utensils had been polished by the loving touch of Naomi's busy hands.

In the center of the table was a woven basket with a curved handle arched across its rim. Inside the basket, covered with a white linen napkin, was a plentiful stack of crisp unleavened bread, the matzoh. On one side of the basket were a bowl of salt water and a bunch of lettuce greens; on the other side was a bowl of freshly ground bitter herbs. Several pitchers of wine enhanced the table. Next to each of the pitchers was a bowl of charoseth, a tasty reddish-brown mixture of chopped apples, figs, raisins, nuts, cinnamon, and wine.

In front of the head place was a silver platter containing items symbolizing various aspects of the Seder. Between the platter and the basket of unleavened bread was the roasted Pesach lamb. It would remain covered until the time for its serving. These essential components had been customary in Jewish households for centuries.

Outside, the sun dipped below the horizon. Several shofar blasts passed back and forth over the rooftops as Jerusalem welcomed the sacred night.

Washing Their Feet

Yeshua occupied the center place at the long rectangular table. His talmidim gathered around him to receive his blessings and listen to his teachings as they enjoyed the feast. His opening statement caught them all by surprise. "With fervent desire, I have desired to eat this Pesach with you before I suffer; for I say to you, I will no longer eat of it until it is fulfilled in the Kingdom of God."

The talmidim looked at each other, then back to Yeshua. What was all this talk about suffering? The Seder was traditionally a joyous celebration. Why would he suffer?

John Mark had heard this expression, "Kingdom of God," before—it was the very night his father had come to believe that Yeshua was the Messiah. Benjamin had quoted Yochanan the Immerser, "The Kingdom of God is at hand." At that time, Yeshua was saying that God was near. But how could he know where God was?

Yeshua prayed over the first cup. The wine had been warmed, its temperature a further reminder of the blood of the Pesach lamb. Lifting his cup into the air, he sang the Kiddush, the prayer of the Cup of Sanctification, setting it apart for God. "Baruch ata Adonai Elohaynu melech ha-olam boray p'ree haggafen." Blessed art Thou, O Lord our God, King of the Universe, who created the fruit of the vine.

This was the first of four ceremonial cups of wine. Taking the cup, he gave thanks, and said, "Take this and divide it among yourselves; for I say to you, I will not drink of the fruit of the vine again until the Kingdom of God comes." There was that expression once more. This was not a traditional toast. After a moment's hesitation, all drank.

The men could tell this Pesach would be unlike any they had previously experienced.

The wine was to be followed by the customary washing of hands. Yeshua rose and walked over to the water jug, which had been filled to the brim before the meal. This was the same vessel that John Mark had carried down the street earlier that day.

Next to the pitcher were the sizable earthen washbowl and a towel. To honor the leader or rabbi of a Pesach Seder, the one presiding was given the privilege of being the first to wash his hands. Yeshua gestured at John Mark to pick up the jug. John Mark poured the water over Yeshua's hands into the clay container while Yeshua washed. Yeshua then dried his hands with the towel.

The men were completely unprepared for what happened next. Yeshua girded his waist with the towel. He took the basin and knelt at the end of the table before Andrew, the brother of Peter, and proceeded to wash his feet! The surprised talmidim watched in silence.

John Mark had been to many Pesach dinners, and he knew this was a totally unprecedented act. Only slaves performed such humble service. He struggled with his thoughts, muttering, "What is happening? This is unbelievable! It defies all reason. Any self-respecting Jewish person would regard performing such an act as altogether demeaning."

The talmidim were embarrassed. No one in authority ever cleansed another adult's feet—unless they were the feet of a relative who was sick or had just died. How could Yeshua, whom they all held in such high esteem, stoop so low?

Peter couldn't bear the thought of Yeshua washing his filthy feet. When Yeshua came to him, he protested strongly. "Lord, you shall never wash my feet!"

Yeshua replied: "Unless I wash you, you have no part with me."

Everyone was struck dumb except Peter, who was exasperated. "Then Master," Peter said, "Not just my feet, but my hands and my head as well!"

Yeshua's head was already bowed as he began washing Peter's feet. Peter's idea now sounded a little silly. Yeshua lifted his eyes just long enough to view the look of consternation on Peter's face. Yeshua's loving care overcame the man's resistance. He uncomfortably yielded while Yeshua finished the humble service.

Downstairs the women could overhear Peter's protests. Naomi whispered to Miriam, "Peter is learning about submission the hard way." Miriam agreed with a smirk.

John Mark moved around the room behind the master. Along with the water, Yeshua poured out his love on each of them. He treated them as a mother treats her children — with tenderness and compassion. He knew their sufferings. He felt their sorrows. He understood how difficult this must be for them.

When Yeshua was finished, he straightened up, looked at John Mark, and sighed gratefully. Finally, he rinsed his hands in fresh water. Taking the towel from around his waist, Yeshua cleaned himself up with the unsoiled part that had served as his waistband, and then draped it over John Mark's arm, thanking him. He was so humble, so loving. John Mark melted with admiration. Yeshua returned to the table and sat at his place of headship.

"Do you understand what I have done?" Yeshua asked them. "You call me 'Rabbi' and 'Lord,' and rightly so, for that is what I am. Now that I, your Lord and Rabbi, have washed your feet, you also should wash one another's feet. I have set for you an example that you should do as I have done for you."

Several of the talmidim squirmed uncomfortably. Following Yeshua's wishes was not often easy. Their master spoke further, "I tell you the truth, no servant is greater than his master, nor is a messenger greater than the one who sent him. Now that you know these things, you will be blessed if you do them."

John Mark realized that Yeshua was not specifically commanding them to wash one another's feet. He was showing them how to serve others. Yeshua had demonstrated loving one's neighbor as one's self. This supreme act of humility punctured the puffed-up pretense and false pride that the political teachers of the Law had appropriated to themselves. Yeshua was indeed a remarkable rabbi.

The Four Questions

Yeshua began the Seder. He reached for the dish of bitter herbs and lifted it for all to see. "We have seen the bitterness of slavery. The bitter herbs are symbolic of this wicked practice. Later, when you taste this herb, allow it to remind you of our ancestors' harsh lives under the oppressive yoke of the Egyptian taskmasters."

No mention of Roman oppression was made, but the parallels between Egypt and Rome were unmistakable. Several talmidim affirmed Yeshua's words with "Amens." Yeshua contrasted the trials of the Hebrew nation to the tenderness of his Father's heart. "How marvelous," he commented, "that God chooses mercy before wrath. He offers forgiveness to people deserving judgment."

Next, Yeshua turned to the bowl of salt water. "The Hebrews prayed to God. He saw their tears. He sent Moshe to them to prepare the way for their deliverance from the hands of their enemies. This salt water represents the tears and toil of our ancestors. God our Father knows our every tear. None are forgotten."

Reaching for the greens, Yeshua sighed deeply. "This is dipped in salt water to remind us of the hyssop that was dipped in the blood of the Pesach lamb and spread upon the lintels and doorposts of the dwellings of every faithful Israelite in Egypt. The color speaks to us of springtime, a time of new life."

Yeshua took a small clump of lettuce and pulled off a leaf. He dipped it in the salt water and ate it. Then he passed the greens around the table for others to do the same. This the faithful men did willingly, even though the taste was sour. They each endured the unpleasant taste as a tribute to their ancestors.

John Mark and Benjamin poured the second cup of wine, the Cup of Judgment. John Mark, as the youngest in attendance, had been appointed to ask the traditional questions. He stood at the end of the table and began with the time-honored query: "Why is this night different from all other nights?"

He followed this with the four questions: "On all other nights we can eat any kind of bread, but why on this night do we eat only unleavened bread? Why on all other nights do we eat tasty herbs, but on this night only bitter herbs? Why do we dip the herbs twice in salt water? On all other nights we eat sitting upright, but why on this night do we recline while we eat?"

Yeshua had a surprise for John Mark. Instead of responding to the questions himself, he asked Benjamin, the head of the household and the senior man present, to answer the four questions.

Honored and pleased, Benjamin thanked the rabbi. He launched into a brief overview of the history of Israel from Avraham until the first Pesach in Egypt. He related how God called Avraham out of idolatry and brought into existence a new nation from his seed. He then told the story of Joseph, which resulted in the move of the Children of Israel to Egypt and their settling in Goshen. Next, the epic of Moshe was told, right up to the night of the first Pesach. The plagues were described. Then came the standards for the selection of the lamb, and after four days in a household, its sacrifice.

At this point in the telling, the specific answers to the four questions of Pesach were answered. The unleavened bread represents the shortness of time before Israel's exodus; the bitter herbs symbolize the bitterness of life in the iron furnace of Egypt; the salt water stands for the bitterness of slavery, as well as the tears of joy for being set free; and the reclining position signifies the leisure posture taken by a person free from oppression.

Benjamin outlined the regulations for the preparation and consumption of the lamb, and the reasons why their ancestors had marked their doorposts and lintel with blood. "The smearing of blood was the act of obedience and of faith that provided a protective covering over the

Israelites. This was the sign given to Moshe by God. Our forefathers in Egypt saw redemption in the blood of the lamb and willingly submitted to God's instructions.

"On that 'night to be remembered,' God spared the first-born son of every household that publicly proclaimed its confidence in the blood atonement of its sacrificed lamb." Looking at his own son, Benjamin concluded with, "The first-born male in a family represents the promise of a heritage."

Yeshua summarized, "From among all the nations, God chose Israel to be His covenant people. He has never broken His promises nor forsaken His Chosen. Israel would have perished long before today without His protection and mercy.

"In the Scroll of Exodus, God made four promises to the Israelites, and he has fulfilled them all to the letter. God said to Moshe: 'Therefore say to the Israelites:

"I am the Lord. I will bring you out from under the yoke of the Egyptians. I will free you from being slaves to them. I will redeem you with an outstretched arm and with mighty acts of judgment. I will take you as my own people, and I will be your God.

"Then you will know that I am the Lord your God, who brought you out from under the yoke of the Egyptians. And I will bring you to the land I swore with an uplifted hand to give to Avraham, to Yitz'chak and to Ya'akov. I will give it to you as a possession. I am the Lord.' Tonight, we celebrate this Pesach atop the holy mountain in the city of David, in the land God promised to our ancestors. God be praised."

Tears welled up in Yeshua's eyes and trickled down his face. He made no attempt to wipe them away. He prayed quietly for several moments. All eyes were set upon him. The talmidim were enraptured. Time stood still. Peace flooded their hearts.

Yeshua was silent, yet it seemed to John Mark that love flowed from him like a fountain of living water. Benjamin's arm went around his son's shoulders. All felt that this Pesach was being celebrated in heaven. Everyone knew God was in their midst.

Everyone, that is, except the one who had distanced himself from the rest. More than once, John Mark noticed that this man was keeping to himself. Almost disinterested in the proceedings, he sat close to the stairway with his eyes fixed on the exit below. At first, John Mark supposed he was ill. But there was something else…he was different from the others. There was something cold about him.

Yeshua gestured at the matzoh. John lifted the basket of unleavened bread. Rolling back the linen cover, he offered it to Yeshua. The rabbi took the matzoh and held it before them. With his fingertips curved around opposing ends of the flat bread and with his thumbs in the center, he applied gentle pressure. The bread broke in two.

Returning the smaller part to the basket, he held up the remainder. Instead of the customary passing of bread for each to break off a section, Yeshua circled the table and broke off individual pieces of matzoh, putting them in front of each of the talmidim. He then blessed the unleavened bread.

The holy man of God looked over the table setting. His eye caught a small egg with a scorched shell. Earlier that day, Rebekah had made her own offering for the meal. She had roasted one of her hen's eggs to adorn the center platter. Miriam had made a circular nest of greens to cradle her child's gift. Yeshua reached over to receive this simple offering from the youngest member of the household.

Pausing again, he spoke with humble appreciation. "The significance of Pesach must always be taught diligently to our children. Small hands have prepared this offering, the hands of a child.

"This egg represents a new beginning—what this very night signifies. Pesach first initiated God's sequence of redemption. Without Pesach there would have been no Red Sea crossing or God's guarantee of an everlasting covenant with Israel."

Yeshua looked at John Mark and Benjamin and smiled. By this time, father and son had long forgotten their earlier reticence. They were proud to have offered their home for this Pesach Feast. Whatever the risks may have been, it was wonderful that this celebration was taking place in their upper room. This was indeed a night to be remembered!

All sang several psalms of David. At last, the Second Cup, the Cup of Judgment, was offered up to God. All participated.

Betrayal

It was time to take the bitter herbs. After reclining again, Yeshua said, "Surely, I say to you, one of you who eats with me will betray me."

It was as if a thunderbolt struck the table. Each of the twelve recoiled in horror. One by one they asked, "Is it I?"

Yeshua said, "It is one of you twelve who dips with me in the dish."

While the others were clamoring over whom it could be, the one of the talmidim who had distanced himself from the proceedings, Judas Iscariot, looked up at Yeshua and asked, "Rabbi, is it I?"

Yeshua looked at him. "You have said rightly."

The other talmidim missed this moment. Instead of each searching his soul in an effort to find the catastrophic blunder, everyone was busy denying any possibility of being the traitor. They argued among themselves who should be considered the most loyal:

"None have sacrificed more than I. I left my wife to follow him."

"I have given up any chance of ever having a wife."

"I have sacrificed my fortune. I deserve a place of honor."

"At least you were once rich."

"I walked away from a thriving business to serve our master."

"There is no more honorable profession than fishing. I feed the masses."

Just then, John Mark observed Yeshua dip a matzoh into the bitter herbs and hand it to Judas Iscariot. Yeshua said, "What you are about to do, do quickly." No one in the room understood what he meant. Since Judas was in charge of the money, some thought Yeshua wanted him to buy some last minute item that may have been overlooked for the meal, or perhaps to buy food for the poor.

Judas took the flat bread with the bitter herb and ate it. His face expressed both the unpleasantness of taste and the hurt of being excused from the Seder. Angrily, he shook his head, turned away, and descended the stairs. John Mark heard the front door shut behind him.

Yeshua resumed teaching, "Greatness is about serving, not about being served." John Mark related this to the foot washing. Indeed, Yeshua had an unusual way of explaining significant values.

There was an awkward silence. Then the men began to eat again and were soon preoccupied with mixing the sweet charoseth with bitter herbs and putting it between two pieces of matzoh. Alone, the herbs were difficult to eat, but with the addition of the charoseth, the bitterness was taken away. The combination was delicious. It was John Mark's favorite Pesach dish.

Then, Thaddaeus performed another traditional part of the Seder, "Our people must remember that the color of the charoseth is much like that of the red clay of Egypt. When we see the wine-stained fruit, we are reminded that our ancestors used mortar made of this earth to secure the stone blocks of the pyramids. Those were days of sorrow. Now is a time for joy." They all voiced hearty approval.

Just as the bitterness could be masked with a special mixture of fruits and nuts, it seemed to these men that the best response to Yeshua's comment concerning treachery was to disguise it with something sweet, so they dug into the bowl of charoseth.

Yeshua shocked them again: "God is about to glorify me," he announced. "And I'm going to glorify God with what I am about to do. My children, I will be with you only a little while longer. You will try to find me. But you cannot go where I am going. What is more important is that you hear a new commandment. You must love one another in the same way that I have loved you. By this, everybody will know that you are my talmidim."

Not grasping the full meaning of Yeshua's words, the talmidim focused on the idea that he would be leaving them. Peter asked the question that was on everyone's hearts. "Master, where are you going?"

Yeshua answered him, "Where I am going you cannot follow me yet, but you will follow me later."

Peter said to him, "Why can I not follow you now?"

The rabbi shook his head. "Simon, Simon," he called Peter, using his former name—a clear statement that Peter was acting like he did before he started following Yeshua. "Satan has asked to sift you as wheat," Yeshua cautioned, "But I have prayed for you, Simon, that your faith may not fail; when you have turned back and realized the error of your ways, you will return to strengthen your brothers."

Peter was perplexed. He furrowed his brow. He replied ardently, "Lord, I am ready to go with you to prison and to death. I would lay down my life for your sake."

But Yeshua knew Peter's weakness. "Would you really lay down your life for me?" he asked. "In fact, before the rooster crows, you will disown me three times." Peter swallowed hard. He was sure that Yeshua was mistaken.

Yeshua asked the talmidim, "When I sent you out without purse, bag, or sandals, did you lack anything?"

"No," they answered.

He said to them, "But now, if you have a purse, take it and likewise a knapsack. And if you don't have a sword, sell your robe and buy one. For I tell you this: the passage from Tanakh says, 'He was counted with the transgressors.' I tell you that this must be fulfilled in me. Yes, what is written about me is reaching its fulfillment."

Everyone knew that this Scripture from the Scroll of Yesha 'Yahu referred to the Coming One. Yeshua had again identified himself as the Messiah!

By this time, the talmidim were thoroughly confused. They conferred among themselves for a few moments and then presented some weapons.

James said, "Look, Lord, here are two swords."

Yeshua said to them, "Enough of that kind of talk!"

Again, they all were baffled.

Breaking Bread

At Yeshua's bidding, Benjamin uncovered the roasted lamb, revealing it for the first time. The moment had arrived for the Pesach Feast to begin. The lamb was cooked to a crispy brown. Surrounded by delicious gravy, it was beautifully presented. This freshly prepared sacrifice, still warm from the hearth, sent out a pleasing aroma.

As prescribed by Moshe in the Scroll of Exodus, the entire animal had been cooked. Nothing was wasted. None of its bones were broken, as this would have disqualified the lamb for consumption. It had to be an unblemished and pure sacrifice unto God.

All ate together, using their fingers, reminiscent of their reclining posture, just as in Egypt. Each of the talmidim was buried deep in thought. Unlike other Pesach celebrations, which were festive, this one was solemn.

After everyone had been served, a share of the main course was given to John Mark and Benjamin. Discreetly, they joined the three women in the kitchen below where the hosts might enjoy their own ceremonial supper.

When the meal was over, Benjamin and John Mark returned to clear the table. They found the atmosphere of the upper room strangely hushed. Looking at Yeshua, John Mark could see his turmoil. Everyone present sensed it. A feeling of dark foreboding came over the group. Something inexplicable was about to take place.

Yeshua stood, looked at the talmidim, lifted his goblet and prayed. Once more he reached into the basket and took the unleavened bread. He looked to the heavens, gave thanks, and broke it. Keeping a piece for himself, he passed the remaining portion to the talmidim for them to perform the same task. Everyone was surprised. This was entirely unorthodox. At Pesach, once the meal was finished, nothing else was to be consumed—except for the last two cups of wine.

Uncomfortably, the talmidim complied. Each followed Yeshua's example and broke off a section of matzoh, then awaited further instructions. When each had received his share, he looked upon them and repeated the blessing for unleavened bread.

"Baruch ata Adonai Elohaynu melech ha-olam asher kidd'shanu b'mitzvotav v'tsivanu al acheelat matzoh."

"Blessed art Thou, O Lord our God, King of the Universe, who hast sanctified us by Thy commandment to eat unleavened bread." This was a blessing similar to the one Yeshua had made earlier in the meal. Except this time, Yeshua added a new declaration:

"This is my body which is given for you; eat this in remembrance of me."

The talmidim were astounded. The only body offered in a Pesach Supper was that of a lamb. How could unleavened bread represent Yeshua's body? They looked at Yeshua. His eyes were cast upward as he sought his Father's face. They turned to Peter, wondering what his response would be. Peter shook his head in dismay and respectfully ate the unleavened bread. The others followed Peter's lead, but remained puzzled.

Yeshua circled to the other side of the table. He stopped at Eliyahu's empty seat. The man of God lifted Eliyahu's serving of wine. It was the time for the third cup of wine—the Cup of Redemption. This cup symbolized the fulfillment of God's promise to deliver His people from oppression.

Everybody could not help but notice that Yeshua chose Eliyahu's cup for this purpose. How unusual. The rabbi prayed again. Then glancing around the table, he caught the eyes of each of his talmidim. His next statement would completely unhinge the minds of his friends:

"This cup is the New Covenant in my blood, which is shed for you."

Several of the men cringed under the weight of his words. Bewilderment covered their faces. Yeshua raised the goblet and took a swallow. Then he passed it to his followers.

John Mark considered this incredible disclosure. He pondered the mystery he now confronted. "Was Yeshua saying that this wine symbolized his own blood?" All knew that the wine was not his actual blood, but Yeshua was now telling them that he would shed his own blood on their behalf.

Every Israelite had been taught about blood. One of God's cardinal rules was not to drink blood under any circumstances. The very idea was sacrilegious. Blood represented life itself! What did Yeshua mean by giving his body and shedding his blood?

John Mark's mind wrestled with these issues. He thought to himself, "When a sacrifice is offered, its blood is drained and then splashed against the altar. Only a Levitical priest is qualified to perform this sacrificial ritual, except at Pesach. For this specific sacrifice alone, the head of each Jewish household is personally responsible for pouring the blood on the family altar where its lamb is sacrificed. Certainly, as a rabbi, Yeshua knew all this better than any.

"But what of this New Covenant he was proclaiming? Just minutes before, as the story of Exodus was retold, all were reminded that God alone could make a covenant and fulfill its requirements."

John Mark continued his internal dialogue. "All these men had witnessed Yeshua's signs and wonders. They had heard him challenge the legalisms of the P'rushim. They had seen him confront the deceptions of the Tz'dukim. He gave sight to the blind. He made the lame walk. They had even seen him walk on water in the midst of the sea! There was no end to his miracles. But drinking blood, especially Yeshua's own blood—this reached outside all boundaries of decency. It sounded like heresy, or some pagan ritual!"

John Mark read the sadness on Yeshua's face. At first, the talmidim just looked down. Then, one by one, they looked up at the rabbi. They were more flustered than ever. True, their understanding of him was incomplete, but they trusted him. They had all followed him for years. No matter what anyone had said about Yeshua, they knew how much he loved them. And they knew that he would never dishonor them or disobey the Law.

Then John Mark's heart was touched with a sudden revelation. Of course! The sacrificial blood! The shed blood of the sacrifice symbolizes the atoning price of sin. He looked around the room. Everyone at the table was contemplating Yeshua's meaning. John Mark could see the searching in their eyes.

Could it be? John Mark became very clear-headed. Yeshua was challenging them to see a great truth. Yes! He was revealing a new promise, one written in his own blood! This was shocking if it was true.

The goblet passed from hand to hand and was lifted to the lips of every one of the talmidim. Each drank from the cup. When all had finished, Yeshua accepted the empty vessel and raised it to God.

Yeshua took a deep breath. Sorrow was written upon his face. Closing his eyes, he bowed his head in prayer. Finally, he smiled and said, "Let us sing praises to God." The second half of the Hallel—a selection of King David's psalms—was sung. Yeshua and the talmidim joyfully declared the wondrous works of God. Their words filled the chamber. Eventually, the last notes of the closing psalm reverberated in the rafters:

> The stone the builders rejected
> Has become the chief cornerstone.
> This was the Lord's doing;
> It is marvelous in our eyes.
> This is the day the Lord has made;
> We will rejoice and be glad in it.
> Save now, I pray, O Lord;
> O Lord, I pray, send now prosperity.
> Blessed is he who comes in the name of the Lord!

As John Mark heard "Hosanna!" and "Save now!" once again, his mind was momentarily transported back to Yeshua's triumphal entry into Jerusalem a few days before. At that time the crowd had hailed him as the Messiah with these very words taken from this passage. Yeshua and his talmidim concluded the psalm:

> We have blessed you
> From the house of the Lord.
> God is the Lord, and He has given us light;
> Bind the sacrifice with cords

> To the horns of the altar.
> You are my God, and I will praise You;
> You are my God, I will exalt You.
> Oh, give thanks to the Lord, for He is good!
> For His mercy endures forever.

John Mark could hear Benjamin praying quietly beside him. His father quoted the prophet Mal'akhi:

> Behold, I send my messenger,
> And he will prepare the way before Me.
> And the Lord, whom you seek,
> Will suddenly come to His temple,
> Even the messenger of the covenant,
> In whom you delight.
> "Behold, He is coming,"
> Says the Lord of Hosts.

John Mark felt the Spirit of God touch him. He was soaring into heaven on the wings of an eagle. His soul was kindled with fire.

Do Not Let Your Hearts Be Troubled

Without warning, Yeshua's voice took on dynamic authority, demanding fresh attention from every person in the room. His words were piercing. He spoke with a passion they had seldom seen. First, he comforted them: "Do not be troubled. You trust God; now trust me too. In my Father's house there are many rooms. I am going there to get a place ready for you. I would not go and prepare a place for you if I was not coming back to take you to be with me. That way, we will be together forever. You know the way to the place where I am going."

Thomas was exasperated, "Lord, we do not know where you are going, so how can we know the way?"

Yeshua answered, "I am the way, the truth, and the life. No one comes to the Father except through me."

The men were astonished. This was another new teaching. John Mark's jaw dropped. Yeshua had just said that the pathway to God was through him alone! How was this possible? Yeshua claimed the very authority of God! Everyone was amazed.

Yeshua continued, "If you love me, you will do what I have asked you to do. I will ask my Father on my behalf to provide you with another Helper, one who will never leave you, the Spirit of Truth. This Helper is Ruach HaKodesh, the Holy Spirit, of whom the prophets often spoke. My Father will send Him in a new way because I have asked. The Holy Spirit will teach you everything you need to know and He will remind you of everything I have told you.

"Peace I leave with you; my peace I give you. I do not give to you as the world gives. Do not let your hearts be troubled, and do not be afraid."

No one knew what to say. Yeshua's words were so overwhelming. After giving his talmidim several moments for quiet contemplation, Yeshua said, "Come now; let us leave."

He looked up at Benjamin and John Mark. Bidding a polite farewell to the family, Yeshua went down the stairs and stepped out into the night. The remaining eleven men hastily grabbed their cloaks and followed close on his heels. Benjamin and John Mark went below and watched as they set out down the street.

The last to leave, Philip, whispered to John Mark, "We're going to the garden near the Mount of Olives."

John Mark's head was filled with exhilarating thoughts. He appealed to his father, "May I go with them?"

Benjamin smiled. "Yes, but keep your wits about you. I don't want you in the middle of any trouble."

John Mark was elated. He shouted, "Thank you!" as he grasped his cloak and bounded out the door.

Something fundamental had changed within John Mark. Now he had spent time with Yeshua himself. His memory had forever frozen the picture of this holy man's visit. Simultaneously, Yeshua was both approachable and awesomely majestic. How could one ignore the clarity in those eyes, the overflowing compassion, the love he expressed with his hands as he gestured and touched, or the soothing sound of his voice when he prayed?

Hearing the Word of God

John Mark cautiously followed Yeshua's band to the Mount of Olives. Once there, they settled in a small circle on the mountainside. John Mark withdrew to a nearby wall. He studied Yeshua. It was as if light was emanating from Yeshua's head and shoulders from under the covering of his white prayer shawl.

He could hear the words clearly. Yeshua gave the men a fresh perspective: "You are the branches on the vine. You will not be fruitful without my help. You must choose to be nurtured by the vine. I am the vine, you are the branches. Whoever lives in me, and asks for me to live in him will be very fruitful. If you are severed from the vine, you will not bear any fruit at all."

This teaching captivated John Mark. It reminded him of the teachings about the vine in the Scroll of Yechezk'el. He thought: "If Yeshua is the vine and we are his branches, then surely he is responsible for the fruit we bear."

Looking directly at all his talmidim, Yeshua spoke: "If you live inside of me, and the words I have spoken live inside of you, then, when you ask for the things you need, they will be given to you. When you are fruitful, My Father is highly honored. God wants you to be fruitful, for this is the sign of those who follow me."

To further emphasize his teaching, Yeshua gestured with his hands. He extended his arms with his palms upraised and his elbows slightly bent. He drew his hands toward his heart as he spoke—as though he were symbolically drawing the men into intimate relationship with himself.

John Mark longed to be one of Yeshua's talmidim. He knew that he wanted to do what Yeshua was asking. Now he knew why Yeshua claimed to be the only way to God. Following Yeshua brought one into a personal relationship with God Himself. John Mark realized that Yeshua was telling them that God hungered for fellowship with humankind!

Yeshua smiled as if he knew what the others were thinking. Leaning his head back, he looked to the heavens. Yeshua's love seemed to fill the starry night. His words were poetic and gratifying: "I love you in the same way that my Father loves me. Come dwell in my love. If you do that, you will share my love, just as I obey my Father and share His love. I am telling you these things because I want my joy to be with you forever. I want this joy to fill you to overflowing.

"Furthermore, I ask that you love one another as I love you." John Mark could not imagine his joy ever being more full than it was at this moment. Every fiber of his being was electrified. Every thought was refreshing. Every breath filled him with the peace of God. He could imagine nothing more wonderful than to love and be loved in the way Yeshua expressed his love for his talmidim.

John Mark's sense of God's vast love burst into fresh and new dimensions. His understanding plumbed new depths and soared to new heights. He kept asking himself, "Why has God chosen Yeshua to reveal His plans to these men and even to my family? This is too marvelous. It is beyond my grasp."

If there were doubts in anyone's mind that Yeshua was the Messiah, these statements confirmed his identity to all. His demeanor was extraordinary—he expressed authenticity and transparency. No double standard. No personal agenda. No self-promotion. In contrast to Temple leaders, his words pointed to the highest principle—a majestic command to love! Not only were people called to love God first, but love was now defined in terms of caring unselfishly for others.

This was bold teaching. None of the scribes in the Temple had ever given instruction such as this. No wonder the cohanim feared Yeshua. He proclaimed love as the undergirding, the very rock upon which Torah was given!

During the years John Mark was raised in the Temple, rabbis taught the tradition of Torah and the necessity to fulfill its every precept. He had studied the Law carefully, diligently applying himself to this endeavor.

However, he increasingly found that obeying the hundreds of rules therein posed an intolerable burden to shoulder.

The Law's requirements were so complicated it seemed each legal obligation overlapped half a dozen others. No individual possessed the wisdom to judge the best law that most adequately applied to all situations. The result was constant inward tension and fear of failure, leading to repeated debates over the Law's countless details.

Yeshua uncovered the hidden snare overlooked by the Temple hierarchy. Despite their quest to maintain the covenant of Moses, Hebrew tradition had passed over the understanding of God's love and compassion that had rescued His chosen ones from Egypt. In its stead, people were taught to put their hope of salvation into obedience to Torah's every letter. Now, Yeshua was giving everyone permission to receive God's love as the fulfillment of Torah, without fear or condemnation. What joy!

Then Yeshua took them deeper still: "Greater love has no one than this: that he lay down his life for his friends." This was a bothersome thought—the rabbi had turned from the joy of friendship with God to thoughts of sacrifice and death. It would not be until the following day that John Mark would begin to understand the full implication of Yeshua's statement.

Their leader spoke again. He returned to an earlier theme. He forewarned his talmidim, "In a little while you will not see me. You will grieve, but your mourning will turn to joy." Concern furrowed the foreheads of the Pesach guests. John Mark felt his throat tighten. Was Yeshua again speaking of his imminent death?

Finally, as Yeshua prayed aloud to God, the talmidim were allowed to observe anew the great intimacy between their leader and Almighty God.

Concentrating his full attention heavenward, he prayed intensely, "Father, I do not pray just for these friends. I pray also for those who will come to know who I am because of their witness. My prayer for all of them is that they will be one, just as you and I are one, Father; and that just as you live in me and I live in You, they will live in us in complete unity. This is so they can tell the world that You sent me, and that You love them just as You love me."

All eyes were riveted on the man of God. John Mark's spirit soared. "What a prayer! Only someone who is truly intimate with God could say such things!"

One thing was sure—John Mark knew he loved Yeshua. He knew at last that he was willing to obey this prophet's every request. With utmost certainty he now believed that everything Yeshua said and did came directly from heaven above.

To be one with Yeshua. To be one with God. Could Yeshua really make such a statement? Could he do this for his chosen ones?

Eventually, the group started to move down the hill toward the Garden of Gethsemane. Peter looked at John Mark. The leader of the talmidim had taken quite a liking to him. Not wanting any harm to come to the lad, he warned him, "You had better be going home, John Mark. There is always the unexpected when traveling with Yeshua. It would be better if you were not seen with us."

John Mark waved reluctantly, "Thank you, Peter. Shalom."

John Mark started to head back to the city, but something stopped him. Looking back after the talmidim and Yeshua, he could see them making their way down through the rocky terrain of the incline. He was irresistibly drawn to the man of God, whose words were more valuable than fine gold.

John Mark longed for more truth. He didn't want to miss anything concerning Yeshua. The young man decided to discreetly follow the others to their garden retreat.

Back to the Garden

Nestled in the shallow valley between Jerusalem, the city on a hill, and the rising slope of the Mount of Olives, was an ancient garden called Gethsemane. Alongside the garden was a small stream, the Brook Kidron. Its gentle trickle of water served as the backdrop for this peaceful place. Here, in the quiet of the garden, Yeshua regularly met with his talmidim for times of rest and prayer.

There was a crossing over the stream used by those who traveled between Jerusalem and the Mount of Olives. The path down to it ran alongside the city's formidable eastern wall. The Temple Mount was located on the high ground immediately behind this extensive fortification. Framed within the wall, leading directly to the Temple, stood the Golden Gate, one of the entrances to the city.

Reaching the path to the garden, John Mark looked back up the slope of the Mount of Olives. He knew from his studies that nearly a thousand years earlier, on this same road, King David had wept over the rebellion of his son, Absalom. Recalling this further heightened John Mark's sense of foreboding. He wondered if something terrible was going to happen.

He had almost caught up with the others when they reached Gethsemane. Rather than intrude, he looked for a well-concealed place among some trees on the upper edge of the garden. Here, he could closely observe Yeshua and his friends. Spreading his cloak on the ground, the self-appointed emissary made himself comfortable. Shortly thereafter, Yeshua separated Peter, James, and John from the rest and headed toward a nearby cluster of olive trees, most certainly to pray with them.

John Mark could easily make out the figures of the talmidim as they walked. He watched the humble man of God, accompanied by the three fishermen from Galilee, retrace familiar steps up the pathway to the secret place where he often retired to pray, passing just meters from John Mark's own hiding place. He could see that these talmidim enjoyed favor with Yeshua.

High overhead, a full moon marked Pesach. Its iridescent glow streamed through the canopy of olive trees. Bent, woody boughs obscured much of the light, casting dark jagged shadows beneath the branches. An evening breeze coaxed a myriad of leaves into motion. Flickering and fluttering above the irregular turf, swaying shapes played out their dark drama on an earthen stage.

The wooded area surrounding Yeshua seemed to mirror the tumult within his own soul. The forces of nature in that arid climate had accomplished their weathering work, twisting and turning the ancient trunks of olive trees into contorted wooden sculptures. Gnarled, ungainly branches spoke of their harsh struggles with life. It reminded John Mark of the way the olive wood was often carved into intricate designs that highlighted the contrast between its dark wavy grain and smooth golden timber.

Rugged roots plunged into dry, sandy soil, seeking out nourishment and moisture from the nearby stream. Leafy arms reached toward the sky to worship their Creator. How profound, thought John Mark, that in the Holy Scriptures these fruit trees figuratively represented the people of Israel!

These wizened trees gave life by yielding a rich, abundant harvest, sharing the very essence of their being to nurture the needs of humanity. The delicious fruit of the olive could be eaten or gathered into large vats where its golden oil was extracted by squeezing its juicy fibers between great wooden presses. This translucent liquid held a myriad of uses—besides food and health remedies, these included lubrication, illumination, and anointing.

Looking out over the valley, John Mark followed Yeshua's gaze along the path of the quiet creek as it flowed down the ravine. Yeshua's eyes swept along the ridge of mountains that climbed southward toward the village of Bethlehem, the ancestral home of the parents who raised him, Maryam and Joseph.

The cliffs around Bethlehem were pocked with caves that sheltered flocks of sheep. Here, shepherds sat in craggy, arched entrances, keeping their nightly vigil. Countless contoured hillsides spanned the distance between the small stable where Yeshua was born and the olive garden where he now rested.

From his point of view, John Mark could discern rocky slopes reflecting the bright moonlight onto a web of timeworn trails cut into steep inclines. Thousands of ancient narrow lanes laced the mountainsides at every conceivable angle. They had been etched over the centuries by the innumerable hooves of foraging livestock. These footpaths appeared as slender streams of light zigzagging over the bluffs. Under the polished luster of evening light, they looked like fishnets of woven silver tossed over an uneven earth by an unseen hand. The countryside was breathtakingly beautiful. But the beauty of this sanctuary would soon be overshadowed.

John Mark heard Yeshua say to his friends, "Sit here, while I go over there and pray." What Yeshua then added frightened John Mark, "My soul is overwhelmed with sorrow to the point of death. Wait here and keep watch with me." The men agreed, but as soon as Yeshua stepped away, they too curled up to sleep on the grassy carpet.

Reaching a place of solitude, Yeshua fell to the ground and clung to a large limestone boulder. Even before his head came to rest on his forearm, he began to weep bitter tears. He called out to God. "Abba, Father, all things are possible for You. Take this cup away from me; nevertheless, it is not what I want that should be done but what You want me to do," he sobbed.

It was obvious that John Mark's concerns were justified, for Yeshua was grappling with an incredible burden. Sometime later, Yeshua struggled to his feet and returned to Peter, James, and John. They were sound asleep.

John Mark grieved quietly as he watched Yeshua's fruitless efforts to awaken his friends. "Simon, are you asleep? Couldn't you stay awake one hour?" But the men were too fatigued to arise and pray. John Mark wanted to go and comfort the lonely man, but decided that since he was not one of the twelve, it would be wrong to do so.

Yeshua returned to his place of prayer. He looked toward the heavens and further poured out his heart to his Father. His pleading became impassioned. It appeared that his strength was waning, as if his very heart was breaking. John Mark groaned as he realized that he was observing Yeshua in an intensely personal crisis.

Again, Yeshua approached his other followers but not one stirred. John Mark edged in closer. The agony he witnessed shook him to his very core.

Yeshua's stress was catastrophic. His breathing was heavy and labored, his body drenched with perspiration. Capillaries beneath his skin actually began bursting under the intense emotional pressure! Hemorrhaging blood vessels leaked scarlet fluid into his sweat. The crimson mixture passed through the pores of his skin, turning it into the color of his own blood. Great scarlet drops fell from his body, staining the boulder beneath him with wet, reddish streaks.

A glimmer of torchlight caught John Mark's eye. He saw the glint of weaponry in the distance! An armed troop was headed toward the garden! Had they come to seize the rabbi and his talmidim? Looking back at Yeshua, he could see him still in deep travail. John Mark was on the brink of stepping forward, when Yeshua got up.

John Mark clenched his fists in frustration as the enemy drew closer. Yeshua roused his friends. "Are you still sleeping and resting? Enough! The hour has come. Look, the Son of Man is betrayed into the hands of sinners. Rise! Let us go! Here comes my betrayer!"

Awakening to the racket of the armed band's arrival, the talmidim were aghast as the soldiers quickly flanked Yeshua. Peter and the talmidim sought to intervene. They stepped up to protect him, but Yeshua commanded them, "Stand back!"

To the further dismay of Yeshua's compatriots, the troop of guards was accompanied by one of their own—Judas Iscariot!

Judas approached Yeshua. John Mark heard Judas call out, "Rabbi, Rabbi!"

Yeshua replied, "Judas, are you betraying the Son of Man with a kiss?" Judas could not look Yeshua in the face. Closing his eyes, he grabbed Yeshua's neck and pulled his head down and kissed him on the cheek. John Mark watched helplessly as Judas slipped back into the crowd, grinning darkly. The talmidim were beside themselves with anger and dread.

John Mark could now clearly make out the entire detachment of Temple soldiers and officials. They carried torches and lanterns and brandished spears and swords. Yeshua stepped forward. "Who is it you want?"

"Yeshua of Nazareth!" they demanded.

Yeshua said, "I am he." As he spoke the entire troop staggered backwards and fell to the ground as though smitten by Yeshua's words. It was as if they were pushed over by an invisible hand. Not one remained standing. John Mark was filled with awe.

When the soldiers regained their feet, Yeshua repeated his request, "Who is it you want?"

Apprehensively, they replied again, "Yeshua of Nazareth."

"I told you that I am he," Yeshua answered.

They trembled for fear he would knock them down once more. Instead, he gestured toward his talmidim, "If you are looking for me, then let these men go."

The talmidim were jumpy and anxious. They realized that their master was under arrest. Some drew their weapons. The guards tensed.

Yeshua's men asked him, "Shall we strike them with our swords?" Without waiting for a reply, Simon Peter, who had concealed a short sword, drew it and swiftly struck Cohen Hagadol's servant, slicing off his right ear. The man howled in pain.

The soldiers started to seize Peter, but when Yeshua spoke, they stopped in their tracks. Yeshua commanded Peter, "Put your sword away! Shall I not drink the cup the Father has given me? No more of this!"

Yeshua bent over, reached out, and touched the man's wound. No one was quite sure what he was doing. After a moment, the injured one quit bellowing. There were excited whispers from both sides, "He has healed him!" The soldiers marveled and were terribly afraid. John Mark gasped in awe. The ear had been completely healed.

Then Yeshua said to the chief cohanim, the officers of the Temple guard, and the elders, who had come for him, "Am I leading a rebellion, that you have come with clubs and swords? Every day I was with you in the Temple courts, and you did not lay a hand on me. But this is your hour, when darkness reigns."

Again, fear swept through their ranks. The soldiers stood frozen—as at attention. But they had to carry out their orders. Mustering up their courage, they took Yeshua into custody and led him away. They were relieved they did not have to restrain him; he went willingly. For a few moments, Yeshua's men were petrified with terror. Then they fled into the night completely demoralized.

In his efforts to see and hear what was being said, John Mark had drawn in closer. His attention was so focused upon Yeshua that he became distracted. He was unaware that he was sticking his head out from the shrubbery, exposing himself to view. Suddenly, two Temple guards nabbed him and picked him up by the collar. The young man's heart leaped into his throat. He had never felt panic like this!

Instinctively, he dropped to the ground and threw his hands up over his head. The guards grabbed at him but only caught hold of his clothing. In the scuffle, his linen shirt came off over his head as his arms slid out through the shoulder openings. Leaving his attackers with nothing in their hands but an empty garment, John Mark ran off into the hills like a frightened deer.

The Sheep Are Scattered

The hour was late. John Mark returned home, doleful and fatigued. He had run aimlessly for miles—partly because of what he had just experienced, but mostly out of anxiety, driven by fear for the fate of Yeshua. Slipping inside the door, he tiptoed his way past the hearth, but to no avail. His father was sitting by the fire waiting for him. John Mark was both embarrassed and relieved to see him.

Benjamin quickly noted his son's partially clothed appearance and his obvious huffing and puffing. His eyebrows raised: "Son, where are your clothes?"

Exhausted, John Mark sat on a wooden stool next to the hearth. His father wrapped him in a blanket. "The Temple guards caught me watching Yeshua in Gethsemane. But that is not the worst of it." He paused, as much to collect his thoughts as to catch his breath. "The guards were not after me. They came for Yeshua! Now they have him in their custody. It was Judas Iscariot who betrayed him and led the guards right to him!"

"No! God help us!" cried Benjamin.

"I am so sorry, Father. I know you told me to be careful, but I wasn't careful enough. The guards jumped me. They grabbed my clothing; I tore myself free and let them have my tunic. I ran to the top of the Mount of Olives. I then circled all the way around to the western side of the city before I reentered the gates. It took me an hour to get home without being seen."

Benjamin took in every word. He looked at his son carefully. "It is good you have escaped. The clothing can be replaced, but you cannot."

In the fading firelight the two men called out to God as they prayed. Their emotions were in turmoil. It appeared that the enemy had taken charge. They pleaded for help. They knew that only God could sort out this twisted situation.

Later that night several of the talmidim returned to Benjamin's door. John Mark had fallen asleep by the hearth. He was awakened by their anguished whispering and the sound of his father trying to calm them. John Mark recognized the stress-filled voice of Andrew: "The master has been taken prisoner by the Temple guards!"

"I know," said Benjamin. "Come in quickly before you are seen."

Sympathetically, Benjamin listened to their tales. Andrew said that Peter and several others were missing. John Mark shuddered. No one knew what to do or where to find these newfound friends. Perhaps the Temple guards had captured them during the skirmish. Maybe they were in jail or dead. God forbid!

Before Andrew had finished, Matthew arrived, agitated and disheartened. Once safe in the upper room, he began to cry. Benjamin did his best to console him. John Mark knew only to pray for them all. After a time, they all fell silent, morbidly depressed.

Later that night, word came with Philip and Nathaniel that Yeshua had been taken to the home of Annas, the father-in-law of Caiaphas, Cohen Hagadol. Annas was the former Cohen Hagadol and one of the most powerful men in Jerusalem.

Philip turned to John Mark and said, "Our colleague John knows some people at Annas' home. He gained access to the interrogation. We hid in the shadows nearby, hoping not to be noticed."

Nathaniel picked up the story from there: "John went in, but Peter was reluctant to enter. He stayed with the guards outside by a fire. While he warmed himself, a young woman accused him of being a conspirator. And can you believe it, Peter denied knowing Yeshua! To make things worse, two more bystanders identified him as a follower of Yeshua. They had seen Peter in the garden, and when he spoke, they recognized his accent as Galilean. Peter disavowed any knowledge of Yeshua to each of them. At that very moment, just as Yeshua had prophesied in this very room, a rooster crowed!"

Nathaniel's listeners turned pale. They remembered Yeshua's warning to Peter just hours before, that Peter would deny him three times before the rooster crowed. Astonishing! How could that be?

"This is a terrible and fearful thing," said Benjamin.

Philip's voice trembled as he resumed speaking. "Peter froze where he stood. He was overcome with grief. The last we saw of him, he was on his knees, in a nearby alley, groaning in distress. As for the rest of us, we escaped. Some have scattered into the hills. Fear has blotted out our faith. Alas! How could we have forsaken the one we loved? But we did, even when we knew how much he cared for us!"

Trying to maintain his composure, Philip went on: "Annas questioned Yeshua about his teaching." Yeshua simply replied, "I have spoken openly to the world; I always taught in synagogues or at the Temple, places where all my fellow Jewish people come together. I have said nothing in secret. Why question me? Ask those who heard me. They know what I said."

"When Yeshua said this, one of the officials struck him in the face and shouted, 'Is this the way you answer the Cohen Hagadol?' Everyone looked at Yeshua for some word either of defense or retribution, but he continued to speak in the same fashion: 'If I said something wrong, testify as to what is wrong. But if I spoke the truth, why do you strike me?'"

John Mark flinched. He remembered Yeshua healing the downtrodden in the Temple. How could they assault this wonder-working man of God?

"Then the priest had him bound," said Philip. "We left when Annas had finished questioning Yeshua. But not before we saw that the men guarding him began mocking and beating him!" Philip began to weep. "It was awful! Forgive us for coming back here, but we had nowhere else to turn."

"You need not ask for forgiveness." Benjamin comforted them, "Anything that concerns Yeshua is important to us. You are welcome here."

Matthew tried to sound hopeful. "The Sanhedrin cannot conduct a trial at night. And even if he is condemned, Rome has not granted the Sanhedrin the authority to condemn anyone to death. They cannot execute anyone. That right is reserved for the governor himself."

As the night wore on, more talmidim came to Benjamin's home for safety and consolation. Benjamin met each man at the door and invited him to the upper room.

The windows were covered. Lamps were lit. Mats were arranged about the floor. But no one rested. The men moaned as they implored God for help. It all seemed so senseless. The sheep had lost their shepherd.

Philip related to the latecomers the punishments inflicted upon Yeshua. All became even more distraught. The talmidim had long worried what would happen if Yeshua were ever taken captive by the cohanim. Now it had actually taken place.

At first light, John rushed in. For a few moments all were relieved to see that he was safe. Confirming their worst fears, he related, "After our master was interrogated at the house of Annas, they took him to Caiaphas' palace."

Philip swallowed hard. Panic set in. John had difficulty expressing himself. He stammered, "Caiaphas has the authority to recommend Yeshua's execution. He hates Yeshua. Everyone knows he's ruthless and crooked. His influence extends to the highest level of Roman rule."

John hurriedly filled in other details. "By the time we got there, Caiaphas had already assembled the council and the entire Sanhedrin for another inquiry. It was a shameful exhibition. Teachers of Torah and elders gathered there to question our master without any regard for their Law. They harangued him and had him beaten unmercifully!"

Nathaniel broke down, unable to control his feelings. John Mark wept alongside as they comforted one another.

"Caiaphas brought in false witnesses," John reported. "He tried to establish some kind of legal basis on which to condemn Yeshua. But there was none. Then two last witnesses came in and testified that Yeshua had once said: 'I am able to destroy the temple of God and rebuild it in three days.'

"Caiaphas demanded, 'What did you mean by that?' Yeshua said nothing. This brought a malicious grin to Caiaphas' face. 'Why don't you defend yourself?' And still Yeshua said nothing.

"Caiaphas had a tantrum. He challenged Yeshua. 'Tell us if you are the Messiah, the Son of God.'"

"'Yes, it is as you say,' Yeshua told them. His voice was quiet and clear. Then he added, 'But I say to all of you: In the future you will see the Son of Man sitting at the right hand of the Mighty One and coming on the clouds of heaven.'

"Cohen Hagadol tried to reply," explained John, "But he was so flustered, he choked. In his rage, he tore his clothes and shouted out an accusation: 'He has spoken blasphemy! Why do we need any more witnesses?' Then I saw Caiaphas spin about and approach the council demanding, 'What is your verdict?' They answered him, 'He is worthy of death!'"

A chill went through those listening to John's story. By now, his sorrow had sunken to the depths of misery. He struggled to continue his description: "They insulted him and spit in his face. They blindfolded him and struck him with their fists. Others slapped him and said, 'Prophesy to us, Messiah! Who hit you?' At Caiaphas' prompting, the whole assembly decided to take Yeshua to the Praetorium at dawn for a Roman trial before the Governor – Pontius Pilate himself. So I came here hoping to warn you. It will be light in a few hours."

The talmidim jumped to their feet in anger. James lamented, "This is the worst of all possible situations. The governor will judge Yeshua in public. And we know that the Tz'dukim and P'rushim will do all they can to sway the crowd. Pontius Pilate has the power to sentence him to death. Most certainly, the Sanhedrin will try to force his hand. This must have been their plan from the beginning—those self-proclaimed paragons of righteousness!"

John Mark was numb. He retreated to his sleeping mat, but rest eluded him. He could tell by the frantic voices of the talmidim that their distress was increasing. He heard everything. Trying to hold back tears, he bit his lip, but he could not help himself. He laid his head back on his pillow. His sobs sent rivulets of saltwater running down his temples that pooled in his ears before streaming down his neck, soaking his mattress. He hardly noticed. All he could think about was Yeshua.

Emotionally drained, the young man drifted off to sleep. A short time later John Mark was jerked back to consciousness, his brief sleep ruined by a disconcerting dream. Dark forces were pursuing him. He was trying to warn Yeshua of the danger in the garden. But it was too late! Suddenly, Temple guards snared him! He tried to shout, but his mouth was gagged, his arms bound.

Gasping for air, fighting for his freedom, he awoke with a desperate cry, "Yeshua!" only to find his face smothered and his limbs entangled under his twisted blanket. Unraveling the covers, John Mark turned onto his back and interlaced his fingers behind his head. The house was quiet. He felt weak. His head throbbed. His face was wet with perspiration from his nightmare of wrestling.

Unfortunately, he knew this dream was not entirely his imagination. His life had done a complete turnabout. In the span of a few short hours he had ascended the lofty heights of the Mount of Olives with Yeshua and his talmidim, then descended to reports of horrors in the harsh depths of the dungeon beneath Caiaphas' house. And now these same talmidim had returned to the upper room with more tales of woe.

Ironically, John Mark's thoughts returned to his treasured Moriah. He still yearned for that little yearling. He had so enjoyed the tender nudge of his innocent friend's wet nose. He missed his little companion, who had been such a comfort to him. Life could be so hard. There were just too many unanswered questions.

As the sun peeked over the skyline, a shaft of light streamed by John Mark's head. Dust particles danced in gentle drafts of warming air. A refreshing breeze began to stir. The smell of the straw soothed his senses. Thankfully, his head started to clear; his thinking grew keen once again. Taking a deep breath, he swung his legs over the side of the cot. He could hear Yeshua's ragged, forlorn flock leaving. They talked of taking up places where they could discreetly view the trial at the governor's palace.

Without warning, Benjamin lifted the flap over the doorway of his son's room. His statement set the young man into motion. "John Mark, we must go to the palace for Yeshua's trial."

He leaped from bed, pleased that his father had asked him to go. Instinctively, John Mark knew this would be a place of potential hazard. They were on their way in seconds.

Man, Monarch, and Messiah

A huge crowd milled about at the front of the Roman Judgment Hall. The talmidim had interspersed themselves within the gathering to avoid detection by Yeshua's enemies. Carefully blending with the crowd, John Mark and Benjamin crept in as close as they could. This was no safe place for any supporter of Yeshua.

"The trial must be held outside," Benjamin informed John Mark. "Pilate is glad that Jewish people cannot come inside the Praetorium. He knows we must avoid ritual defilement if we are to obey the requirements for Pesach. The governor despises our customs."

Just then, Yeshua was ushered outside between two guards. They directed him before Pontius Pilate. The Roman Governor was the first to observe that the accused had already been brutally thrashed. The crowd fell silent when they saw the prisoner's badly bruised face. His clothing was splattered with blood. Obviously, the Judean hierarchy had already found Yeshua guilty and punished him before turning him over to Pilate for further judgment.

John Mark whispered, "How can they call themselves spiritual leaders? Yeshua is not guilty of anything. Our cohanim are dishonoring the Law of Moshe!"

Benjamin responded under his breath, "Shhh. I know. This is a blatant affront to our judicial system." He grimaced. "Now the cohanim will seek to persuade the governor to put Yeshua to death. For the cohanim to consummate their conspiracy, a sentencing has to occur."

Trumpets blew. The crowd fell silent. Pilate opened the proceeding. "What charges do you bring against this man?"

"If he were not a criminal, we would not have handed him over to you," the priests replied craftily.

Pilate appeared puzzled. The cohanim had deliberately avoided answering his question directly. He thought for a moment and decided to sidestep a confrontation. "Then take him yourselves, and judge him by your own law."

"But we have no right to execute anyone," the religious leaders objected.

Pilate acted surprised, "Oh, so you want me to have this man killed? On what grounds?" he asked.

"We have found him subverting our nation," they shouted angrily. "He opposes payment of taxes to Caesar and claims to be Messiah, a king!"

The crowd stirred anxiously, whispering among themselves. "Had Yeshua proclaimed himself King of Israel? When did this happen?"

Pontius Pilate stalked back into the Praetorium while everyone waited outside. A few moments later, much to the ire of the cohanim, a Roman guard came out and took Yeshua inside. John Mark surmised that Yeshua was being questioned privately.

"This is very dangerous," said Benjamin, trying to gain a glimpse of what was happening inside the palace. "Pilate does not really know what he's up against. I fear all the more for our rabbi."

After some minutes, Pilate emerged and returned to his rostrum. Confidently, he addressed the chief cohanim and the crowd. "I find no basis for a charge against this man."

"Thank God," breathed both Benjamin and John Mark.

But their hopes were quickly dashed. Provoked by instigators, the crowd insisted on judgment:

"He stirs up the people all over Judea by his teaching!" cried a priest.

"He started his lies in Galilee and has brought his rebellion to Jerusalem!" a moneylender yelled.

Pilate was caught off guard. "Is he a Galilean?" he asked in surprise.

"Yes, he comes from Capernaum!" several people responded.

"That is King Herod Antipas' jurisdiction," said Pilate seeking an escape. "Herod is in Jerusalem for your religious feast. Let him deal with it."

"The governor is shunning responsibility," Benjamin groaned. "This is awful. There's no telling what Herod will do. He's not even Jewish.

He's an Edomite, serving at the pleasure of Rome. What if he sees Yeshua as a threat to his throne?"

"Oh no," whispered John Mark.

Before anyone could raise a protest, the prisoner was taken away. The crowd followed Yeshua and the Roman guards a short journey across the city. Within minutes they had reassembled at Herod's palace.

Herod stumbled out onto the porch of his home, rumpled and drowsy.

"I think we woke him up," said John Mark.

Benjamin remarked, "This is truly an odd situation. Herod and the cohanim hate each other, but the cohanim are being forced to seek his cooperation."

At first, Herod seemed grouchy, but his attitude changed when he learned whom the prisoner was. Drawing himself up to his full height, the portly prince assumed an authoritative posture and played to the crowd.

"We have always been fascinated by the deeds of this nonconformist," he quipped. "Now we have finally gotten to meet him. Perhaps we can make him to perform some miracle."

With that, John Mark and Benjamin realized that Herod was not interested in justice at all. The two became increasingly distressed when Herod and the cohanim began peppering Yeshua with leading questions and threats. They were especially vicious in their inquisition, which quickly turned into a slanderous tirade.

"Look upon King Herod!" they ordered Yeshua.

"Assert your claim to his throne!" taunted Caiaphas.

"Are we to bow to you?" asked King Herod. "Show us your magic."

Yet, through it all, Yeshua remained silent.

Finally, Herod grew contemptuous. "Let us accord him the dignity he deserves," sneered the puppet monarch. He directed his troops to dress the prisoner in a gorgeous robe.

"Hail, mighty king!" scoffed Herod. His men joined in and mocked Yeshua with other insults until they were all laughing. Still, Yeshua gave no response. John Mark and Benjamin were heartsick.

"Enough of that," ordered Herod. "Take him back to Pilate. This is a waste of my time." The Roman soldiers obediently led Yeshua back to the Praetorium.

A short time later, the whole assemblage returned to the pavement before the Hall of Judgment. Pilate was none too glad to see their prompt return. John Mark could see that the procurator was frustrated.

John Mark looked about, wondering where Yeshua was being held.

Pilate addressed the crowd. "It is the governor's custom at this Hebrew feast to release one prisoner. At this time, we hold a notorious murderer called Barabbas, who deserves to die. I'm sure you don't want me to release such a dangerous man. So who would you have me set free, Barabbas, or Yeshua who is called the Messiah?"

Benjamin was excited, "Pilate is trying to free Yeshua! He knows that it is out of envy that they have handed our rabbi over to him." John Mark and Benjamin saw a glimmer of hope. They prayed that Pilate's sentiments would influence the people.

Debates broke out throughout the audience. Barabbas had an unsavory reputation. Sensing their position was being weakened, the cohanim g'dolim jumped forward. The high priests again shamelessly accused Yeshua of grievous crimes. Then they rallied the audience to free Barabbas.

Caiaphas directed one of his cohanim to address the crowd. A young priest stepped forward and said, "Barabbas has not harmed any of us. He is Rome's enemy, not ours! This Yeshua, on the other hand, breaks our sacred Law by performing his false miracles on the Sabbath! He defiles our Temple and insults the priesthood of Aaron! We choose to free Barabbas!" Most of the listeners agreed. Their sentiments had been swayed.

Dreading the answer, the governor tried again, "Which of the two do you want me to release to you?"

"Give us Barabbas!" Soon it became a chant. "Give us Barabbas! Give us Barabbas!" Caiaphas smiled as he eyed the Roman governor. The Cohen Hagadol had outmaneuvered him. Pilate was disgusted. John Mark and Benjamin were crestfallen. Pilate sent for his captive. He was not going to yield without a fight.

Yeshua came forth again, this time dressed in a purple robe with a crown of thorns squashed onto his head. He was a spectacle of horror. It only took one look at Yeshua for John Mark to see that the accused man had been further abused and beaten. His face was puffy and covered with new welts and ugly abrasions. Fresh blood stained his cheeks and clotted his beard. Upon viewing their master's broken frame, his talmidim drew back, wincing in revulsion.

"Look at this man!" Pilate called to the swarm. "You brought him to me as one who was inciting the people to rebellion. I have examined him in your presence and have found no basis for your charges against him. Neither has Herod, who sent him back to us. Your Yeshua has done nothing to deserve the death penalty. Therefore, I will punish him some more and then release him."

This ploy fell on deaf ears. The cohanim and many of the P'rushim began to chant and agitate the audience. "Crucify him! Crucify him!" The crowd picked it up.

"Crucify! Crucify! Crucify!" Their voices soon reached fever pitch. They wanted blood!

Pilate raised his hands to silence the crowd. "Why? What crime has this man committed? I have told you, I find no grounds for the death penalty. I will have him chastised and then release him."

The cohanim insisted, "We have a law, and according to that law he has to die because he claims to be the Son of God. He's a blasphemer!"

John Mark knew that in their culture, sonship meant the same thing as being equal to the Father. If Yeshua was truly the "Son of God," then he must be the Messiah himself. This was something the cohanim would never accept.

When Pilate heard this, he became pale. He realized he was losing control of the trial. Everyone could see fear written on his face. Benjamin and John Mark were disturbed. The governor retreated into the palace. Soon Yeshua was summoned within.

A few minutes later, Pilate returned followed by Yeshua, who was being shoved along by Roman guards. Pilate declared, "I am going to set him free. I am not bound by your law!"

A hush descended over the crowd. Caiaphas whispered to one of his cronies, persuading him to speak, "If you let this man go, you are not Caesar's friend! Whoever makes himself a king speaks against Caesar!" Immediately the crowd seized upon these words and roared in agreement.

Benjamin was appalled. "That devil Caiaphas no longer appeals to our Law, but to Rome's!" he whispered intensely.

Pilate was at a loss. He stretched out his hand and pointed to the tortured man being held by guards. Sarcastically, Pilate said, "Behold your King!"

Recognizing that the governor was seeking pity for Yeshua, the crowd would have none of it. They bellowed their disapproval. "No! No! Crucify him!"

Thoroughly perplexed, Pilate appealed, "Shall I crucify your King?"

The chief priests answered, "We have no king but Caesar!"

Pilate was amazed. He knew that was a lie. John Mark and Benjamin were equally shocked. Shame on the cohanim! This was an insult to the Most High God!

Amidst the uproar, Pilate called for a basin of water. "I am innocent of this man's blood," he asserted loudly. He washed his hands in front of the mob, and then cried out, "It's your fault!"

Benjamin and John Mark knew that Pilate had given up.

"Release Barabbas!" Pilate ordered his men sourly. "Scourge the King of the Jews and crucify him!"

The trial was at an end. John Mark and Benjamin buried their heads in their hands and wept as the mob wildly celebrated its triumph.

Roman Justice

Benjamin and John Mark returned home to report the dreadful outcome of the last trial. "Roman guards have taken Yeshua to the dungeon," said Benjamin grimly. "No doubt our master is being spat upon, verbally assaulted, and beaten with fists. He will then be flogged with a multi-strapped whip with metal spurs attached, cruelly designed to rip open his flesh. He has been sentenced to be crucified."

Upon hearing the description of this sadistic torture and the terrible judgment, the women broke down and cried uncontrollably for several minutes. Fortunately, little Rebekah was at a neighbor's house and did not witness their anguish.

Knowing the ordeal Yeshua was enduring, John Mark's father instructed his family, "Now let's get a hold of ourselves. We must be strong and courageous."

After the initial shock subsided, Benjamin said, "Those who have studied Tanakh all their lives have condemned the very one they claim to seek. And our people who hailed him just days ago have turned on him and demanded his death. Actually, they condemn themselves. They do not believe that Yeshua is that Prophet spoken of by Moshe, nor that this is the day our prophets foretold would come to the nation of Israel."

Naomi grabbed a medicine jar and insisted, "I want to take this ointment to ease our master's wounds."

"I hope they will permit us to see him," said Benjamin.

As soon as they opened the door, they were jolted by the clamor in the streets. "Yeshua is already on his way to his death. We are too late!" cried Miriam.

"Let us make haste, and pray like you never prayed before," said Benjamin, plunging into the pandemonium outside.

When they caught up with the procession, they found that Yeshua was being forced to drag through the streets of Jerusalem the wooden beam upon which he would be crucified.

Naomi and Miriam caught their first glimpse of the man. As part of his public humiliation, Yeshua had been stripped totally naked. Only the shreds of a tattered loincloth and the satiric crown of briars remained. His appearance was appalling. He was frightfully disfigured, his skin laid raw, his face swollen and discolored, his form marred beyond human likeness. Their hearts sank.

Throngs lined the streets of Jerusalem. Some voiced encouragement to the beleaguered rabbi. Others jeered. Fortunately, most quietly gawked at the man of sorrows. The four grieved as they joined the march.

It was then that Benjamin remembered that his presence was required elsewhere. He told John Mark, "I am needed at the Temple. Stay with your mother and grandmother. They'll need you."

He added, "Don't forget to meet me on the steps behind the altar at the hour of the sacrifice." John Mark knew it was a son's duty to be at the altar at mid-afternoon for the Great Sacrifice of the Lambs by the temple priests.

By now, Yeshua had left through the north city gate. He faced an uphill trek. His destination was a barren mount overlooking the city. He eyed the pathway ahead, pausing to catch his breath.

A Roman guard cuffed him, "Keep moving!"

Yeshua climbed the twisted trail.

Like a random assortment of bleached bones, the crumbly rock on the mount's upward slope had been badly eroded by abrasive weathering, leaving large gouges and pockmarks on the pale limestone surface. Just below the summit, on the side facing Jerusalem, protruding ridges of chalky stone gave shade to several shallow recesses. From a distance, the shadows within these hollows resembled the eye and nose cavities of a human skull. Thus the mount was known by its Aramaic name, Golgotha—the place of the skull.

Yeshua struggled arduously toward the top of this hill. Here was his execution site—outside the walls of the City of David, well-removed from the Temple he so deeply revered. His walk on earth was drawing to a close. He was to end his days upon this mount of death—a convicted criminal, an exile, an outcast.

Yeshua reached the top of Golgotha. His head burned with searing pain from the crown of mockery's thorns that had been maliciously jabbed through his scalp. Blood dripped down from its puncture wounds, coagulating in his hair and beard, congealing on his face—altering his appearance into a grotesque mask of suffering.

Yeshua crumpled to the ground, his beleaguered body strapped to the timber. Mercilessly, Romans soldiers seized his arms and legs and savagely nailed them to the rough-hewn beams with large metal spikes. Each hammer blow sent shock waves of agony through Yeshua's entire body. The spectators winced with every strike. Then, the soldiers raised the wooden cross bearing the man of God into its upright position, lifting his bruised and bloodied frame high for all to observe.

Yeshua had been crucified, one of the most perverse kinds of execution ever devised. John Mark could now see just how horribly disfigured Yeshua was. He could barely stand to look at him. It was a haunting sight. Ironically, a sign posted over Yeshua's head read, "King of the Jews."

The profile of Yeshua on the cross, reminded John Mark of words in the Torah. In the Scroll of Deuteronomy, it says that anyone who is hung upon a tree is cursed! It occurred to John Mark that his friend was now hanging upon the limbs of a tree. How terrible that the good Yeshua could be so defamed! Two criminals were also crucified, one on each side of him. All three would share the shame of a lawbreaker's death.

Yeshua struggled to speak. Incredibly, he said, "Father, forgive them, for they know not what they do." John Mark could not believe his ears. How could Yeshua speak kindly of his executioners? How could he ask God's pardon for those who were causing him so much pain?

Yeshua then prayed over the remnant of his followers, including his own family, several women of Galilee, and many others who had come with him to Jerusalem. Only a band of men were present; most were curious Romans. Quite a few of Yeshua's supporters stayed away from the crucifixion for fear that any association with him might lead to a similar fate—imprisonment, torture, or at the very least, personal disgrace.

Despite his weakness, Yeshua slowly lifted his head and caught the eyes of his mother and his disciple John. Both were standing near the foot of the cross. He addressed them, "Woman, here is your son," and to John, "Here is your Mother." They wept openly.

Naomi comforted Yeshua's mother and prayed for her. Now she understood why Yeshua had told her the previous night that his mother would be needing support.

Roman guards stood in the shadow of Yeshua's body and taunted him. They hurled insults and wagged their heads:

"Is this the one who claims to know God? What a sorry sight."

"Hey, Yeshua. Where's your God now that you need Him?"

"If he trusts in the Lord, let the Lord rescue him."

They ridiculed him and demeaned the faithful. As was their custom during crucifixion, the soldiers parceled out the victim's personal property among themselves. There was a seamless mantle coveted by all the soldiers. Not wanting to tear the beautiful garment, they chose not to divide it into smaller pieces. There was no thought of offering the tunic to his family or his friends.

Thus, the guards cast lots for Yeshua's last earthly possession—a piece of cloth. They had unwittingly fulfilled another Scripture, the twenty-second Psalm of King David, pointing to the Messiah's true identity.

John Mark frowned at the bitter irony of it.

Stepping into Eternity

At noonday, the sun was mysteriously concealed from the city of David, steeping and submersing Mount Zion in supernatural darkness. For the next three hours, Jerusalem held its breath. Everything was eerily calm. Then, without warning, the weather turned violent. Dark, dusty storm clouds swept over the city. It was toward the end of this wind-blown assault that John Mark suddenly realized the Great Sacrifice of the Lambs was about to take place at the Temple. He needed to join his father.

Yeshua had all but given up his spirit by the time young John Mark had to leave. He could see the vitality draining out of this man he loved. He knew that the end was at hand. He did not want to be there to witness his death. It was just too painful to behold. He bid his family good-bye and left the hill of horror.

Giving one long last look back as he made his way, he could see the three crosses silhouetted against the dismal sky. Everything John Mark had ever trusted or believed about his friend was being tested in the fires of affliction.

John Mark had trembled uncontrollably while Yeshua contorted on his cruel spikes, gasping for air. How could this crucifixion have ever happened? Events seemed oddly orchestrated, yet beyond human comprehension. And John Mark was powerless to stop them. It seemed as if his life was turning inside out.

John Mark reasoned, "Yeshua could have held the king's scepter. Instead, he was jeered at his own execution. His enemies had won the victory. What a waste. His miraculous acts are now destined to become but a distant memory, quickly fading away. No one will even remember his name . . ."

Finally, John Mark reached the Temple. With such strange happenings and mayhem in the heavens, he was deeply relieved to find his father waiting at the gate, surrounded by the unnatural gloom that blanketed the city.

After briefly discussing the ghastly events at Golgotha and reports of the hopeless suicide of Judas Iscariot, the two carefully made their way through the courtyard. They stopped next to the stairs between the brass altar and the Temple. Once there, John Mark could not help but go into more detail about the grisly execution. Even though Benjamin thought he had known what to expect, as his son described the events his burden grew heavier and his shoulders sagged.

Two priests passed right in front of them, holding aloft flaming ceremonial torches in an effort to combat the darkness. Embossed gold reliefs carved into the eastern wall of the Temple reflected the flickering firelight. Father and son hardly noticed.

Soon, other priests descended the stairway from the Temple Porch into the courtyard. The onlookers separated before them, yielding the right-of-way. After the assembly passed them by, Benjamin and John Mark hastened up the steps to gain a better view.

Upon reaching the top of the stairs, they were as close to the entrance to the Holy Place as permitted. Benjamin's eyes fastened on the ceremonies below. John Mark however, fell on his face, like Job of old, in a posture of abject humility before God. His heart was breaking. He pleaded and prayed for the life of his friend.

* * *

Suspended between heaven and earth, atop the Mount of the Skull outside the city walls of his beloved Jerusalem, hung Yeshua. Separated from his Father above and his family and friends below, his body burned in agony. His hemorrhaging blood stained the ground beneath his feet.

Searching the blackened skies, he sought the comfort of his Father in heaven, but he could find no respite. The heavens were unresponsive, sullen, and brooding. No aid was offered. Yeshua cried out for relief: "My

God, my God, why have You forsaken me?" using the very words that David spoke a millennium ago, when he was a fugitive prior to being crowned Israel's king.

Adding insult to injury, many unsympathetic onlookers jeered and joked, twisting the meaning of his words. "Look, he's calling for Elijah!"

There was no doubt among Yeshua's talmidim on Golgotha that these words taken from David's psalms were a prophesy meant for this very moment in time. But, as with King David, only silence met Yeshua's plea.

The parallels were clear; Yeshua was a direct descendant of David. And like David, he lived the life of a solitary shepherd preparing for the time when he would be released to fulfill God's plan. Both were rejected by men but accepted by God.

Yeshua was a living enigma. He spoke in parables. He spent time with the outcasts of society. He hated hypocrisy. He flustered the scribes. Despite his awesome gifts, Yeshua did not boast. He was humble. His authority did not come from physical stature — he was no larger or stronger than any of his talmidim. He led, yet he had no reputation as a leader. Instead, he earned obedience and loyalty like no other Israelite by proclaiming and embodying the realities of the Kingdom of God. Without ever raising a weapon, he had won the hearts of thousands.

But in the end, the outspoken majority of his fellow countrymen called for his crucifixion.

"It Is Finished"

Later that evening, John Mark would hear his mother describe what had transpired on the Mount of the Skull after he joined his father at the Temple. She told her son how heart wrenching it had been to witness Yeshua's bleak ending. Her account confirmed what John Mark already knew in his spirit . . .

While she described the closing moments of the master's life, she placed her hands on her throat empathetically. "Yeshua gasped, 'I thirst!' Nearby, the Romans had a few stalks of hyssop tied together and a vessel of sour wine used to dull the pain. A centurion soaked the long reeds in the rosy-tinted vinegar, saturating the tips."

Reenacting the scene, Miriam raised her hands and stared off into the distance. "The guard lifted the soggy bundle up to the sufferer. The liquid brushed his lips. He opened his eyes. After this ever-so-brief taste of relief, Yeshua turned his head to the side. This caused the juice to smear about his mouth. Reddish streaks of moisture dripped from his chin, burning the raw skin where the guards had ripped portions of his beard from his face."

Miriam began to cry. Knowing that she must tell all the horrible details, and appreciating John Mark's abiding love for Yeshua, she forced herself to go on. "His body was collapsing under its own weight. He couldn't breathe. It must have been crushing his heart. His blood leaked out of open wounds, pooling on the ground. In a final courageous effort, he arched his back and panted for air, exposing the crimson stripes where his flesh had been laid open across his ribs and shoulders. Fighting to inhale, he looked to the sky and cried out, 'It is finished!'"

"I know it's strange," Naomi interjected, "But it sounded to me like a proclamation of victory!"

Miriam folded over in grief. She fought to maintain her composure. "Then, he gasped his last and surrendered his life: 'Father, into your hands I commit my spirit.' He bowed his head. From out of nowhere, a blast of wind swirled about his body. We felt the presence of his spirit moving among us! A shiver passed through each of us. We were speechless. All was still.

"There was a centurion at the foot of the cross. He saw it all. He heard Yeshua ask God to forgive those who tortured him. He had witnessed his suffering. You could see the surprise on the soldier's face as he observed compassion from a man stripped of all dignity. It was the centurion who broke the silence. He said, 'Truly this Man was the Son of God.' From the lips of a pagan, truer words were never spoken. We, the living, beat our breasts in sorrow. I can scarcely describe the grief we have felt today."

Miriam was bereft as she finished her tale of woe. "Finally, Roman guards came to break Yeshua's legs, their way of ending his ordeal by causing him to completely collapse and suffocate on the cross. But, it wasn't necessary. It was clear he was dead. Just to be sure, a guard pierced Yeshua's side with a spear. Strangely, both blood and water came out of the wound!" Miriam broke down. She could no longer speak.

Naomi finished the account, "We prayed for God to restore his life. We could not believe that heaven would allow such an injustice. If we could see his sorrow and hear his pleas, could not our Heavenly Father? Where was God?"

Have You Seen The Lamb?

The women's account of the happenings on Mount Golgotha had been given. Little did they know of simultaneous events unfolding before John Mark and Benjamin, who were witnessing fantastic miracles of immeasurable proportions upon the Temple Mount.

*　*　*

John Mark lay prostrate, his father Benjamin alongside him, praying at the edge of the limestone porch between the brass altar and the Holy Place. A spontaneous, supernatural perception ignited his soul. He knew the hand of God was moving in him and around him. Goose bumps covered his body. All his senses were alerted.

Overhead, a bank of clouds rushed toward the center of Jerusalem, spreading across Mount Zion. Instantly, the heavens burst open. The sky tore apart with a shearing sound that severed the very fabric of the firmament. Lightning exploded in the air. The earth was jolted by shock waves, as if shuddering in grief from a great loss.

The clouds erupted with a screech. The cohanim standing before the great altar of the Temple were paralyzed with fear. At that very moment, a priest had been poised to sever the jugular vein of the first of thousands of sacrificial lambs. Terrified by the trauma overhead, the hand holding the blade at the throat of the sacrifice dropped the killing instrument. Those assisting the priest also released their grip on the animal, afraid for their lives.

The lamb leapt free while the cohanim stood there trembling. No one noticed the yearling as he trotted to safety. All eyes searched the heavens in abject fright.

Suddenly, an even deeper darkness obscured Jerusalem. The earth groaned, growled, and moaned. No noise had ever been heard like this. This was an earthquake unlike any that had ever been experienced, straight from the bowels of the world; its magnitude declared that creation itself was profoundly stricken. The upheaval left everyone shaken.

John Mark clung to the stairs. He knew that this was the stunning event he had anticipated. Even though he had sensed it coming, it was no less incredible. He blinked his eyes as he tried to adjust to brilliant flashes in the darkness.

A lightning bolt struck the Temple's high tower. Sparks sprayed off the rooftop. A blast of wind slammed against the doors of the Temple, flinging the entryway open. Looking down the lengthy corridor to the far end of the Holy Place, John Mark and Benjamin beheld the implausible. Their eyes were transfixed on the curtain at the back of the chamber.

This great partition, a hand-breadth thick, hung illuminated by the golden lampstand whose seven large flames appeared like rays of filtered firelight dancing on angry puffs of air. A supernatural wind ruffled the massive folds of the magnificent tapestry. Golden beams of iridescent light reflected off the velvety undulations of the curtain, the sacred divider that stood at the center of the innermost, most exclusive, location in the entire world—God's own Dwelling Place.

The wind lapsed. For a moment, all was calm. Then they beheld the most astounding event imaginable. How could this be? Right before their eyes, starting from the top of the curtain high overhead, the impenetrable veil of separation began to slowly, inexorably tear. It was ripping in two from top to bottom!

The floor of the Temple quaked and quivered. The walls swayed before them as John Mark and Benjamin witnessed the intricately woven tapestry split all the way down the middle. They could hear the heavy fabric shredding and see its jagged edges unfurl and flutter inside powerful, invisible currents of air.

Suddenly they saw it! The Most Holy Place, revealed! The very place where the Presence of God once had shone in all His splendor! Benjamin covered his eyes, fearing the wrath of God, unable to believe what he was seeing. John Mark was transfixed, oblivious to the chaos all about, his attention riveted on the spectacle before him.

What came next was also inexplicable. It must have been a vision granted by God Himself that John Mark might further appreciate the unparalleled moment in which he was living. He knew he was entirely awake, not dreaming. Instantaneously he was transported in the Spirit to the Tabernacle in the wilderness ages ago. In front of him was the Most Holy Place, where in all its majesty stood the Ark of the Covenant—now also miraculously unveiled. Beacons of pure white light shimmered off its polished surface, showering the Tabernacle with brilliance.

John Mark was enthralled, enraptured. He beheld the lustrous sheen of the inner chamber of the Most Holy Place, the Mercy Seat of the Most High God! He stood where Moshe had stood — in the Presence of God!

Immediately, John Mark was conveyed again through time to the immense Most Holy Place of King Shlomo's Temple, built almost a thousand years before. He found himself in God's earthly throne room of old, a gleaming domain of pure gold, radiating the glory of God. Yet again, before him stood the long lost Ark of the Covenant!

Lightning arced overhead, illuminating the golden cherubim, protectors of God's holiness, stationed upon the Mercy Seat. Unlike the Tabernacle in the wilderness, Shlomo's Temple contained two more cherubim, so massive that they appeared to soar over the head of the young man. With wings outstretched, they spanned the entire room. So large were these cherubim that their wingtips touched the walls on either side of the hallowed alcove.

The earth shook and rolled once more. Suddenly, John Mark was drawn back into his own time. He returned to the edge of the Temple Porch where he was still staring past the torn curtain into the Holy of Holies where the Ark of the Covenant had once stood.

John Mark asked himself, "What just happened?" Then he was staggered by an overwhelming realization. "I have been in the Presence of God!"

He was aware this awesome succession of experiences and emotions had occurred in a split second. His spirit rejoiced, "Hallelujah! Glory to God Most High!"

Then he had a revelation that terrified him through-and-through. He was certain this was the exact instant of Yeshua's death. The Son of David had just died.

But oddly, the terror passed as quickly as it came, and John Mark found he was not sad. He need not mourn. Joy filled his whole being. Immediately the Temple filled with a Presence he recognized as that of Yeshua. Then he saw God's blessed glory sparkling like morning dew, sprinkling the sacred chamber with a golden holy mist.

John Mark blinked in astonishment. He rubbed his eyes and looked again. The curtain was indeed torn! The Most Holy Place was unveiled! And he had seen it happen. The supernatural light of the Presence of God enveloped the Temple, spreading across Mount Zion. Beams of glowing glory shot into the heavens!

"O wonder of wonders!" John Mark whispered in total awe and adoration.

His spirit was transformed. He was reminded of the silent moments of the previous evening's Pesach. At that time, the Presence of God had filled the upper room, and all were full of glory and overcome with joy unspeakable.

John Mark's mind searched for some explanation. He remembered, "Entry to the Most Holy Place requires a blood sacrifice. There has to be a sacrifice." He wondered, "Where is the blood?"

Lightning lashed out.

Remembering the Pesach, he cried out loud, "There must be a blood offering! The blood is the atonement for sin!"

Thunder clapped. His every nerve was charged with acute awareness.

He declared aloud, "Only the sacrificial lamb can take away our sin!"

Dozens of lightning bolts shattered the sky over the Temple Mount, temporarily blinding him. John Mark cried out to God: "What is it Lord? I must know! Please tell me! Where is the lamb?"

But there was no need to ask again. He felt the truth well up inside him, overflowing his mind: because of Yeshua's death, nothing stood between him and God!

In yet another epiphany, the image of Yeshua hanging on the rugged timbers flashed through John Mark's mind. He saw a drop of blood fall off the slumped brow of Yeshua. His eyes followed it as it fell slowly through the air and splashed into a large crimson puddle on the hard cold stone of Golgotha. He realized that Yeshua had been drained of blood like an animal on the Temple Altar. Then he saw the simple truth. "There is the sacrifice! There is the blood! Yeshua is the lamb!"

Benjamin had so often said when he repeated the words of Yochanan the Immerser. "Behold the Lamb of God, who takes away the sin of the world!"

John Mark leaped for joy. Divine rapture flooded his soul. He knew the truth! Yeshua was innocent, like the lamb. He understood it now. With all his might he shouted: "Yeshua is the lamb! Yeshua is the Lamb of God!"

Suddenly, grief washed over John Mark. He lamented, "O God, our Messiah is dead. How can this be?" He crumpled in despair on the Temple stairs.

Up until this moment, because of the extraordinary phenomena all about him, Benjamin had not fully appreciated the turmoil in his son's life. But now, he could truly see John Mark's pain as he sobbed on the stairs. Benjamin reached for his son to reassure him.

John Mark grabbed his father and held on for dear life. "Oh, Father! Oh, Father! I understand it now. Yeshua just died."

"I know," said Benjamin, clutching his son.

"Yeshua is the Lamb of God!" voiced John Mark.

Benjamin was completely dumbfounded. This was the third time John Mark had declared that Yeshua was the Lamb of God, but it was just beginning to sink in. His son was having a supernatural revelation of earth-shattering proportions. Benjamin knew that indeed, God had placed His hand upon John Mark's life.

* * *

On a hill overlooking Jerusalem, wind tossed the bloody, matted hair on the lifeless body of Yeshua as he languished upon the tree of death that the Law decreed a curse for any who were hung upon it. As foretold by the Prophet Yesha'Yahu, Yeshua had taken on himself that curse. He had taken on himself the sins of all humanity. He had taken them upon his own perfectly innocent being.

Resurrection Power

As John Mark and Benjamin learned later, Nicodemus and Joseph of Arimathea, members of the Sanhedrin who were sympathetic to the cause of Yeshua and had rejected the charges against him, arranged for his lifeless body to be taken down from the cross. It was washed, covered with myrrh and aloe, wrapped in fine linen, and laid to rest in a tomb carved inside a cave that belonged to this same Joseph. The entrance to the tomb was then closed with a large rock, which was rolled into place to secure the portal.

The cohanim feared that Yeshua's body might be stolen by his close followers, enabling them to fabricate a resurrection. At the request of these priests, Pontius Pilate ordered the tomb sealed with the official Roman emblem, forbidding entry. To break the seal was to defy the Emperor. To further guarantee the security of the vault, Pilate posted two Roman guards at its entrance.

Three days passed. At dawn on this first day of the week, the day after the Sabbath, the talmidim were jolted from their fitful sleep by yet another violent earthquake. Distraught, and fearing that the Judean hierarchy might arrest them and sentence them to the same fate as Yeshua, they had remained in the upper room, where they continued to grieve the death of their master. The atmosphere in the house was grim. The latest tremor added to their apprehension. Wisely, Benjamin kept the doors locked.

Despite the miraculous things they had experienced and seen with their own eyes on the steps of the Temple, it took ongoing effort for John Mark and Benjamin to remain strong in their faith. They busied themselves with the numerous needs of the talmidim. Besides, venturing in and out of the house was risky for their guests.

On his way down from the upper room, John Mark heard a woman's voice from outside the house. "Let me in," she whispered. "I have great news."

He stepped to the door. Opening it, he found Mara of Magdala, whom Yeshua had notably delivered from seven demons, standing with two of her friends at the front gate. When the young man let them in, she grabbed his arm with unexpected firmness. "Our master's body is gone. We don't know where it is!"

Immediately John Mark felt his stomach knot. He escorted her to the upper room. Reaching the top of the steps, she announced to all present, "The tomb is empty!"

Peter swiveled around. Overcoming his surprise, he challenged her, "What do you mean empty? The entrance is sealed."

"Well, it's unsealed now," Mara responded. "The stone has been rolled away." Mara paused, then added, "And we saw an angel."

"An angel?" asked Peter, his mouth agape.

"Yes, but we didn't see him until after the guards took flight. We had hoped to anoint him with perfumes and spices, but after this morning's earthquake we found the guards lying on the ground in shock, trembling in fear. That alone was a sight to behold. We tried to question them, but we could make little sense of what they said. All anyone could gather was something about a great shaking and that an angel had moved the enormous stone. Once the guards gathered their wits, they ran off.

"Then we heard a voice and turned around to see an angel sitting on the stone that had previously covered the tomb. He said to us, 'Do not be afraid, for I know that you are looking for Yeshua, who was crucified. He is not here; he has risen, just as he said. Come and see the place where he lay.' The angel pointed us to the tomb. We looked inside and Yeshua's body was not there. Then the angel said, 'Go find Peter and the talmidim and tell them that the Lord is risen.'"

"I don't believe it!" said Peter. The other talmidim dismissed her story as well.

"Then go," said Mara, somewhat annoyed, "See for yourself!"

Peter hesitated for a moment then bolted for the stairway. He glanced over his shoulder to see if John was following. Both darted down the steps in a blur, leaving the other talmidim behind.

John Mark looked at the women and then spoke to his friends. "We'll see about this!" He hastily grabbed his sandals, then paused mid-stride, hoping to gain his father's permission.

Benjamin consented, "Don't be long." He knew it would be futile trying to change his son's mind. John Mark was gone before his father could say another word.

As he dashed across the city, his mind filled with questions. "Maybe the women have seen an apparition. They must be mistaken or confused. What could have happened to the guards? Where is the body if it is not in the tomb?"

Arriving at the burial site just moments after the talmidim, John Mark saw the cave entrance was indeed unsealed, the stone pushed aside. Peter and John had ventured within. John Mark moved in to get a closer look. At that moment, the two emerged from the dark recess.

"He's not here," said Peter.

"The tomb is empty," added John. "Nothing in there but burial linens."

John Mark decided to go inside. Yeshua's tomb was carved out of a solid rock wall. To enter, one had to step over a drainage ditch. This trench doubled as a channel for a very large limestone disc that had covered the entrance.

The low entry led to a small inner room. Once inside, centered in the wall to the right, John Mark observed, a doorway that gave access to an adjacent, similarly sized space. The side room had a ceiling tall enough to allow him to stand up straight. Two rock hewn ledges protruded from each side of the chamber, both about knee height. Each was wide enough to hold a body. It was on the ledge to his right that the corpse of Yeshua must have been laid. But now the room was vacant.

As John Mark looked around for some explanation, closer inspection revealed, alongside the stone shelf that had held the corpse, the linen shroud for Yeshua's interment. It had not been unwrapped. The herbs were still enclosed, distributed around the form of the missing body. The handkerchief with which Yeshua's face had been covered was neatly folded and placed more than an arm's length from the linen cloth.

When John Mark came back out of the cave, he seemed dazed. He walked over to join the others sitting on a low wall at a nearby wine press. He was totally deflated; his emotions overwhelmed him. He collapsed in a heap, holding his head in his hands. His companions consoled him.

John Mark could not begin to imagine what had happened to Yeshua. "Why would anyone take his body?"

"Or remove him from his burial shroud?" added John incredulously.

By this time Mara had caught up with them. Catching her breath, she knew by the look on their faces what the men had found.

"See!" said Mara triumphantly. "He is risen!"

"This doesn't prove anything," Peter retorted.

"Except that the body is gone," said John skeptically.

"What's going on here?" muttered John Mark, staring at the empty tomb.

The Witnesses

The rest of the day was filled with reports too incredible to believe.

First it was Mara of Magdala again with another wild tale. She told the talmidim, "Late this morning, I saw a man at the tomb whom I thought was the groundskeeper. But when he spoke to me, I realized it was the master!"

Taking her story as fantasy, each of the talmidim rejected it in utter disbelief.

Peter returned to the upper room after dark. John, who had come back hours before, demanded, "Where have you been?" Peter was practically jumping up and down, so the talmidim knew he had something important to share.

But first, Peter insisted that they listen to Mara again.

"I know you must think that I am out of my mind, or that I seek to deceive you," said Mara, "but I assure you that I saw him. I talked with him. I even touched him."

"Tell us again, who was it you saw?" asked Thomas skeptically.

"Yeshua, of course!" she said.

Nathaniel paled. "Oh, we're seeing ghosts now?" He turned to his peers and winced. They made faces.

"Nonsense!" said Matthew. "I don't believe it."

"No, it was not a ghost," countered Mara. "I tell you, Yeshua is alive!"

Several of the talmidim groaned. "Enough of this!" said Nathaniel.

"Can't you see the woman is overcome with grief?" said Philip dismissively.

"Her tale cannot be supported by anyone else's witness," said James.

"We want to hear what Peter has to say," said John.

Mara sat down. She had done her best to relate her miraculous encounter. It was senseless trying to convince people who had already made up their minds.

Peter held up his hands, trying to restore calm. The room quieted down. They had already heard about Mara's so-called "meetings with Yeshua" and were sure that he had something to disclose that would discredit the woman's fantasies.

Before anyone could ask, Peter's words rocked them to the core. "I saw him too!" he declared.

Everyone gasped.

"I am told there are some others who have seen him as well."

"Peter, have you taken leave of your senses?" asked Matthew.

"I have never been more sure of anything in my life," replied Peter.

"I've heard enough!" said Thomas, throwing his hands up in the air. "You can't prove one word of what you're saying. I'm going home!" He turned heel and stormed out of the house.

That did not stop Peter. "My friends, I saw him!" he insisted, irked that they did not believe him.

With that, an uproar ensued. Angry voices competed with one another trying to rebuff the claims of Peter and Mara.

Above the din Peter shouted, "I saw our master!"

Nathaniel responded testily, "And I suppose he asked you about your wife?"

The other men jeered Peter. "O come on, Peter. This has all been painful enough without your ill-timed antics."

Peter jumped onto a bench. "Listen to me my brothers! What is wrong with you?" he shouted. "He's alive!"

"Peter, if you think this is going to make us feel any better, then you are deceived," said Andrew. "Now you're seeing ghosts like Mara of Magdala."

Everyone laughed self-consciously.

"This is not a joking matter," said Matthew. "We are trying to cope with Yeshua's death."

"Who would joke about a thing like that?" rejoined Mara.

"This is crazy!" said Thaddaeus, speaking for the rest of the talmidim.

Suddenly, a loud rap on the door startled everyone. It was too late for a social call. Perhaps Thomas had come back, or God forbid, the Judeans had overheard their debating and found their hideaway.

"Peace Be With You"

John Mark scrambled down the stairs and opened the door to find Cleopas and Simeon, two men well known to them all. They were bursting with enthusiasm.

"We saw him!" they exclaimed. "We saw Yeshua alive tonight!"

John Mark was taken aback. This could not be a coincidence. "You did?"

"Yes! On the road to Emmaus!"

John Mark urgently beckoned the visitors, "Follow me." He rushed them to the upper room where the talmidim were arguing and announced, "Here are two more who claim to have seen our master." Everyone hushed.

"We saw him!" they chimed together.

Pointing at the newcomers, Peter spoke emphatically, "There! You see?"

"You see, what?" Thaddaeus replied angrily, rebuffing their report.

John Mark turned to the newcomers, "Peter tells us that he has seen him too!"

"Now wait just a minute!" Matthew interjected. "Who exactly do you say you have seen?"

"Yeshua!" Cleopas responded, "We even talked to him!"

"Have you all lost your minds?" asked Andrew. "What is your proof?"

John was flustered. Staring at Cleopas, he began asking questions: "When did this happen? How do you know it was Yeshua? Maybe you saw a ghost."

Cleopas' hands and head were shaking as he tried to explain. "Listen! We walked with him. We talked with him. We've traveled half the night just to bring you the news."

"Baruch HaShem, Bless the Name of God!" exclaimed Mara of Magdala, feeling vindicated.

Benjamin brought order to the room, "John Mark, please get these travelers something to drink." He said to the newcomers, "Sit down. Relax. Start from the beginning."

Everyone listened carefully while Cleopas related significant details of their encounter. "We left Jerusalem late this afternoon. We were glad to be leaving the city, considering the deplorable events that have taken place. On the road to Emmaus, we met a stranger. Neither of us recognized him. He asked us about the news from Jerusalem. It seemed as if he knew nothing of the crucifixion. But, as he talked, he revealed profound insights from the Scriptures. He spoke as a man who had intimate knowledge of God.

"He acted as if he was planning on traveling by himself after dark. We feared for his well-being. There are robbers on the road, so we invited him to join us for dinner and even suggested he stay at the inn. He agreed.

"At the meal, he took the bread, blessed it, broke it, and gave it to us. Instantly, our eyes were opened and we realized this was Yeshua. Somehow we had been in his presence for hours and had not known it was he. We were stupefied. The next thing we knew, he vanished from right before us!"

John could not contain himself, "Are you saying that a dead man walked and talked and broke bread, and then just up and disappeared?"

Simeon looked at Cleopas and said, "Did not our hearts burn within us on the road and while he opened the Scriptures to us?"

"He explained his life, death, and resurrection," said Cleopas.

An uncomfortable stir ran through the room at the mention of resurrection.

"Everything he said was from the Law and the Prophets. He even told us . . ." Cleopas stopped in mid-sentence, his mouth open.

Without warning, Yeshua appeared in their midst. "Shalom aleikhem! Peace be with you!"

Everyone gasped. Some of those present emitted low moans of terror. Others were also frightened, thinking it was an apparition. John Mark's heart skipped a beat. Yeshua was not ghostly. He was himself, and clearly alive!

And he said to them, "Why are you troubled, and why do doubts rise in your minds? Look at my hands and my feet. It is I myself! Touch me and see. A ghost does not have flesh and bones, as you see I have." When he had said this, he opened his hands to show his wrists and palms. The nail prints were vivid.

He asked them, "Do you have anything here to eat?" Everyone laughed nervously. They could not help but be amused at the startling contrast between the reality, yet impossibility of it all. Benjamin called downstairs for food

Within moments, the women appeared with a tray of delicacies. Upon seeing Yeshua, they stared with breathless awe.

Receiving the tray of food, Benjamin offered their guest broiled fish and some honeycomb. Yeshua took it and ate.

He said to them, "This is what I told you while I was still with you: Everything must be fulfilled that is written about me in the Law of Moshe, the Prophets, and the Psalms, the entirety of Tanakh."

Then he said, "Remember what I also told you: The Messiah will suffer and rise from the dead on the third day, and repentance and forgiveness of sins will be preached in his name to all nations, beginning at Jerusalem. You are witnesses of these things!"

John Mark grew excited; Yeshua was opening their minds so they could understand the Scriptures! No one said a word. All resistance to Yeshua's resurrection crumbled. How could one disagree with a living testimony?

Again bidding them peace, Yeshua said, "Shalom aleikhem." Having heard this, the people in the room began to calm down. Each person in the room knew that he or she was being personally addressed. John Mark perceived that Yeshua was preparing them for a momentous announcement.

"As the Father has sent me, I am sending you." John Mark did not know where Yeshua was sending him or the others, but he was willing to go. No matter what the cost, he would be a follower of Yeshua! He believed!

With a gesture, Yeshua breathed on those in the room and said, "Receive the Ruach HaKodesh, the Holy Spirit."

While Yeshua was exhaling, each of them experienced a remarkable transformation. The peace they felt was not just an emotion; it was a transcendent essence that permeated their entire beings. Several of them were overcome with tears of joy; the remainder were bathed in absolute serenity. John Mark knew that the Presence of God was saturating the upper room again. But this time, it was far more intense.

John Mark and Benjamin looked at one another. They understood what Yeshua had just done. The Holy Spirit, Ruach HaKodesh, found throughout Tanakh, was theirs, given to them by Yeshua himself! Hallelujah!

Then Yeshua said, "If you forgive anyone his sins, they are forgiven; if you do not forgive them, they are not forgiven."

Unbelievable! Yeshua had just empowered them with the Ruach HaKodesh to proclaim the forgiveness of sin! Only God could forgive sin. This was beyond reason.

John Mark felt his life had reached its zenith. First, he had been a witness to mighty miracles. He could hardly keep track of them all. Now Yeshua stood before him, risen from the dead! He was moving and gesturing, breathing and speaking, showing them the nail scars in his hands and feet while bidding them to touch the marks. He ate their food. He did what he said he was going to do. He bestowed the Ruach HaKodesh upon them and commissioned them to proclaim His life-changing message worldwide!

The next thing they knew, Yeshua was gone, vanished in the same manner Cleopas and Simeon had described. For several minutes nobody spoke. No one dared break the silence.

Finally, Peter looked at John. "Now can we tell them what happened on the mountain?"

John shook his head approvingly. "We wanted to tell you before, but Yeshua swore us to secrecy. Believe me, neither John, James, nor I ever dreamed we would see Yeshua after his death, even though he told us repeatedly that it would happen."

John said, "Because you have seen the risen Yeshua, we can tell you."

Peter looked knowingly at John Mark. He realized the two talmidim were referring to the undisclosed secret they nearly divulged the afternoon they prepared for Pesach.

The others in the room were bubbling with curiosity. "Tell us what?"

"Yeshua made us promise not to tell this to anyone until after his resurrection," said John. "Of course, at the time, we did not even know what he was talking about, or that he was going to be resurrected! It is all so incredible. It happened the day that Peter, James, and I went up on the mountain to pray with him. Do you remember when Yeshua rebuked Peter?"

"Which time?" said James. They all chuckled. Peter could not help but laugh as well.

John continued recounting, "It was six days after Yeshua reprimanded Peter for letting himself be used by Satan." The room became very quiet. This was no joking matter. "We saw Yeshua manifest the very glory of God. His clothes turned brighter than the sun. The light was so blinding, we had to shield our eyes from the brilliance."

"If I had not just seen Yeshua, I would not believe you," said Matthew, his voice trembling.

Peter could not contain himself. He blurted, "We saw Moshe!"

"And Eliyahu too!" added James.

Benjamin responded first, "Moshe? Eliyahu?" The listeners hung on every word.

"That's right!" insisted James. "Standing on the mountain with Yeshua!"

John continued, "The three of them spoke of his death, which he was about to accomplish here in Jerusalem."

There were gasps of amazement. The talmidim began to ask questions. But Peter raised his hands to silence them.

John Mark saw Peter, who had behaved so foolishly only hours before, take on a new air of authority. "But that's not all. A bright cloud overshadowed us.

Suddenly a voice came out of the cloud saying, 'This is my beloved Son, in whom I am well pleased, Hear Him!' We fell on our faces in fear. The next thing we knew, Yeshua came over and touched us. When we looked up, only Yeshua remained."

"As we walked down the mountain," said James, "He made us promise, 'Tell the vision to no one until the Son of Man is risen from the dead.' Frankly, although I gave him my word, I never expected to see it come to pass."

"Every word you have just heard is true," said John. Peter agreed.

Whispers of "Amen" filled the room. In the quiet that followed, each man offered a deeply personal prayer recalling his days with the master. Many wonderful revelations from Yeshua's teachings came into focus. John Mark knew that everyone was experiencing the same miracle—all had witnessed the irrepressible hand of God at work. And none could contain the desire to bear witness to him.

Peter prayed so fervently that all were in awe, "God our Father, I thank you that we were eyewitnesses of Yeshua's Majesty on the sacred mountain. For he received honor and glory from You when Your voice came to him from the Majestic Glory. And I thank You that by this, the words of the prophets throughout the ages have been confirmed."

In the twinkling of an eye, John Mark realized he was being prompted by Ruach HaKodesh to continue the prayer. "Avinu Elohim, Father God, I thank You that on that holy mountain, Peter, John, and James witnessed the fellowship of Yeshua with Moshe and Eliyahu. Moshe, the prophet that God used to usher in the first Pesach in Egypt, and Eliyahu, the unseen guest at the Pesach table, the harbinger of our Messiah's coming, with whose cup in this very place Yeshua proclaimed a new covenant. The promise of Pesach is now revealed full circle, fulfilled. The first Pesach and this Last Supper are *echad*, one!

John Mark paused briefly as his words took root, concluding, "Yeshua is the Lamb, our Pesach Lamb—our sacrifice for sin."

"Baruch HaShem! Bless His Name!" echoed the talmidim.

"Hallelujah and Praise God. Glory to Yeshua our Messiah, the Lamb of God," voiced Benjamin.

"We have seen the Lamb."

Epilogue

For forty days, Yeshua was seen by hundreds of witnesses, many of them in Jerusalem. Others, including his talmidim, saw him as far away as Galilee, where he fulfilled his promise to meet them. There, he again walked and talked and ate with his friends.

He was born to a Jewish family, circumcised on the eighth day and was instructed as a son of the Commandments. He lived a faithful life, worked as a carpenter, and taught as a rabbi. But more than an Israelite, more than a builder, more than a spiritual leader, he was blameless before God. And because he had no sin, he was destined by God as the chosen Pesach Lamb. He presented himself as the perfect offering of atonement—an unblemished sacrifice for the redemption of our souls.

The curtain separating humankind from the Holy of Holies has been torn. He is the Messiah, God's own Son, the fulfillment of God's Covenant with Israel.

And Yeshua did many other miraculous signs in the presence of his talmidim, that you may believe, and that by believing you may have eternal life in His Name. Shalom aleikhem! Peace be with you!"

He was oppressed and afflicted,
Yet he did not open his mouth;
He was led like a lamb to the slaughter,
And as a sheep before her shearers is silent,
So he did not open his mouth . . .
Yet it was the Lord's will to bruise him;
And cause him to suffer,
And though the Lord makes his life
A guilt offering for sin,
He shall see his offspring,
He shall prolong his days;
The will of the Lord
Shall prosper in his hand . . .
Therefore I will give him a portion
Among the great,
And he will divide the spoils with the strong,
Because he poured out his life unto death,
And was numbered with the transgressors.
For he bore the sin of many
And made intercession for the transgressors.

ISAIAH (YESHA 'YAHU) 53: 7, 10, 12
(a. 700 B.C.E.)

Family Tree

PART I

ELISHAMA
(Paternal Grandfather)
Biblical

NUN
(Father)
Biblical

DEBORAH
(Mother)
Fictional

JOSHUA
(Older Brother)
Biblical

RACHEL
(Younger Sister)
Fictional

PART II

NAOMI
(Maternal Grandmother)
Fictional

BENJAMIN
(Father)
Fictional

MIRIAM
(Mother)
Biblical

JOHN MARK
(Older Brother)
Biblical

REBEKAH
(Younger Sister)
Fictional

Glossary

Adonai	My Lord
Amen	It is true, So be it
Avinu Elohim	Father God
Avraham	Abraham
Bar Mitzvah	Son of Commandments
Baruch HaShem	Bless the Name (of God)
Bethlehem	House of bread
Binyamin	Benjamin
Cohen, Cohanim	Priest, Priests
Cohan hagadol, h'gadolim	The high priest, priests
Dani'el	Daniel
Echad	One
Efrayim	Ephraim
Eliyahu	Elijah
'Ezra	Ezra
Hosanna	Save now
Ketuvim	Writings (Tanakh Part 3)
Mal'akhi	Malachi
Matzoh	Unleavened bread
Moshe	Moses
Naftali	Naphtali
Neviim	Prophets (Tanakh Part 2)
Pesach	Passover
P'rushim	Pharisees
Rabbi	Teacher

Glossary

Ruach HaKodesh	The Holy Spirit
Re'uven	Reuben
Shalom	Peace
Shalom aleikhem	Peace be with you
Shekinah	The Glory of God
Shofar	Ram's horn
Shlomo	Solomon
Sh'mu'el	Samuel
Shim'on	Simeon
Talmidim	Disciples
Tanakh	Torah, Neviim, Ketuvim
Torah	Law (Tanakh Part 1)
Tov meod	Well done
Tz'dukim	Sadducees
Ya'akov	Jacob
Yechezk'el	Ezekiel
Yesha 'Yahu	Isaiah
Yeshua	Jesus
Yirmeyahu	Jeremiah
Yochanan	John
Yochanan Markon	John Mark
Yosef	Joseph
Y'hudah	Judah
Yissakhar	Issachar
Yitz'chak	Isaac
Z'vulun	Zebulon

www.ingramcontent.com/pod-product-compliance
Lightning Source LLC
Chambersburg PA
CBHW071155070526
44584CB00019B/2795